~~therapy: a handbook~~

Open University Press
Psychotherapy Handbooks Series
Series Editor: Windy Dryden

Child and adolescent therapy: a handbook

Edited by
DAVID A. LANE
and
ANDREW MILLER

Open University Press
Buckingham • Philadelphia

Open University Press
Celtic Court
22 Ballmoor
Buckingham
MK18 1XW

and
1900 Frost Road, Suite 101
Bristol, PA 19007, USA

First Published 1992

A catalogue record of this book is available
from the British Library

Library of Congress Cataloging-in-Publication Data

Child and adolescent therapy: a handbook/edited by David A. Lane
and Andrew Miller.
    p.   cm.—(Psychotherapy handbooks series)
    Includes index.
    ISBN 0-335-09890-8 (pbk.)   ISBN 0-335-09891-6 (hb)
    1. Child psychotherapy. 2. Adolescent psychotherapy.   I. Lane,
David A., 1947-   . II. Miller, Andrew, 1946-   . III. Series.
    [DNLM: 1. Psychotherapy—in adolescence. 2. Psychotherapy—in
infancy & childhood.   WS 350.2 C5357]
RJ504.C466   1992
618.92'8914—dc20
DNLM/DLC
for Library of Congress   92-18914
                                                            CIP

Typeset by Colset Private Limited, Singapore
Printed in Great Britain by Biddles Limited, Guildford and Kings Lynn

Contents

The editors and contributors

NIGEL BLAGG is Principal Consultant with Nigel Blagg Associates, a firm of Chartered Psychologists based in Taunton, Somerset. Previously, Dr Blagg was a Senior Educational Psychologist with specialist research interests in school phobia, learning problems and cognitive development. His publications include *School Phobia and its Treatment* (Routledge, 1987), *Can We Teach Intelligence?* (Lawrence Erlbaum Associates, USA, 1990) and a modular programme for schools, collectively known as the *Somerset Thinking Skills Course* (Simon & Schuster, 1988–92).

MARIA CALLIAS is a Lecturer in the Department of Psychology and of Child and Adolescent Psychiatry, Institute of Psychiatry, and Clinical Psychologist at the Maudsley-Bethlem Royal Hospitals, working in the Children's Department. Her current research is on problematic peer relationships in young children.

PHIL CHRISTIE is a Chartered Psychologist and Director of Child and Educational Services for the Nottingham Regional Society for Autistic Children. He has previously worked as a Residential Social Worker, Child Psychologist, Teacher and Principal in schools for children with autism. His particular interests include behaviour management and early communication skills.

DANYA GLASER is a child and family psychiatrist and teacher at Guy's Hospital and in a community clinic. She has a developmental and community paediatrics background. Her major clinical, research, and teaching interest and activity have been in child abuse and family therapy and include published research, a book on child sexual abuse and review articles. She has contributed actively to UK policy-making in the field of child sexual abuse. She also has a particular interest in child abuse and neglect prevention and treatment internationally with continuing special connections with Israel, Turkey, Argentina and Germany including visits, workshops and lectures.

PETER GRAY is currently Principal Educational Psychologist for Nottinghamshire LEA. Prior to working in Nottinghamshire, Peter was Associate Tutor at the

University of London Institute of Education (Department of Educational Psychology and Special Educational Needs). He has worked for a number of LEAs as an educational psychologist as well as spending some years teaching in East London. He is editor of *Educational and Child Psychology* and has written a number of articles on aspects of professional practice.

NEIL HALL currently works as a tutor at the University of Birmingham, teaching on the professional training course for educational psychologists. He is also the senior psychologist for Birmingham City Council's Social Services Department: in this role he coordinates the community-based work of a team of eight other specialist psychologists. He has published on working with child-abusing parents and psychological and health-related aspects of child abuse. His doctoral research is concerned with investigating the development of repression in young children. Along with two colleagues, from the Child Protection Project where he has also worked for the past five years, he is writing a text on assessing children at risk.

ROY HOWARTH is Consultant Psychiatrist in the Islington Community Child and Adolescent Psychiatry Unit in London, where his interest is in delivery of service. He is also currently head of Clinical Service in the Department of Psychological Medicine at the Hospital for Sick Children, Great Ormond Street, where his interests are in the psychiatry of chronic physical illness and cognitive-behavioural approaches to the management of symptoms.

DAVID A. LANE has worked with vulnerable children for over twenty years. As Director of the Professional Development Foundation he has published widely and presented workshops and organizational change programmes designed to improve the quality of service to children. He was the recipient of the National Freedom of Information Award for his pioneering work in the 1970s on open access to files for children and parents. He is a Visiting Professor of Psychology at Syracuse University, Honorary Senior Lecturer at University College London, and Honorary Senior Fellow at City University. Previous books include *The Impossible Child* and *Bullying in Schools* (both published by Trentham Books).

MONICA LANYADO is Course Co-ordinating Tutor of the Child and Adolescent Psychotherapy Training Course at the Scottish Institute of Human Relations, Edinburgh. She is also consultant to Harmeny School, Balerno, a primary residential school for children with special needs. She has published papers on a variety of therapeutic themes in the *Journal of Child Psychotherapy*, the *Journal of Social Work Practice*, and *Maladjustment and Therapeutic Education*. Her research interests are the study of the mother–infant relationship and the treatment of sexual abuse.

ANDREW MILLER is Course Director, Educational Psychology, at the Child Development Research Unit, University of Nottingham and has previously worked as a teacher and educational psychologist in a number of local authorities. His research interests include parental involvement in children's development, teacher belief systems and the management of difficult classroom behaviour, and systems for effective professional development. Previous books include *Planning and Managing Effective Professional Development* and *Psychological Services for Primary Schools* (both published by Longman).

ELIZABETH NEWSON is Professor of Developmental Psychology at the University of Nottingham. Apart from her continuing two-generational research on childrearing styles and their sequelae (with John Newson), her major research themes lie in the pervasive developmental disorders (identification and intervention), and in creating a 'language of partnership' between professionals, parents and children. She has received many research grants from the Department of Health to study aspects of autism.

JOHN NEWSON founded the Child Development Research Unit with his wife Elizabeth Newson at Nottingham University in 1967. Well known for their refinement of the interviewing method in order to investigate successive generations of parental attitudes, Professor John Newson has also specialized in early infancy and has undertaken observational research on interactions between babies and their caregivers.

JIM NOAKES is the Headteacher of the Northern Area Education Support Service for children with emotional and behavioural difficulties, Warwickshire. Most of his teaching career has been spent in East London where he has taught in special and comprehensive schools. He has worked with Peter Gray in a multi-disciplinary team structure within an educational psychology service. Together with Andy Miller they organize the 'New Directions in Behaviour Support Work' national conferences for EBD support services that are held annually at Nottingham University.

WENDY PREVEZER is a Speech and Language Therapist. She is currently evaluating 'Musical Interaction' as therapy for children with a range of communication difficulties, within the Speech and Language Therapy Service in Nottingham. Previously (1986–91) she worked as a Music Specialist at Sutherland House School for Autistic Children, and maintains links with the school on a consultancy basis. She also gives lectures and workshops on using music to facilitate communication.

MARTIN SCHERER has worked in residential schools, childcare, remand and assessment centres for children and young people showing emotional and behavioural disabilities and delinquent behaviour. He was a headteacher at Chelfham Mill School. He has undertaken postgraduate research in psychology and published several papers and is co-editor of *Disruptive Behaviour* (1990). He is currently managing director and senior consultant of ABACA'n Consultants.

RUTH M. WILLIAMS is a Lecturer in Clinical Psychology at the University of London, Institute of Psychiatry and Honorary Top Grade Clinical Psychologist at the Bethlem Royal and Maudsley Hospital. For the past ten years, Mrs Williams has specialized in cognitive behaviour therapy in this Department, having had training with Beck in Philadelphia. Recently, Mrs Williams has applied this type of therapy to helping survivors of major disasters.

WILLIAM YULE is Professor of Applied Child Psychology at the University of London Institute of Psychiatry. After qualifying in clinical psychology, he spent six years in educational and epidemiological research before returning to the Institute. He has researched into training parents of autistic children; training teachers to use behaviour modification in classrooms; longitudinal studies of children's disorders; the effects of lead on children's development; children's fears; and post traumatic stress disorders in children.

Preface

Major changes are happening in child and adolescent therapy. The contexts in which therapists work, the range of problems tackled, and the models of intervention adopted are changing increasingly rapidly. Traditionally, therapy books have taken an approach that presents either different theories or different problems. This book presents diverse practice in multiple settings. It looks at the changing agenda for therapy, and the evaluation of interventions.

Six areas of practice that do represent particular challenges to therapy are examined. A developmental model for promoting communication for non-speaking children is presented. A powerful model of play therapy is provided that is applicable in a variety of contexts. It has been pioneered with children facing violence, neglect, terminal illness and impoverished environments. Child abuse presents major challenges to therapists and these issues are considered. School phobia in particular confronts the boundaries between therapy and control: recent work in this area is presented. Conduct disorders have always represented a major headache for therapists but the problem of bullying and victimization in schools has caused consternation for victims, parents, professionals and politicians. The challenge for therapists is discussed. The management of trauma following disaster has become an important area in recent years. Therapists working in the field are faced with managing experiences sometimes beyond their comprehension.

The consideration of challenging areas of practice leads to the settings in which therapy takes place. The most restrictive form of therapy is the therapeutic community. Staff and clients work and live together, and solve problems of living through their interactions. The problems and justifications for this approach are debated. The Child Guidance Clinic, linchpin of child service for more than fifty years, has been the subject of increasing criticism. The prospects for this service in the 1990s require timely consideration. Most therapy now takes the form of multi-disciplinary teamwork. This perspective presents its own difficulties and these are considered. Finally the challenge that community-based therapy presents is explored.

We hope that this books reflects the excitement and confusions that currently impact on therapy services.

PART I

The changing agenda

Child and adolescent therapy: a changing agenda

MARIA CALLIAS, ANDREW MILLER,
DAVID A. LANE AND MONICA LANYADO

This book examines the changing face of therapeutic services for children and young people in the early 1990s. As such it is concerned with both the nature of therapy itself – the techniques, their effectiveness, the ethical implications of their use – and the way in which professional services are structured and set within a societal context. It is not the intention of the book to provide a primer of the range of psychological problems and adverse circumstances to which young people may become prone nor do the chapters set out one by one the therapeutic approaches that professionals might employ. In many ways these functions are well served by earlier publications (Daws and Boston 1977; Rutter and Hersov 1976; 1985; Morris and Kratochwill 1983).

Instead, this book takes as its starting-point the fact that a revolution is taking place within many of the professional services whose members provide therapeutic services to young people. The strongest manifestation of this is the rapid succession of legislative changes being made in relation to funding within Health, Education and Social Services Departments and the new statutory duties being imposed on members of these services. Expectations of the types of services offered by these agencies are also changing within society in general. A public climate now exists in which those who fund and consume such services are demanding a greater say in the setting of their priorities, a process that was originally held firmly within the grasp of the professionals. The changing climate is also reflected in the greater prominence given to ethical issues and the requirement that the effectiveness of therapeutic interventions be subjected to more rigorous evaluation. The need for therapeutic services to be more sensitive to issues surrounding cultural diversity, and to examine critically their practice in relation to minority groups and the disempowered, is also becoming more widely recognized.

This combined chapter is an attempt by four clinicians from different theoretical orientations to give a balanced overview of child and adolescent therapy today. While acknowledging our different and at times conflicting approaches to the work, there is nevertheless a creative core of good practice which is clearly of help to our clients and which can be generally respected across the somewhat artificial divides of varied theoretical perspectives. We all have to respond to criticisms of our work and bad practice within our respective orientations. It is through these responses which should be a spur to further thought about the work, as well as through experience gathered from our clients, that the body of knowledge of child and adolescent therapy grows.

While progress has been made in some quarters, great challenges still remain for therapists to demonstrate that they understand characteristics, contexts and outcomes. This applies to a range of problems, which new generations of young people continue to present to therapeutic services. However, types of difficulties and problems have not remained static and, without a doubt, the most demanding and contentious area of professional work to have developed since the early 1980s has been in response to the increased reporting and detection of the sexual abuse of children. Another area now requiring the attention of professional services is provision for the young (and adult) survivors of mass disasters. These areas have generated a great deal of reflection by therapists, who have had to look carefully at their own response to their clients.

Within professional services themselves rapid changes have also been taking place. These have been partly in response to the forces already outlined. They have also derived from a consideration of whether services can or should concentrate their efforts on attempting to deal with the aftermath of traumatic circumstances, or alternatively act to prevent the occurrence of some of these in the first place. A number of chapters take up this theme. Interventions are described that illustrate; for example, work directly with children and parents and those who act *in loco parentis*; examples of agencies adopting a preventive approach through a community focus; and work with the organizational structure of schools. Clearly, the fact that these extensions to professional practice are taking place suggests that a broad definition of the term 'therapy' is required if discussions are to reflect current practice and to encompass the broad range of activities being employed by services charged with promoting the psychological well-being of young people. The question of how we define therapy is discussed on p. 5.

The development of theory and the attempts to derive practice from theory continue. There are a number of problems surrounding the relationship between theory and practice. Several chapters in this book will look at the way in which psychological theory informs the activities carried out by therapeutic services. For example, Christie and colleagues in Chapter 3 take a theoretical perspective from developmental psychology and demonstrate its practical implications for working with autistic children. Blagg (Chapter 6) describes research into the outcomes of approaches towards the treatment of school phobia that derive both from psychodynamic and from behavioural perspectives. Newson (Chapter 4) provides an account of how a therapeutic intervention may be developed to meet an expressed need by drawing on a number of theoretical perspectives where no one approach alone appears to offer a fully appropriate method.

This chapter considers first the definition of therapy and then the major theoretical perspectives that have formed the backdrop to the development of therapeutic interventions. It then looks at the range of organizations and professional groups that are involved, either centrally or as an adjunct to their main duties, with the provision of these therapeutic services. It considers how children are referred for help and the implications of that process. Some examples of current practice are described to illustrate the range of work undertaken in child therapy. Finally, the chapter outlines the ways in which therapeutic services will need to respond in terms of their organization and style of operation if they are to provide an effective contribution within and beyond the revolution that is all around them.

What is therapy?

Psychotherapy or psychological therapies are generic terms for the wide range of interventions that rely on personal actions of therapists of any theoretical persuasion to alleviate the distress of a person seeking or being brought for help with particular emotional and behavioural problems and to improve their functioning in everyday life (Rutter 1985; Kazdin 1988). More specifically, the five main goals in present-day interventions for children's problems are to reduce overt problems, to promote normal development, to foster autonomy and self-reliance, to generalize therapeutic gains and to foster the persistence of improvements (Rutter 1985).

This is of course a theoretically neutral definition. It would not necessarily be accepted by those who see therapy as an endeavour designed to explore the child's 'inner world'. It is also a politically neutral definition which does not take account of the view sometimes expressed that therapy is a process in which those with power modify the behaviour of the powerless. In the latter case therapists are believed to act as agents of social control rather than as the benevolent providers of services as implied above. It is true to say that any attempt to define child and adolescent therapy will run into the difficulty that it will not be accepted by some practitioners in the field. It is part of the changing agenda of child therapy services that such diversity of opinions now exist.

The diversity in definitions of therapy extend to the range of interventions adopted. The means of intervening, for many clients, remains primarily interpersonal contact and verbal interaction, but now includes a wide range of other interactions such as play, teaching of new skills, rehearsing activities with the child and reinforcing new or desired behaviour. Toys, puppets, games, stories and other materials are often used as aids, as are art, drama and music. These procedures may be carried out by therapists in special settings or groups; in triadic models of therapy, therapists may guide parents, teachers, nurses, peers or others in more day-to-day contact with the child to try out new ways of relating in special sessions, or by changing some aspects of their everyday interactions. The stereotypical notion of child therapy as a one-to-one process which is carried out only in a clinical consulting room is no longer current.

Over 230 alternative psychosocial treatments have been identified by Kazdin (1988); these range from specific techniques to whole schools of therapy encompassing broad philosophies with numerous strategies and specific techniques. Most of these therapies have been described at some level but very few have been evaluated. Nevertheless, most therapies are the descendants of a few theoretical and philosophical schools which have dominated practice (Johnson et al. 1986). These differ in the way they define problems, and strategies and techniques of intervention but all aim to bring about change in some aspects of the thoughts, feelings or actions of the person who has sought or been brought to treatment. The more prominent of these various schools will be reviewed.

The psychoanalytic practitioners of child therapy

Much of the therapy offered to children and adolescents is provided by core professional groups such as psychiatrists, psychologists, social workers and occupational therapists. The theoretical positions taken by members of these core professions vary widely. There is in addition the distinct professional group of child psychotherapists who have undergone five years of postgraduate training in psychoanalytic psychotherapy and are recognized as a separate profession working in the main, within the National Health Service. The profession is small with two hundred and forty members and seventy trainees (in 1991), who mostly work in the south of England. This is in the main due to the fact that nearly all training schools until recently have been based in London, and child psychotherapy posts outside the south-east of England have been scarce. The recent establishment (in 1990) of a Scottish training school in Edinburgh is the first step in widening the geographical spread of child psychotherapists in Britain.

The child psychotherapy profession has been in existence since 1949, having been established as a separate profession as a result of a British Psychological Society Study Group into Child Psychotherapy. The Association of Child Psychotherapists (ACP) was founded at this time and is the organization which regulates the training and standards of the profession.

The psychoanalytic training undertaken requires personal analysis throughout the training period, individual supervision of three intensive cases (three to five times weekly), supervision of a variety of once weekly and less intensive cases, and attendance at seminars on theory, observation and practice for four years. There is a register of qualified child psychotherapists; the ACP has recently been recognized by the Department of Trade and Industry as the designated authority to uphold comparative standards of training within the EC in 1992, when therapists from Europe will have the right to practise in the United Kingdom. This group is small but has been an influential force in the development of child therapy services. Their recognition as a 'Designated Authority' ensures that they will retain influence throughout the 1990s.

Although known as child psychotherapists, the training in fact spans the age range from mothers and babies to late adolescence. The five training schools offer a choice of Kleinian, Anna Freudian, Independent or Jungian orientations to the work. As well as training therapists to offer intensive treatment when appropriate, a core part of the training is in once-weekly work, work with parents and less frequent consultation work or brief therapy. This results in both a depth and breadth of treatment options being offered although all within the psycho-analytic tradition. Most child psychotherapists work in the public sector and the need to make a scarce resource stretch as far as possible has resulted in recent years to a move away from the intensive work in which they were trained. In addition they are undertaking an increasing amount of consultation and short-term work, and are unlikely to have more than one intensive case going on at a time. The bulk of their caseload is likely to be once-weekly work in the context of parallel work with the parents undertaken by a colleague.

This issue of the interrelationship between the form of training and the pressure of resources is not restricted to analytic therapies. It raises the broader question of whether it is appropriate to train practitioners to work in ways which do not reflect the reality of service provision.

Child psychotherapists would argue that much of the value of their long and intensive training period lies in the unique opportunity it provides to study and work in depth with patients. This lasting experience becomes a wellspring of knowledge and insight which enriches briefer and less intensive work during many years of clinical practice (Miller et al. 1989). Thorough and intensive training also provide the therapist with the staying power to remain in close emotional contact with the distressing problems that their patients bring over long periods of time. Professional burn-out is reduced as a result.

Traditionally child psychotherapists have been based in Departments of Child and Family Psychiatry and Child Guidance Clinics, but more recently they are found working in special care baby units, paediatric wards, general practice, special schools and children's homes.

The most comprehensive description of the way in which child psychotherapists work can be found in Daws and Boston (1977), in which Boston says:

> When carrying out individual treatment the child psychotherapist attempts to help the patient to understand his or her own situation and, in particular, any unconscious difficulties which may be contributing to current diffi-culties. The therapist is, in other words, concerned with the patient's 'inner world' – the subjective picture of people and things we all carry round within us, sometimes without even being aware of it, and which may or may not adequately correspond to outward reality.
>
> (Daws and Boston 1977)

Unconscious anxieties, conflicts and fantasies are some of the key psychoanalytic concepts which underlie the work of the child psychotherapist. These internal processes within the child's inner world interact with significant factors in the child's external world, such as the quality of care that the child experiences while growing up, and the impact of traumatic events on his or her life. Theories of what constitutes an ordinary developmental process, with all its consequent awkward phases, underpin the concept of emotional disturbance. A relatively smooth passage through childhood is seen as laying the foundations for adult mental health.

Although Freud had always seen the roots of the psycho-neuroses in his adult patients as being in childhood, the first known psychoanalytic treatment of a child, aged 5 (conducted by Freud through the child's father) was a case study, 'Little Hans', which was written to provide support for theories of infantile sexuality (Freud 1909). In many ways it is of course very different from the way such a treatment would be conducted today (see Wolpe and Rachman 1960 for a detailed critical review). During the period between the First and Second World Wars, Melanie Klein (1932) and Anna Freud (1966), while differing sharply on a number of fundamental issues, nevertheless argued that children could be effectively helped by direct psychoanalytic treatment. Klein believed that psychological processes during the first year of life were crucial to understanding later development. She described two fundamental ways of relating to the world throughout the life cycle which arose from these very early experiences, which she called the paranoid schizoid and the depressive position. These she thought of as processes coming from within the child's mind (Segal 1973).

Anna Freud did not agree with this formulation, and continued to believe, as her father did, that the degree of resolution of the universally experienced Oedipus complex (which was at its height between the ages of 3 and 5) was the chief determinant of the emotional health of the individual. This complex related to the child's love and hate relationships with his or her parents and focused on three-person relationships as opposed to the two-person relationships of Kleinian theory. Anna Freud described detailed sequential phases of normal development in life which are ordinarily largely outgrown. Pathology was seen as being due to difficulties in progressing through these phases. These contrasting theoretical orientations lead to differences in therapeutic technique and emphasis. The conflicts between the Kleinian and Freudian schools of thought have been largely reconciled by establishing separate trainings within the main psychoanalytic institutions.

Jungian thinking has in the main developed separately forming its own psychoanalytic institutions. Jung (1966) introduced the concepts of a collective unconscious and primordial images called archetypes. He felt that Freud overemphasized the importance of the sexual instincts and he differed in his approach to treatment to that of Freud. More recently, Jungian training has been recognized by the Association of Child Psychotherapists. Current thinking with regard to the treatment of children and teenagers is illustrated by Fordham's work (1969).

After the Second World War, evidence on the devastating effect of separation and loss on children, particularly when evacuated, led some thinkers to pay greater attention to the impact of the environment and quality of care given on the development of the infant and child. Bowlby (1988), James and Joyce Robertson (1989) and Winnicott (1965) are particularly influential in this respect. They worked from the basis of observation of 'ordinary' children as well as the observations of emotionally disturbed children undergoing psychoanalytic treatment.

Bowlby's contribution was within the area of attachment, separation and loss, in which he drew heavily on an ethological perspective. He put love (attachment) relationships at the centre of clinical considerations, and vividly described the possibly traumatic results of separation of children from those that they loved (Bowlby 1988). Winnicott drew on his many years of experience as a paediatrician in a well-baby clinic to formulate his concepts about the 'good-enough mother', creativity and play. These concepts were central to his theories about human development as well as at the heart of his approach to his patients (Winnicott 1965; Philips 1988).

Winnicott and Bowlby belong to the third main stream of psychoanalytic thought, the Independent Group. While Winnicott and Bowlby have had the most significant influence on independent psychoanalytic practice with children; other major contributors to this school of thought are Balint, Rycroft, Fairburn and Guntrip (see Rayner 1991).

Post-Kleinian development has seen the emergence of Bion (1962) as a powerful influence. His theories, which relate to the development of the mind as an apparatus for thinking informed by experience, have provided a model of early infantile states of mind as well as psychotic states of mind (Bion 1962; Shuttleworth 1984).

There are many differences in theoretical orientation as described above, but there are aspects of method and technique which all analytically oriented child psychotherapists have in common. Some of the most fundamental concepts relate to the setting in which therapy takes place, the transference relationship between therapist and client, the use of interpretation to bring about change in the client's inner world, and the process of containment of anxieties.

Psychoanalytic therapists argue that careful consideration must be always given to the setting in which psychoanalytic psychotherapy takes place. A regular time and place is established for the therapy, and these are kept as constant as possible throughout the therapy. The aim of this is to provide a predictable and reliable setting which can help the work by minimizing extraneous distractions, such as changes of play materials or attendance at varying times of the day. Efforts are made to ensure that there are no interruptions of the client's time with the therapist and that carefully selected toys provided for the child are kept constant. Breaks in therapy due to holidays or unavoidable absences of the therapist are notified to the client several weeks in advance. These measures are in recognition of the way in which therapy becomes emotionally important to the client and is therefore missed during breaks in the regularity of the sessions. Arranging the therapy sessions in this way encourages the growth of the relationship with the therapist and the recognition that the sessions provide a dependable and safe setting in which the client's feelings are taken seriously.

Psychoanalytic therapists believe that anxieties are expressed by clients in disguised form, the presenting problem for which help is initially sought. This disguise is the result of psychological defences which clients have erected over the years in order to survive. Effort is made to provide a safe setting so that what is often felt to be unacceptable or unbearable by the client can be explored. The therapist seeks to maintain an attentive, non-directive approach which will encourage clients to feel able to express themselves freely. A secure therapeutic setting enables hostile and angry feelings as well as tender and painful ones to be explored within the firm limits provided by the therapist.

The concerns from therapists of other persuasions and some clients is that rather than provide a safe arena, the setting becomes a rigid demonstration of the therapist's power through the over-interpretation of the client's behaviour (Taylor 1991). The rigidity in any system which demands that clients conform to the therapist's notion of a safe area is something that child psychotherapists have addressed. The notion of the safe area can become a fixed system in which the Child Guidance Clinic is seen as the only place in which therapy can take place. A reluctance to work in the community was noted by some critics. Increasingly, practitioners have accepted these criticisms and have moved away from a rigid approach towards a more flexible mode of operation. This has required a widening of the concept of a safe place and change in therapeutic techniques.

The process of working with the child depends upon the therapist's ability to interpret material which elucidates the child's inner world. The thoughts, dreams, fantasies and feelings (verbal and non-verbal) that clients bring to the therapist are received and worked on within the therapist's mind through the interrelated therapeutic processes of containment and the transference relationship, and the use of interpretation.

As described below the process of containment and the use of interpretation are informed by the quality of the relationship which develops between the therapist and client. This relationship is known as the 'transference relationship' and is of central importance in the psychoanalytic process.

The clients are seen as relating to the therapist in their habitual way of relating to people outside therapy, with all the attendant difficulties that have lead to the need for treatment. The way in which relationships with their mother and father, as well as other significant people in their past have been subjectively experienced by the clients, affect the way in which they expect all relationships to work. This is what is meant by the 'transferring' of important past relationships into the present, in this instance, into the therapeutic relationship. Efforts can then be made to understand the anxieties and conflicts of the client's inner world based on the careful observation and direct experience of the current transference relationship. This relationship is not static but is actively changing throughout treatment. In this way a second chance is offered in therapy for the client to re-experience anxieties and conflicts from the past, in a setting that can facilitate new solutions and healthier development in the present.

'Interpretation' is the technique used by psychoanalytic psychotherapists to offer formulations about the client's inner world. Intellectual explanations about the client's difficulties are frequently not sufficient to bring about change in the inner world. However, interpretations carry emotional significance as they are based on the often intense experience of the transference relationship: the timing of interpretations is very important. Care is taken to ensure that the interpretation is given when it is most likely to be helpful to the client and is put in ordinary language. It is a straightforward communication from the therapist to the client.

The term 'containment' is used to describe the way in which all manner of painful as well as positive aspects of an individual's emotional life can be communicated and held within the mind and heart of another attentive human being. In ordinary circumstances the mother does this for her developing child, when she attempts to understand and respond to his or her communications. In later life friends and marital partners try to help each other in the same way. This important process helps previously distressing or poorly understood experiences to become more tolerable and comprehensible. In this way it is possible to promote the growth of an individual's capacity to contain their own anxieties as a result of having someone else do this for them, when they needed this type of help.

What the therapist offers when such processes in everyday life have been overwhelmed or unavailable is the willingness to enter into a relationship in which the possibility of containing such anxieties is provided. It is the intensity and distressing nature of the feelings that may need to be expressed, that leads to the requirement that child psychotherapists as a central part of their training, undergo their own psychoanalysis. This is to help them to have the personal resources to cope with the emotional demands of the work, and to minimize professional burn-out.

One of the ways that passionate and chaotic feelings can be contained for the client is through the therapist's efforts to formulate interpretations. These verbalizations are the end product of a lengthy thought process within the therapist while they are struggling to understand the powerful feelings that their clients share with them. Interpretation and containment are intrinsically linked in their capacity to promote emotional growth during therapy.

Psychoanalytic theory and practice are seen as mutually informing each other. Observations from the consulting room can challenge theory, while theory can provide a working hypothesis for clinical practice.

Other theoretical perspectives influencing UK work

Criticism of the models which dominated child therapy services surged from the 1950s onwards. They came from a number of sources (see Lane 1990), but of particular significance was the attack on the child guidance movement itself:

> the child guidance clinic, linchpin of the child guidance service, is an expensive, ineffective and wrongly conceived institution. . . . Its clinical orientation causes it to pay only minor regard to the problems of the school, the teacher and the classroom.
>
> (Tizard 1973: 22)

Similar problems emerged in the USA, and criticisms of clinic based services also led to an expanding range of options (see Apter 1982; Apter and Goldstein 1986; Kazdin 1988).

Services have of course responded to the criticism, sometimes by denying them, but often by changing the focus of the service. The criticisms did, however, provide an impetus for the development of competing ideas and new service provision. The extent to which psychoanalytic practitioners could operate outside of their 'safe space' in the clinic was a major challenge during the 1980s. The increasingly diverse contexts in which child psychotherapists work is evidence of their response (Daws 1989; Judd 1989).

Individual psychoanalytic and other psychodynamic psychotherapies were the first therapeutic approaches to become established in children's services and still play a prominent role (Wilson and Hersov 1985). It was not only designated child psychotherapists who used psychoanalytic ideas but also other core professionals. Other movements also emerged as ideas from adult therapy influenced child practitioners. Non-directive play therapy and counselling (Axline 1947) grew out of the Rogerian client-centred approach with its interest in self-concept and interpersonal relationships rather than the inner unconscious conflicts of interest to child psychotherapists. However, much play therapy took place in confined clinic settings and therefore increasingly faced similar criticisms. Alternative models of play therapy emerged. The models developed in Nottingham are particularly relevant and are discussed in detail by Elizabeth Newson in Chapter 4.

As criticisms of service provision increased the question of treatment effectiveness became more influential. The two became parallel concerns and unfortunately the argument became primarily a battle between proponents of psychoanalytic and behavioural schools. An 'Evaluation War' rather than a careful assessment with the client as the central focus developed.

Questions of treatment efficacy were not seriously addressed until the end of the 1950s when strong doubts were expressed about the value of psychotherapy for children's psychological and behavioural distress (Levitt 1957; 1963). Behavioural approaches began to gain ground in the 1960s, when psychologists began to apply interventions based on learning theories, especially operant principles, more widely to the problems of children, including handicapped children whose difficulties were not amenable to verbally mediated therapies (Rachman 1962; Yule 1984). Being strongly rooted in psychological research traditions, high store was set on demonstrating that the techniques being used were indeed responsible for the changes observed.

The early behavioural interventions applied models from experimental psychology based on classical and operant conditioning. The emphasis was placed firmly on the interaction of the environment with the individual. The notion of the child's 'inner world' was abandoned. This was unacceptable to psychoanalytic practitioners, and others as well. There was a hard-nosed attitude by many behaviourists who made little attempt to address the concerns of critics. The language of 'stimulus and response' used had minimal appeal for any but convinced exponents. The success of early demonstration projects did lead to greater use of the ideas, but a less dogmatic approach to the language, and a more effective use of the role to be played by changing environments rather than people, did lead to a dramatic increase in the use of the ideas. Many variants based on behavioural ideas became standard practice, in particular parental involvement schemes. The increasing involvement of behavioural psychologists with real world community-based problems, and a willingness, indeed a preference, to work in the context where the problem was occurring was responsible for its acceptance (see Lane 1990). Miller and Burden (1992) have looked at the development of behavioural approaches. In Chapter 6 Blagg considers its application in the areas of school phobia.

More recent major theoretical developments have occurred from psychological traditions in the form of cognitive and cognitive-behavioural treatments which aim to modify patterns of thinking in relation to problems. With children, three variants have developed in relation to different problems: social cognitive problem-solving (Pellegrini 1985), cognitive behaviour therapy focusing on self-instruction and self-control for impulsivity (Kendall 1984) and for depression (Kazdin 1990).

The fourth main approach, family therapy, introduced systemic conceptualizations by a major shift in focus away from the individual child pathology to seeing problems as residing in the whole family and thus to treating the whole family unit.

Early family therapists combined systems theory concepts with their existing psychoanalytic background (Barker 1986; Dare 1985) while more recently behavioural and cognitive approaches to family therapy are being integrated with systemic approaches. Psychological and family approaches are now widely accepted as playing central roles in psychotherapeutic endeavours for children (Rutter 1985). The 1980s have seen the increasing influence of ecological and broad system thinking (Apter 1982; Topping 1983). The move towards a general systems view rather than simply a family systems view has led to programmes which attempt to modify whole environments. Miller and Burden (1992) consider systems thinking in the context of work in schools.

Growing out of different traditions, psychological interventions differ on a number of key issues including the conceptualization of the problems, goals and focus of intervention, the main therapeutic agent – especially the relative role of the therapist–client relationship and techniques, duration of therapy, who is seen, and the therapeutic settings. For example, psychodynamic therapy and non-directive counselling share the view that the relationship between the therapist and client is at the heart of the therapeutic process. In contrast, in behavioural and cognitive approaches, the relationship is viewed as necessary but not suffi-cient with specific strategies and techniques playing a key role and receiving more attention. At the ecological end of the spectrum, relationships form just one part of a comprehensive approach which includes environmental modification.

Since the mid-1960s there have been rapid conceptual and technical advances especially within the behavioural (Yule 1984; Ollendick 1986) and family therapy traditions (Speed 1984; Barker 1986) as well as in the broadening of work under-taken by child psychotherapists. Despite persisting differences, changes over time have also led to blurring so that some therapeutic strategies and tactics are now common to many treatment approaches (Rutter 1985). These include a greater emphasis on short-term focused therapy using specific techniques of change, better defined goals with an increasing focus on overt behaviour, and a focus on the present rather than the past as evidence suggests that such approaches are more effective than ill-defined long-term open-ended approaches. Residential treatment is used more sparingly and more selectively ensuring that families are involved in treatment wherever possible (Topping 1983; Hersov and Bentovim 1985).

These changing concepts of treatment have been integrally linked with changing notions of the nature of psychological disorder (Rutter 1982). Early views of disorder as disturbed intrapsychic personality processes by psycho-analysts or as no more than conditioned responses by early behaviourists have been superseded by the recognition that the child is a complex active, thinking and developing person living in a social world.

The child's existence within a web of social relationships especially within the family is reflected in the development of family therapy, parent training and school-focused interventions. Treatment issues, such as the situation specificity of many child problems and treatment effects as well as problems of generalizing and maintaining treatment gains from special settings, have strengthened the emphasis on home and school based interventions and awakened an interest in the characteristics and circumstances of families and parents in relation to treatment efficacy (Wahler 1980). More recently, the importance of the child's wider social relationships has become recognized with interventions for poor peer relationships (Frosh and Callias 1980; Spence 1989).

The view of the child as an active, thinking person has led to therapeutic developments focusing on cognitive interventions and developmental theories (Rutter 1982; 1985). It is, however, developmental theory based firmly on study of child behaviour rather than an adaption of adult work to children.

Psychodynamic therapies are underpinned by an understanding of developmental processes, but developmental issues have not been central to some behavioural and other interventions which have focused mainly on the methods of bringing about change. Nevertheless, developmental aspects have been implicit in the conduct of some behavioural interventions and are being addressed more explicitly (Lane 1974; 1990; Yule 1990; Herbert 1991). Christie and colleagues provide an example of a model explicitly informed by developmental theory in Chapter 3.

Despite some common ground, recent overviews of the current state of affairs indicates that different approaches tend to be practised by different professional disciplines (Rutter and Hersov 1985). Because of divergent attitudes and skills in evaluative research, there is variability in both the extent to which different therapeutic approaches are evaluated and the nature of evaluation conducted. This poses problems for finding out whether what we do with the intention of facilitating positive change for psychologically distressed children and their families does indeed work or not (Rutter 1985; Kazdin 1987; 1988). This seemingly straightforward scientific question is in reality a complex one encompassing not only scientific issues and controversies but also social, ethical, practical and resource issues which pervade our clinical practice as well as decisions about which problems and which interventions to investigate and whether and how research findings influence practice. This close fusion of professional identity with theoretical allegiance also compounds the difficulty in questioning by research the validity of what we do. Callias addresses these issues in Chapter 2.

Finally, it should be noted that psychological problems are not always treated by psychological methods. Medical biological treatments such as the use of drugs (Taylor 1988) or special diets are used with some problems such as hyperactivity (Taylor 1986b). Sometimes the main intervention for very troublesome, delinquent or handicapped children is residential placement usually with the intention of providing custodial care as well as some milieu and other therapy. The complex interaction of these elements in a residential context is tackled by Scherer in Chapter 9 and Jones (1992).

The provision of therapeutic services for children

If these are the theoretical perspectives that inform therapeutic services and if these services are indeed facing particularly challenging circumstances, it is necessary to examine their present structures and methods of functioning before subsequent chapters raise in more detail the issues that will impinge upon the structures.

There is no single unitary service staffed by one specific professional group. Instead there are multi-professional teams, such as child guidance, and child and adolescent therapy services, that exist to assess problems and provide interventions of a therapeutic nature, and there is the work undertaken by individual professionals such as teachers, social workers and school nurses where this work is only a part, and perhaps a relatively minor part, of their overall duties. The three major public sector domains – Health, Education, and Social Services – account for the bulk of the work. But the National Society for the Prevention of Cruelty to Children (NSPCC), charitable concerns such as Banardos and National Children's Home (NCH), specialist units in university departments, profit-making establishments and individuals in private practice also make a significant contribution. This section will attempt to provide a brief overview of the scope of the field by asking which young people become involved with which agencies, by what means and with what intended purposes. Local policies and terminology vary somewhat but what is described is an attempt to capture general threads that run through provision.

There is little doubt, however, that the legislation of the early 1990s concerning health, education authorities and social services departments will lead to significant changes in many of their structures.

Health authorities

Therapeutic interventions within the Health Service are available from community child health services, hospital paediatric teams – often involving clinical psychologists – and child and adolescent psychiatry services. Less widespread is the provision of in-patient psychiatry units for young people.

Community child health services cover two main areas of activity: a pre-school remit and school health services. Within the pre-school service, personnel such as general practitioners, health visitors and community medical officers are involved in health surveillance, that is, the various health checks, screening, follow-up and individual casework. At a second tier, community paediatricians and community medical officers provide a service into which the first group may refer children for more detailed assessment and management. Referral in to this service may also be made by parents, social workers, nursery teachers and others.

Clearly, a broad range of children's difficulties are identified at these levels. In addition to physical illnesses, developmental disorders and delay, a number of children displaying behavioural and emotional difficulties are identified. Therapeutic interventions at this level may consist of parent counselling and the giving of advice on child management. Depending on the particular presenting problems, this may be the sole intervention or it may be in conjunction with such provision as speech therapy, physiotherapy or occupational therapy. Where behavioural or emotional difficulties appear to be particularly severe, a third tier which includes child psychiatrists and child psychotherapists may be referred to for specialist assessment and/or treatment. Although the degree of distress being displayed by young children or their caretakers will obviously guide the practice of referral, in many ways the criteria for determining the most appropriate tier for interventions aimed solely at emotional and behavioural difficulties are the most relative and dependent upon the skills and interests of the personnel within any particular team.

The school health service is an on-site provision located within health clinics and schools. It is staffed by community paediatricians, community medical officers and school nurses. A wide range of agencies and individuals refer into this service, which offers a co-ordinating role, some treatment and referral onwards. Within the diverse set of problems that this service deals with, children with emotional and behavioural difficulties may be treated by, for example, counselling provided by a school nurse or referred on to personnel and agencies such as psychiatrists, child psychotherapists, psychologists and social workers. Again, there is not a nationally agreed and explicit set of criteria by which these referral routes are chosen. Ultimate destinations tend to be influenced by local factors such as the particular interests and skills of team members and the known availability of other local experts.

Child guidance/child and family therapy/child and adolescent therapy services/psychiatric units

These services were once the linchpin of provision; their changing fortunes have been documented by Howarth in Chapter 10. Unfortunately patterns of provision vary widely here as well. The multi-disciplinary team can consist of any combination of the core professions: child adolescent psychiatrists, educational psychologists, clinical psychologists, child psychotherapists, psychiatric social workers, psychiatric nurses, educational therapists, occupational therapists and specialist teachers. For some services schools provide a major focus of activity, in others, community based referrals dominate with only a small role for school support work.

Examining the referrals to a small child psychiatry clinic over a one-year period, Thomas and Hardwick (1989) found that 63 per cent of referrals identified a single behaviour disorder (such as stealing, phobias and sleep disturbance) and 37 per cent were for multiple behaviour problems where no single disorder could be identified as the most significant. In terms of referring agencies, by far the biggest group was that of general practitioners who accounted for 64 per cent and, of the total referrals for the year under examination, 88 per cent were treated by means of family therapy whereas the remaining 12 per cent received individual psychotherapy with a child psychotherapist.

The pattern in other clinics can be quite different.

Local education authorities

Therapeutic work in local education authority (LEA) provision may be divided into four broad areas: first, in those special schools that cater specifically for children with emotional and behavioural difficulties, second, in the work of educational psychologists and peripatetic teachers who support schools, especially mainstream schools, third, in the formal and informal pastoral work carried out within schools, and fourth, in certain curriculum areas within mainstream schools.

Special placements

Special schools for 'maladjusted pupils' form a major part of the existing provision. They vary widely in their conceptual base and are also strongly represented in the private sector. Scherer explores some of the history in this area in Chapter 9.

Theoretical orientations vary greatly. There can be some examples of strong adherence to one approach, for example behavioural at Chelfham Mill school in Devon, or psychodynamic at the Mulberry Bush Therapeutic Community in Oxfordshire. Many claim to be eclectic employing some behavioural principles, perhaps within a form of token economy system together with a non-directive counselling approach.

Access to these schools, provided either locally or by the private sector, is by means of a Statement of Special Educational Need which local authorities are mandated by the Education Act 1981 to draw up under certain conditions. The notion of assessment based on the child's need rather than category of handicap was very much seen as a key advance on previous thinking. Children's needs were seen as more complex than could be described by a label such as 'maladjusted'. Yet in practice the tension existed between constructing statements which defined the needs irrespective of the provision available and those which defined needs in order to access available provision. Given that provision remained primarily categorical, statements were seen by many as ineffective or at worst a mechanism of social control (see Lane 1990 and Ford et al. 1982 for a discussion of this).

The Warnock Report as long ago as 1978 proposed the conceptual shift embodied in a terminology that moved away from 'maladjusted children' and towards 'children with emotional and behaviour difficulties'. It remains to be seen whether this will lead to a real shift in the attitudes and policy decisions that affect these children and young people or whether it will be a case of today's acceptable euphemism again becoming tomorrow's pejorative label. The arguments surrounding the introduction of the Children Act 1989 with its emphasis of 'children's needs', and the evidence from the Fish Report (1985) perhaps indicate how little has changed. Fish found in one large authority that separatist provision still represented a dominant mode in spite of the integrationist image that pervaded the 1970s and 1980s. The Children Act 1989, by placing the emphasis of the need in the child, pays, perhaps, only lip-service to the impact of environments.

Professional support to mainstream schools

Educational psychologists have in many LEAs traditionally performed a gatekeeping role to special educational establishments, a role that many within the profession have not always seen to be the most useful contribution that psychologists can make (Miller and Burden 1992). Since the Education Act 1981 an increasing amount of work has focused upon making recommendations to LEAs about ways in which children with special needs may be supported within mainstream schools. In some authorities this role also involves a relatively recent professional group, behavioural support teachers (see Gray and Noakes, Chapter 11). Thus yet another group of professionals are added to the range that might confront a child or parent seeking therapeutic help. In the work of these two groups, behavioural and counselling perspectives may again be found with some practitioners also showing some commitment to methods deriving from family therapy and others becoming involved in the wider area of organizational development (Schmuck et al. 1980).

In practice, even allowing for a notional commitment to 'statements', access to these services comes less through formal referral systems and more as a result of negotiations about priorities with school staff on regular visits to their establishments. Underlying this shift in working patterns is the important recognition that work initiated in this way, rather than by some referral letter mechanism, makes clear the 'ownership' of problem behaviour in schools. The theoretical shift underlying this change in practice is away from what was once an automatic assumption of individual pathology and towards a more social interactionist view of the creation of deviance within institutions (Hargreaves et al. 1975). Within this broad perspective, the therapeutic intervention may be delivered totally or partially by school teachers with the support of therapists working with outside agencies.

Pastoral care in schools

Since the mid-1960s there has been an enormous growth in systems for pastoral care within the secondary sector of education. These vary both in their level of resourcing within individual schools and in the degree to which staff have received additional specific training for posts which include a pastoral care remit. Primary schools, especially those which identify most closely with a 'child-centred' philosophy, have typically seen the pastoral role as residing with the classroom teacher, perhaps with back-up from the headteacher and, more latterly in some local authorities and schools, with community or home–school liaison teachers.

At secondary level, this function is often fulfilled by means of form tutors, teachers who have a regular contact with a class group, sometimes following the same group through their whole school career. These tutors will take an overall responsibility for general welfare of the group and may also deliver part of a school's personal and social education curriculum. They may also undertake counselling with individual pupils.

Senior pastoral care staff, as well as carrying out managerial and organizational duties, often provide a more extended counselling role with those pupils judged by their teacher colleagues to have particularly serious or demanding difficulties. The particular forms of counselling most favoured by staff carrying out these roles, if they have received training in this area, derive fairly directly from Carl Roger's work.

A few pioneering local authorities have made budgets available for school counsellors who are both trained and are members of staff who carry out no teaching or other role in the school, thus going some way to avoiding the lack of independence perceived by pupils when a staff member has to be responsible both for applying a school's disciplinary procedures at the same time as purporting to offer confidential counselling to some pupils.

Yet other authorities have gone much further and have established specialist services within schools able to provide ongoing in depth work with pupils. The more effective of these (for example the work of Lister, featured in a BBC TV documentary ('Bullies', *40 Minutes*, 30 November 1989), and also in Lane 1990) provide a central focus for a variety of professionals working together to deal with individual and system change. The least effective act as receptacles for the schools' problems.

Curriculum aspects

Many schools and local authorities have been extensively involved in the development of personal and social education (PSE) curricula. These vary enormously in content and degree of detail but most share a concern with issues such as social skills, education for parenthood, personal health and vocational matters. Of most interest to the discussion of therapy for young people, are the aspects that deal with such issues as resolving conflicts, acting assertively but not aggressively, and developing a sensitivity to the difficulties of others and an empathy for their positions. Although school work that examines such issues may lack the resourcing, in terms of staff expertise, time and group size, to deal with pupils with extreme difficulties, there would appear to be major benefits from an approach aimed at all pupils in its potential as a preventive measure and in its avoidance of the possibly stigmatizing effects of external or internal referral.

A major concern for educators involved in these matters is presented by the stipulation that the National Curriculum must account for most of the time available in schools, thus squeezing the remaining amount of time that must be shared between PSE, which is not mandatory, and other demands on resourcing.

Social Services Departments

Access to Social Services provision comes via referral to an Area Social Services Office, and on-site community based establishments. Into these offices are received referrals from a wide range of sources, from members of community, child health services, schools, court liaison officers, Childline, local politicians, from children and families themselves and from anonymous sources.

The typical procedure following a referral is for workers to collect as much initial information as possible in order to decide whether involvement from Social Services is appropriate. This information would then be considered by a group whose task it is to decide upon the degree of intervention necessary. For children and young people at risk of, or suffering abuse, national and local child protection procedures are instigated. For other 'complex' cases, attempts are made to put together 'support packages', whereas on more 'routine' cases the best form of intervention within existing resources is worked out in conjunction with families.

Specialist personnel

Social Services Departments possess a range of provision, in the form of personnel and establishments, from which therapeutic interventions may be available. For instance, some social workers are designated to work specifically in child protection cases. These 'child protection officers' have much reduced caseloads to enable them to work co-operatively with NSPCC staff. Similarly, other specialist workers are constituted into teams, juvenile justice teams, and their task is to set up alternative programmes to custody for young offenders. In these circumstances, therapeutic involvement may be offered in conjunction with other interventions such as school support, encouraging interests and hobbies, work experience and voluntary activities.

Specialist establishments

In addition to specialist input from social workers, placements in a number of establishments is possible. Social Services nurseries offer placement priority to pre-schoolers with a parent or parents under stress. Day care workers from these nurseries are also available to carry out family work in some circumstances. Residential placements, in children's homes or family centres, allow personnel, under the Family Support Scheme, to work intensively with young people or families for up to twenty-eight days or longer in cases of voluntary care.

A major thrust of the Children Act 1989 is to increase the responsibility for parents and professionals to act in partnership in all these aspects of assessment and provision made within Social Services Departments.

The complexity of services provided by social workers is summed up in the phrase 'from the cradle to the grave'. The balance between generic and specialist roles in social work has been a matter of debate prior to and since the major reforms of the 1970s. For some social workers specialization in therapeutic work has provided an important area of activity. Even within generic teams important work may be undertaken of a therapeutic nature. There is more than a little truth in the complaint that when highly paid specialists (psychiatrists, psychologists and psychotherapists) cannot cope the matter is referred back for a generic social worker to pick up the pieces.

The complexity of the services available and the equally varied methods of referral makes it difficult to provide a clear picture so that clients and professionals can understand the system and find their way around it. In the authority for which one of the authors worked, there was an ongoing process of revision of the directory of services. The need for an ongoing process was because services which existed had been found to have been omitted. Those that no longer existed were found to be included. Personnel changes ensured that contact names were inaccurate, and procedural shifts meant that the method for gaining access to a service would vary over time. There was no attempt in the directory to deal with the problem that personnel changes could result in an entirely different form of service being offered under the same name. The idea that if you referred a child for help to a service of a designated title, then you had an accurate idea of the help likely to be offered, was idealistic in the extreme.

A method for classifying therapeutic services

That services calling themselves the same thing, and even therapists professing the same orientation, in reality provide different services has bedevilled the whole enterprise of deciding what works.

It is perhaps possible to classify services in terms of the procedure by which someone becomes a client and by the focus of the intervention; these are placement, referral, assessment, individual, systems and ecological approaches. The classification has implications in terms of the power relationships involved. The models are now described in detail.

Placement In placement models a professional agent is able to obtain access directly to a service provision without recourse to a formal assessment process. Placement-led services became very popular in the 1970s as pressure from schools and courts led to a demand for quick entry procedures to a provision to deal with an immediate crisis. Any assessment that took place was a post hoc process. These models were heavily criticized by Inspectors (HMI) and community groups, since they seemed to be predominately provided for Black students. Similar complaints emerged in the USA. The criteria by which 'clients' were placed or released were vague, and the basis on which interventions were designed related primarily to a notional view of what that client group in total needed. The power in the relationship was decidedly one sided. Placement was seen as based on a social control model of power.

Referral In referral models access to services operated through a gatekeeper. The gatekeeper used professional knowledge to determine when, where, how and if a service was to be provided. The client, as someone without that expertise, could not determine the referral, although could to a limited extent agree with or reject any offers made. Assessment played a varied role in referral since it might take place following an elaborate process or as a result of a chat between professionals. But a report through the auspices of a gatekeeper was necessary before access could be gained to a service. Power was shared between professionals in the process. Some of those professionals would share the power of the decision-making process with clients, but that was a gesture on their part rather than a right. Referral was seen as based on a professional or 'expert knowledge' model of power.

Assessment Assessment models were present in the referral model but the movement towards client rights which emerged in the 1970s in the USA and 1980s in Britain changed the emphasis. Clients were now to be seen as partners in an assessment process which was intended to identify needs and determine the appropriate intervention in the least restrictive environment in which it could be provided. Thus community provision was preferred to residential. Clients were to have access to reports, and could offer reports of their own to the assessment process. Although both the statements in Britain and individualized plans in the USA were intended to equalize the power relationships, community groups complained that professionals subverted the process back to a referral system (ILEA 1985). 'What is the point of saying anything when you will do what you want anyway?' In principle assessment systems were intended as a social exchange (or partnership) model of power.

Individual The client once placed was the focus of the intervention. The theoretical model used might be concerned with the child's 'inner world', or with the 'modification' of behaviour, but it was the child who had to change. Placement was the power base to the models since they were primarily concerned with individual change, although some also acted to change the child's family, but either way the pathology was theirs.

Systems   Systems-based interventions were concerned with dysfunctional groupings. These might be family units, and primarily were so, but could be peer groups, or other natural systems. The emphasis was on helping such groupings to be less dysfunctional. Systems methods were primarily referral based, although some assessment-based work was undertaken (increasingly so in recent years). However, the nature of some systems-based work depended on the therapist's expert knowledge which was not shared with the client. The client would be offered prescriptions for change. Some of those prescriptions (for example paradoxical methods) deliberately mislead the client into acting against the stated wish of the therapist, whereas the real intention was to get the client to act in opposition to the prescription.

Ecological   In ecological system-based approaches, the intervention might take place with an individual or a whole organization. The models used tend to be based on organizational systems models, although some family system work has been adapted to this frame. Behaviourally based systems models have also featured in ecologically oriented approaches. Ecological approaches are rare in practice but are becoming more influential. Ecological models are virtually always assessment based.

Comparing the effectiveness of different interventions

A brief review of a sample of some British evaluative studies gives a flavour of the wide range of clinical problems currently being addressed and some indication of what works. It is split into two sections. The first section looks at broadly based studies involving either a range of interventions, or interventions with complex problems. The second section looks at specific problems or single model interventions.

Multiple and complex interventions

The survey starts with an influential study widely regarded as a model of comprehensiveness. Few studies can match it.

A large and most ambitious treatment study was carried out by Kolvin et al. (1981) to compare the effectiveness of different treatment approaches with two age groups of problem children in ordinary day schools. Approximately 4,300 children in twelve schools were screened using several instruments to identify those showing neurotic, antisocial, academic and/or peer relationship difficulties. The 270 juniors (7–8 year olds) who scored above cut-off points were regarded as at risk for psychiatric disturbance and learning difficulties and the 322 seniors (11–12 year olds) were identified as definitely 'maladjusted'. These children were randomly assigned by school class to one of three treatment conditions or a no-contact control group. All treatments were represented in all schools. Treatments were selected to represent behavioural and psychodynamic orientations, direct and indirect therapist contact with children, and the use of therapists of different training. All interventions were short term, of about ten weeks' duration. The psychodynamic approach focused on thoughts and feelings in Rogerian group non-directive play therapy sessions with the juniors or non-directive group psychotherapy discussions with the seniors. The second approach differed for juniors and seniors. The juniors received nurture group work in which teacher-aides were trained to provide a healthy mother–child interaction characterized by warmth, interest and acceptance and to be firm where necessary. Behavioural learning principles were incorporated to help children learn new skills and overcome problem behaviour. With seniors, teachers were taught behavioural principles of management to apply to classroom problems. In the third approach, parent counselling and teacher consultation, specially trained social workers consulted with teachers over the management of particular children and provided short-term casework support to families dealing with a range of social and financial problems as well as child issues. Children were reassessed at the end of treatment and followed-up eighteen months later (three years from baseline) by clinicians who did not know their treatment condition.

The results are complex but important. First, the answer to the basic question of whether therapy in school settings is better than no therapy is yes; most interventions were more effective than none on at least some measures. However, treatments differed in effectiveness generally as well as on different measures and the two post-interventions assessment points. The more direct interventions were generally more effective (nurture work and play group for juniors; group therapy and behaviour modification with seniors) than others with emotional and behavioural problems, but no effects were found on attainments. The pattern of results differed over time: first, some treatment effects were immediate on some measures but washed out over time; second, other differences between groups were greater at follow-up than immediately after treatment; and finally, with some treatments and measures, improvements became apparent only eighteen months after treatment. The effect of child characteristics, sex and nature of problems (neurotic or antisocial) on outcome were examined as well as some therapist characteristics. This well-designed and complex study highlights many of the issues involved in interpreting evaluation studies. Because it is methodologically sound and clearly presented, the issues that require further study are evident.

Another important but much less comprehensive school-based study focused on a more circumscribed education problem, reading, comparing the relative efficacy of an experimental intervention, with a more conventional intervention and no treatment controls (Tizard et al. 1982). Children were randomly allocated to one of three conditions: the first group's parents were asked to listen to their child from books sent home daily from school, the second group received tuition from a remedial teacher at school and the third group had no extra help. The group whose parents listened to them read made the greatest gains and were reading at an age-appropriate level. Although the study did not explore individual differences or the process of what parents did in any detail, it did show that a simple strategy could make a major difference to the attainments of a high-risk group.

Most intervention studies, however, have examined effects from one theoretical perspective (a more traditional approach) and have tended to be descriptive (Topping 1983). The development and use of behavioural approaches for teachers in a variety of school settings has proved a popular area for intervention (Whedall 1987). Some of the projects have included an attempt at evaluation. The teacher–child interaction project is one example of this (Berger et al. 1987). It was designed to enable teachers to learn behavioural principles to implement with problem children in their own classes. The intervention comprised course work and specific guidance in implementing these skills with a problematic child in their class. Twenty volunteer teachers were randomly assigned to two groups: one group received training immediately; the other group was a no-intervention waiting list control group for one term and then received training.

The effectiveness of the intervention was evaluated by direct observation of teachers and of both selected difficult children and other randomly chosen children in their classes, teacher feedback and case study reports. Teachers were enthusiastic about the project and there were several successful individual interventions. The observational measures showed small improvements due to training over and above the gains made by the control group. Sleeper effects were observed in the first group to receive training in that behavioural improvements continued after the training ceased. This project also raises methodological and substantive issues that require further investigation.

Child psychotherapists have found it particularly difficult to devise evaluation studies which provide acceptable ways of measuring the improvement (or lack of improvement) of their patients over time. This has often been a bone of contention with colleagues from other theoretical persuasions. The profession is now beginning to respond to these justifiable criticisms and the first evaluative studies are starting to emerge. A study of the efficacy of psychoanalytic psychotherapy with thirty children who were adopted or in care, has recently been published (Lush et al. 1991). These children were mostly in once-weekly therapy with the majority having nine months' to one year's treatment. Treatment often stopped at an unsatisfactory point as far as the therapist was concerned, frequently for reasons external to issues which pertained to the treatment. These children were followed up during the two years after they ended therapy. On a scale from one to five, which was rated 'blind' by a psychotherapist external to the treatment programme, twenty-five of the children showed at least some improvement during the follow-up and most children showed considerable improvement. As these children provide such great difficulties in the therapy situation and doubts are often expressed about the wisdom of even attempting psychotherapy with them, this is important research.

Sometimes evaluative research has gone beyond the 'single theory' model and compared the relative efficacy of existing educational provision based on different philosophies for children with special needs. For example, autistic children attending schools with an emphasis on education and behavioural management made greater gains in one study than those attending school with a less structured psychotherapeutic approach (Bartak and Rutter 1973; Bartak 1978). Although such research lacks the control of ensuring no biases in the placement of children, or the fidelity of interventions, it provides some evidence on relative efficacy for the children in each setting and clarifies issues for further investigation.

A further complex but important task is that of evaluating the efficacy of specialist services within the education system for children who present with very serious difficulties in the classroom. The work of Islington Education Guidance Centre (Lane 1975) raises many of the issues in evaluating a coherent but complex approach to intervention, especially with the very small highly visible and disruptive group of children whom teachers find impossible in class and who have remained untouched by the usual special treatments (Lane 1978; 1990). Such children were defined as having difficulties of at least two years' standing and to have failed to respond to specialist interventions of at least one year's duration. Careful examination of the records showed that such children had the same number of problems as other difficult children but differed in being seriously non-compliant and hostile on the Bristol Social Adjustment Guide. They also experienced a wide range of serious adverse life events and psychosocial stresses. Interventions with these children were based on a model of negotiated change requiring the participation of all the people involved throughout from the problem definition stage to termination of intervention. The child was included throughout and had open access to records. A school-focused analysis of the problem from the perspective of each participant began the problem-solving approach of specifying and defining the problems. This led to explanations of the problems and then to agreed strategies for change. These usually complex strategies comprised specific goals and techniques drawn from a wide range of theoretical approaches, though mainly from the broad range of cognitive-behavioural approaches.

These contracted programmes of intervention were applied in classrooms and sometimes in special sessions at the Education Guidance Centre when the child needed to learn special new skills, such as social skills or anger control. Evaluation of outcome raised important questions about appropriate measures of success and of suitable contrast or alternative interventions to test the comparative efficacy of this approach. Despite these difficulties, there is reasonable evidence that this strategy of intervention was effective. First, 95 per cent of children were regarded as sufficiently improved after treatment by their schools. Second, compared with an alternative approach with comparable impossible children on measures such as rate of referral to other services, this group fared better; 25 per cent were referred compared with 66 per cent of the contrast approach. Third, a further study of convictions over a ten-year period showed a much lower rate of convictions for this approach compared with controls involved in various other programmes. Finally, in order to understand the processes and ingredients of successful outcome, the records of fifty children who responded to therapy were compared with a group of fifty others who had similar problems on the Bristol Social Adjustment Guide (BSAG) initially but did not respond to treatment. No strong patterns emerged from the factor analyses except for the common pattern of behaviour predicting subsequent behaviour and the events that subsequently impinged on the children were seen as critical. The latter finding highlights the central role of key-workers and teachers as facilitators of positive events and experiences in therapeutic interventions in school settings.

Projects in other service settings have also received increasing attention in the literature as interest has increased in children referred for intervention with behaviour problems. School non-attendance is one area that has received considerable attention but reports of the treatment of school refusal and truancy have been mainly single case studies or descriptive (Hersov and Berg 1980; Berg 1985; Burke and Silverman 1987). In one larger-scale study, a series of consecutive referrals of school refusers in a particular geographic area were successfully treated by an educational psychologist using a behavioural intervention based on a careful functional analysis and co-ordinating the efforts of the child, family and school (Blagg 1977; Blagg and Yule 1984). Although it was not possible to compare this approach with others by prospectively assigning children randomly to different treatments, comparisons with similar children treated in neighbouring areas by either in-patient hospitalization or home tuition, showed the behaviourally treated group to be far more successful at attending school a year later.

In a study on the management of persistent truants appearing before magistrates, children were randomly assigned to either an adjournment procedure or the more usual supervision order (Berg et al. 1978). The adjournment procedure was more effective in returning more children to school and keeping them out of trouble. A few adjournments two-to-four weeks apart were usually sufficient to restore attendance. Child characteristics played a part too; good responders to the adjournment procedure were less psychiatrically disturbed or conduct disordered than those who responded poorly (Berg 1985).

The studies above have indicated the increasing emphasis given to the context in which the problem occurs. Change within the system, not just in the individual, is a frequent outcome in such studies.

This emphasis has also been paralleled by concern not only with the family as a system in family therapy studies but also with the role of parents as partners in the therapeutic endeavour.

There are now several examples of research on helping children indirectly by working with parents with problems as diverse and widespread as conduct disorder and incontinence (Herbert and Iwaniec 1981), problem children (Scott and Stradling 1987), non-accidental injury of their children (Smith and Rachman 1984; Nichol et al. 1988), dealing with the problem behaviour and fostering development of their autistic children (Howlin and Rutter 1987) or mentally handicapped children (Callias and Carr 1975; Callias 1987), or specific problems such as the sleep difficulties in young children (Clements and Hand 1985; Richman et al. 1985; Scott and Richards 1990), and parental partnership for learning problems (Widlake 1992). These studies illustrate how varying research strategies have been used in different contexts.

In a controlled investigation of the role of individual behavioural parent training at home for parents who were on the at risk register for abusing their children (Smith and Rachman 1984), intervention was offered to all families becoming known to one social services office in addition to the social worker's customary role. These families were compared with families referred to a neighbouring area for the customary intervention. This study highlighted the difficulties of conducting rigorous research, including independent assessments, with needy but often chaotic and suspicious families where the problem of gaining and maintaining co-operation throughout the assessments and interventions are paramount. Nevertheless, the study was able to show diverse outcomes for the small number of co-operative families in both groups, and to estimate how far the special focus on improving parenting played a part. It also highlighted key ethical and methodological issues for systematic comparative intervention research when children's safety is at risk (Smith et al. 1984; Dunn Smith 1989).

In a home-base intervention study for autistic children, a combination of behavioural and counselling approaches were used in individually designed interventions to help sixteen families, mainly mothers, with their more able (IQ over 60) autistic sons. The main emphasis was on advice on management to reduce the behavioural problems and to foster language and other aspects of their development but included advice and support over wider practical and emotional needs of the family (Howlin and Rutter 1987). The same therapist visited these families at home over an eighteen-month period. Visits were made at least once a week for two to three hours for the first six months, reducing to two or three a month over the following six months and tapering off to monthly by eighteen months. The intervention was evaluated, first, by single case methodology to monitor the individual interventions, and second, by comparing this group with a control group of similar families, who received less intensive treatment, on a number of observational and interview measures of the child's development and problems and of parental satisfaction with treatment. Individual programmes were effective in their aims. Group comparisons showed that the intensively treated group had fewer intrusive problem and rituals and improved social responsiveness. The language of the treated group was better too in that fewer boys were mute, and those who spoke used their language more meaningfully and socially. However, there were no differences on measures of general development and, years later, the boys were in similar placements. Despite the demands on them, parents felt more satisfied with most aspects of their treatment and contact with services.

Behavioural approaches have played a prominent role in advising parents of mentally handicapped children on fostering development and to ameliorate problems (Callias and Carr 1975; Callias 1987). Evaluation has been mainly of single cases. Some evaluation of group parent training has been attempted by means of assessing the success of projects carried out by parents as well as some comparison with a waiting list control group (see Callias 1987). Most parents were enthusiastic and many were successful with their projects.

An example of an attempt to evaluate an ongoing service is the retrospective analysis of all the behavioural interventions carried out by parents advised by psychologists as part of a broad-based community service (Callias and Carr 1975). Despite the limitations of analysing less systematic data than would be available in a prospective study, this study provided useful information about the nature of problems causing concern to families and the extent of desired change achieved. The project also began to identify characteristics of the child and family as well as of the intervention that seemed to be associated with improvements, clarifying issues that could be tackled more systematically in a prospective study.

While parent training and partnership work has expanded, it has also attracted a research base to support it. Family therapies have seen a similar dramatic rise in provision, but there are a few systematic studies of family therapy. To evaluate the effects of a short-term intervention with families where one parent had died on longer-term outcome of bereavement, families were randomly assigned to treatment of about six sessions of family work within three to five months of the bereavement, or to no contact (Black and Urbanowitz 1987). Families were seen together at home with the aim of promoting mourning and increasing the children's ability to understand and deal more adaptively with their loss. Of the forty-five families offered treatment, thirty-three completed the first interview but only twenty-two completed the four to six sessions of intervention. They were compared with twenty-four to thirty-four controls one year and again two years later when the control group had diminished to eighteen. The treated group were coping better at one year and also at two years although group differences had diminished, not only because the control group had improved too, but also because the most distressed control group families at one year had dropped out by two years.

The effectiveness of family therapy for anorexia nervosa and bulimia was examined in a consecutive series of eighty adolescents and young adults. After their weight had been restored to normal on a specialized in-patient unit, they were randomly assigned to family therapy or supportive individual therapy ensuring that the groups were stratified on the basis of age and chronicity of illness (Russell et al. 1987; Dare et al. 1990). Family therapy was significantly more effective with the subsample of younger adolescents with shorter duration of illness. Older subjects and those with longer standing difficulties did less well, though there was a tendency for older subjects to do better with individual therapy than family therapy.

The various studies above do illustrate the breadth of current work and areas of effective work. The diversity in the results also points to the need for a more informed approach to matching need with intervention.

Single and specific interventions

In spite of the increased use of multiple and complex interventions in recent years, treatment studies which have focused on more traditional, specific and discrete problems such as sleep difficulties have continued to flourish.

A study of behavioural treatment of children's severe night-time problems resulted in improvement in 77 per cent for a series of thirty-five young children whose parents attended a special clinic (Richman et al. 1985). This study demonstrates good outcome for those who took up treatment with most failures occurring in families who terminated before completion. As the authors indicate, the findings cannot be generalized to the general population of children with sleep problems as only half the referred families came; the remaining families were equally divided into those who never came, improved without formal intervention, failed to attend after assessment, or sought other treatment. (For a psychoanalytic approach see Daws 1989).

In a more controlled study comparing interventions for sleep difficulties in ninety infants under 18 months of age, families were randomly allocated to one of three conditions, a written advice booklet, with support visits from health visitors, the booklet on its own, or no intervention (Scott and Richards 1990). In addition, comparisons were made with a non-waking group given specific guidance; they emphasized that there were numerous ways of coping with the problem and generally described them. At the end of the study there was an overall decline in sleep problems but no significant differences were found between the three problem groups of infants who, as a group, still had more sleeping difficulties than the control group of good sleepers. Distressed mothers felt supported by the visits.

In contrast, in an Australian study, differential treatment effects were found in a similar control trial. Random assignment of forty-five families of 9-month to 5-year-old children with night-waking and sleep disruption was undertaken. The interventions were a written guide giving clear behavioural management together with an interview and telephone contact, the guide on its own, or waiting list control for four weeks (Seymour et al. 1989). The guide with contact group did best although both treated groups improved. Treatment gains were maintained at longer-term follow-up. (Follow-up comparison data are available for the intensive treatment condition only, since the main intervention was subsequently offered to the other groups whose problems persisted).

Taken together these studies suggest that more focused and specific advice on how to deal with sleep difficulties are more likely to result in improvement for families who are able to implement the approach. General advice and contact are experienced as supportive by parents but is not more effective than control conditions for improving the child's problems.

Another example of a specific focused intervention was the test of the hypothesis that profoundly handicapped children who stimulated and injured themselves would do so less if they were able to engage in more constructive simple play (Murphy et al. 1985; 1986). Although they did not learn to play constructively on their own, rates of self-stimulation were lower while children were being taught to play, and when they were able to activate toys to make interesting tactile, auditory or visual responses, by simple actions.

Specific focused studies have also been used with enuretic children (Shaffer 1985). In recent years the 'bell and pad' method has become a standard treatment of choice, but not all children are treated effectively by the method. More recently, studies of children attending special clinics have investigated child and family factors associated with poor outcome (Dische et al. 1983) and reasons for failure or drop-out from treatment (Fielding 1985). Treatment failures are associated with maternal anxiety, disturbed home background, failure to wake to the alarm (Dische et al. 1983) and frequency and urgency of needing to empty the bladder (Fielding 1985), whereas drop-out was related to greater parental intolerance of wetting (Fielding 1985).

The treatment of hyperactive boys has included medication and diet in addition to psychological therapies. In a controlled double-blind study to clarify the contribution of medication to the treatment of psychological difficulties, there was a series of consecutive clinic referrals of hyperactive and/or conduct disordered boys (Taylor et al. 1987). Thirty-eight of sixty-four families accepting assessment agreed to participate in the trial (ninety refused assessment, and five out of the sixty-four were unsuitable). Each boy acted as his own control and was put on methylphenidate titrate to therapeutic levels and placebo in random order. Treatment was evaluated on a range of interview, questionnaire and laboratory measures which were administered before treatment, and at the end of each condition. Overall, hyperactive boys improved on medication but conduct disordered boys did not; more change was detected on broader measures than on laboratory tasks. There were considerable individual differences in responsiveness. Long-term effects of medication were not examined.

The role of food additives and diet in hyperactivity has been difficult to establish (Taylor 1986b). A controlled trial of the effects of an exclusion diet on hyeractivity indicated that some of a series of highly selected children improved when incriminating foodstuffs were removed from their diet (Eggar et al. 1985). The study design was a sequential one using a standard order of procedures but testing the particular foodstuffs implicated for each child. The child began on a very restrictive diet. If behaviour improved, putative allergens were added one at a time. When harmful substances were identified, they were subjected to placebo-controlled blind trial. This phase showed increases in disruptive behaviour to be greater with these foodstuffs than placebo for some children.

Single case study was for many years the mainstay of child therapy research. The use of 'single case' studies remains of value. A number of single case studies have usefully demonstrated and evaluated new approaches to problems. These include the use of a complex set of strategies for treating the problems of a hyperactive boy (Hogg et al. 1986); highlighting the difficulties of treating obsessive-compulsive adolescents who are also conduct disordered (Bolton and Turner 1984); demonstrating how to take account of family difficulties in the behavioural treatment of a young boy's faecal retention (Phillips and Smith 1986), a way of combining in-patient and parent work (Holbrook 1978) and treating peer relationship difficulties of clinically referred children in small groups (Callias et al. 1987).

New approaches developed in response to particular problems within the single case study format can be evaluated further in larger studies in different settings with children who show similar difficulties. This was the approach adopted for children showing peer problems in an infant school setting (Frosh and Callias 1980).

These selected examples of evaluative research demonstrate the variety of problems and approaches that have been studied on larger samples of children and families as well as individual cases. The main thrust of studies has been to show that a new approach works in general or with particular groups of psychological problems.

An important feature of the group studies is that many of them have been carried out with children whose problems were serious enough to warrant clinic referral. Studies conducted in school settings were also with children whose problems fell in the serious range on screening measures. While elegance of experimental design still bears an inverse relation to the severity of problem (Ross 1981), clinical studies are becoming methodologically more sophisticated, and, equally importantly, address the issues that are pertinent to the client groups. A wider range of research designs are represented to control for the passage of time or to compare the intervention of interest with other approaches. Comparisons are often made with existing service provision. Such comparisons have some limitations as the comparison is not between a new or more intensive approach and others implemented equally, but include the differences inherent in research and clinical contexts. These differences include the new approach being a special project implemented with the enthusiasm, resources, uniformity and rigour of researching something new and the comparison being ongoing services which are vulnerable to variation, day-to-day pressure, competing demands and the need to spread limited resources to offer some service to many families rather than to few (Callias and Carr 1975). On the other hand, stark differences between the effectiveness of new and old, as in the case of school refusal (Blagg and Yule 1984) must lead on to further research to elucidate the factors involved and to influence practice. It may be that it is possible to define a first choice of treatment, with back-up of alternative services for failures and for those children for whom school refusal is one aspect of more complex problems.

Child and adolescent therapy: practice, settings, issues and challenge

Clearly, the impact of traditional concerns with theoretical origins and evaluation of interventions based on defined problems will continue. There are, however, a number of important areas which have received much less attention yet which are now central to the actual practice of child and adolescent therapy.

Therapy for children and adolescents now addresses the very broad range of problems indicated in this introduction. Emotional and behavioural problems still represent about 90 per cent of the activity of therapists, but the contexts in which that activity is practised extend well beyond the clinical setting. That extension was inevitable if more than the minority of children currently receiving specialist help were to be reached. The change is not, however, a grudging acceptance of resource constraints but a positive commitment to new means of service delivery. The major development in the 1980s was the recognition that the therapist can act as a resource to the carers in daily contact with the child. Sharing skills has become a reality.

If we are working in varied contexts with widening ranges of problems and through partnership with others, then questions of quality and rights will feature more strongly in our work.

The complexity of the child–therapist relationship, recognized by earlier practitioners in the field, will still need to be addressed. We do need to learn how to manage our own pain at being with the children in their pain. But it is not just our pain that confronts us. If we are partners with other carers in a process of change, then their needs will also have to be addressed. How do we learn to work genuinely in a multi-disciplinary context? Within those partnerships the rights of the parties will need to be faced and in particular the rights of the child as client.

As Scherer (1992) pointed out, a set of recent legal judgments and legislation has established the rights of the child. Children are not incomplete adults or the property of their parents. Parents and practitioners do have a duty to protect them, but children do have an independent right to seek confidential advice and treatment.

The rights of children are now recognized as including issues of gender, race, class and disability. Concern with such rights has featured in the therapy literature for some fifty years. However, increasingly, it has been argued that there is an important difference between models of therapy that see culture as integral in all situations and those that use it as a fallback explanation for someone who is different from a dominant cultural norm. It is clear from legislation in both the USA and UK that practitioners must not discriminate, and also that positive images of different cultures should be encouraged. Yet this approach while welcomed does not address the fundamental criticisms expressed by those who feel that the therapeutic endeavour is itself intimately linked to racist ideas (Keise et al. 1992). As yet we have to address the latter point, although therapists are now actively exploring issues of discrimination and positive image.

Running through each of these themes is the central issue of accountability. We are now as professionals to be seen as accountable to our clients, the courts, the research literature, and our colleagues. The concept of total quality in child and adolescent therapy is beginning to emerge. Lane and Miller (1992) have argued that we can, in part, apply the type of quality standard guidelines that have been used in industry. Some of the questions asked in such quality reviews are worth considering as they apply to child and adolescent therapy.

Is the service designed to satisfy the client's needs?

1 Is there a method to identify client needs?
2 Is there a method to allocate services to satisfy those needs?
3 Is there a method to ensure that the service provided is the most appropriate to meet the need?

Is someone responsible for ensuring that quality service is provided?

1 Is there someone who has a specific responsibility for ensuring that the service provided does operate in accordance with the agreed standards?
2 Is there a review system to ensure that the results of internal quality audit are implemented?
3 Is there a process for handling shortcomings in service provision so that complaints by clients are appropriately managed?

Are the considerations involved in setting up the quality system explicit?

1 Is there a document that sets out the aims of the service, the values and beliefs that underpin it, and the methods used to ensure quality control?

Are the systems of communication clear?

1 Does the documentation specify the service provided to each client?
2 Does the documentation provide the basis and justification for service provision?
3 Does the documentation specify who does what to whom?

Are methods for continuing professional development included in the service?

1 Is there a system to identify the need for professional development?
2 Is there a certification system to ensure that skill levels are maintained and enhanced?
3 Is there a statistical procedure for performance management that adequately reflects the contextual demands of the client base and the organization within which they are met?

Conclusion

Our vision of child and adolescent therapy services for the future will increasingly have to address these issues. We look forward to the emerging role of the therapist. We see this as a focus on a network of partnerships that work towards prevention and intervention for child and adolescent problems. Creating those partnerships in ways that empower clients provides the challenge for therapy in the 1990s.

These are exciting and depressing times for child and adolescent therapy. We trust that some flavour of the times is expressed in this book.

References

Apter, S.J. (1982) *Troubled Children, Troubled Systems*, Oxford: Pergamon Press.
Apter, S. and Goldstein, A.P. (1986) *Youth Violence Program and Prospects*, Oxford: Pergamon Press.
Axline, V. (1947) *Play Therapy*, Boston, Mass.: Houghton Mifflin.
Barker, P. (1986) *Basic Family Therapy*, 2nd edn, Oxford: Blackwell Scientific.
Bartak, L. (1978) Educational approaches, in M. Rutter and E. Scholper (eds) *Autism: A Reappraisal of Concepts and Treatment*, New York: Plenum Press.
Bartak, L. and Rutter, M. (1973) Special educational treatment of autistic children: a comparative study; I: Design of study and characteristics of units, *Journal of Child Psychology and Psychiatry* 14: 161–79.
Berg, I. (1985) The management of truancy, *Journal of Child Psychology and Psychiatry* 26: 325–31.
Berg, I., Consterdine, M., Hullin, R., McGuire, R. and Tyrer, S. (1978) The effects of two randomly allocated court procedures on truancy, *British Journal of Criminology* 18: 232–44.
Berger, M., Yule, W. and Wigley, V. (1987) The teacher–child interaction project (TCIP): implementing behavioural programmes with troublesome individual children in the primary school, in K. Wheldall (ed.) *The Behaviourist in the Classroom*, London: Allen & Unwin.

Bion, W.R. (1962) *Learning from Experience*, London: Maresfield Reprints.

Black, D. and Urbanowitz, M.A. (1987) Family intervention with bereaved children, *Journal of Child Psychology and Psychiatry* 28: 467–76.

Blagg, N.R. (1977) A detailed strategy for the rapid treatment of school phobias, *Bulletin of the British Association of Behavioural Psychotherapy* 5: 70–5.

Blagg, N.R. and Yule, W. (1984) The behavioural treatment of school refusal: a comparative study, *Behavioural Research and Therapy* 22: 119–27.

Bolton, D. and Turner, T. (1984) Obsessive–compulsive neurosis with conduct disorder in adolescence: a report of two cases, *Journal of Child Psychology and Psychiatry* 25: 133–9.

Bowlby, J. (1988) *A Secure Base*, London: Routledge.

Burke, A.E. and Silverman, W.K. (1987) The prescriptive treatment of school refusal, *Clinical Psychological Review* 7: 353–62.

Callias, M. (1987) Teaching parents, teachers and nurses, in W. Yule and J. Carr (eds) *Behaviour Modification for People with Mental Handicaps*, 2nd edn, London: Croom Helm.

Callias, M. and Carr, J. (1975) Behaviour modification programmes in a community setting, in C.C. Kiernan and F.P. Woodford (eds) *Behaviour Modification with the Severely Retarded*, Elsevier, N. Holland: Associated Scientific Publishers.

Callias, M., Frosh, S. and Michie, S. (1987) Social skills training of young children in a clinical setting, *Behavioural Psychotherapy* 15: 367–80.

Clements, J. and Hand, D.J. (1985) Permutation statistics in single case design, *Behavioural Psychotherapy* 13: 288–99.

Dare, C. (1985) Family therapy, in M. Rutter and L. Hersov (eds) *Child and Adolescent Psychiatry: Modern Approaches*, 2nd edn, Oxford: Blackwell Scientific.

Dare, C., Eisler, I., Russell, G.F.M. and Szmukler, G.I. (1990) The clinical and theoretical impact of a controlled trial of family therapy in anorexia nervosa, *Journal of Marital and Family Therapy* 16: 39–58.

Daws, D. (1989) *Through the Night*, London: Free Association Books.

Daws, D. and Boston, B. (1977) *The Child Psychotherapist and Problems of Young People*, London: Wildwood House.

Dische, S., Yule, W., Corbett, J. and Hand, D. (1983) Childhood nocturnal enuresis: factors associated with outcome of treatment with an enuresis alarm, *Developmental and Medical Child Neurology* 25: 67–81.

Dunn Smith, J.E. (1989) Child abuse, *Newsletter for Child Psychology and Psychiatry* 2(3): 3–9.

Eggar, J., Carter, C.M., Graham, P.J., Gumley, D. and Soothill, J.F. (1985) Controlled trial of oligoantigenic treatment in the hyperactive syndrome, *Lancet* 1: 540–5.

Fielding, D. (1985) Factors associated with drop-out, relapse and failure in the conditioning treatment of nocturnal enuresis, *Behavioural Psychotherapy* 13: 174–85.

Fish Report (1985). *Equal Opportunities For All?* London: ILEA.

Ford, J., Mongon, D. and Whelan, M. (1982) *Special Education and Social Control Invisible Disasters*, London: Routledge & Kegan Paul.

Fordham, M. (1969) *Children as Individuals*, London: Hodder & Stoughton.

Freud A. (1966) *Normality and Pathology in Childhood*, London: Hogarth Press.

Freud, S. (1909) Analysis of a phobia in a five year old boy, in *Standard Edition of the Complete Works of Freud*, vol. X, London: Hogarth Press.

Frosh, S. and Callias, M. (1980) Social skills training in an infant school setting, *Behavioural Psychotherapy* 8: 69–79.

Hargreaves, D.H., Hester, S.K. and Mellor, F.J. (1975) *Deviance in Classrooms*, London: Routledge & Kegan Paul.

Herbert, M. (ed.) (1991) *Clinical Child Psychology Social Learning, Development and Behaviour*, Chichester: Wiley.

Herbert, M. and Iwaniec, D. (1981) Behavioural psychotherapy in natural home settings:

an empirical study applied to conduct disorders and incontinent children, *Behavioural Psychotherapy* 9: 55–76.

Hersov, L. and Bentovim, A. (1985) In-patient and day-hospital units, in M. Rutter and L. Hersov (eds) *Child and Adolescent Psychiatry: Modern Approaches*, 2nd edn, Oxford: Blackwell Scientific.

Hersov, L. and Berg, I. (eds) (1980) *Out of School: Modern Perspectives in Truancy and School Refusal*, Chichester: Wiley.

Hogg, C., Callias, M. and Pellegrini, D. (1986) Treatment of a seven year old hyperactive boy with educational problems, *Behavioural Psychotherapy* 14: 145–61.

Holbrook, D. (1978) A combined approach to parental coping, *British Journal Of Social Work* 8: 439–51.

Howlin, P. and Rutter, M. with Berger, M., Hemsley, R., Hersov, L. and Yule, W. (1987) *Treatment of Autistic Children*, Chichester: Wiley.

Hughes, J. (1986) *Cognitive Behaviour Therapy with Children in Schools*, Oxford: Pergamon Press.

ILEA, (1985) *Response to the Fish Report for Educational Social Work Service*, London: ILEA.

Johnson J.H., Rasbury, W.C. and Siegal, L.J. (1986) *Approaches to Child Treatment: Introduction to Theory, Research, and Practice*, Oxford: Pergamon Press.

Jones, M. (1992) Children with special educational needs compounded by severe challenging behaviour, in D.A. Lane and A. Miller (eds) *Silent Conspiracies*, Stoke-on-Trent: Trentham Books.

Judd, D. (1989) *Give Sorrow Words*, London: Free Association Books.

Jung, C.G. (1966) *The Collected Works*, ed. G. Alder, M. Fordham and H. Read, London: Routledge & Kegan Paul.

Jung, C.G. (1971) *Psychological Types*, Princeton, N.J.: Princeton University Press.

Kazdin, A.E. (1987) Treatment of antisocial behaviour in children: current status and future directions, *Psychological Bulletin* 102: 189–203.

Kazdin, A.E. (1988) *Child Psychotherapy: Developing and Identifying Effective Treatments*, Oxford: Pergamon Press.

Kazdin, A.E. (1990) Childhood depression, *Journal of Child Psychology and Psychiatry* 31: 121–60.

Keise, C., Kelly, E., King, O. and Lane, D.A. (1992) Culture and child services, in D.A. Lane and A. Miller (eds) *Silent Conspiracies*, Stoke-on-Trent: Trentham Books.

Kendall, P.C. (1984) Cognitive–behavioural self-control therapy for children, *Journal of Child Psychology and Psychiatry* 25: 173–89.

Klein, M. (1932) *The Psycho-Analysis of Children*, London: Hogarth Press.

Klein, M. (1961) *Narrative of a Child Analysis*, London: Hogarth Press.

Kolvin, I., Garside, R.F., Nichol, A.R., MacMillan, A., Wolstenholme, F. and Leitch, I.M. (1981) *Help Starts Here: The Maladjusted Child in the Ordinary School*, London: Tavistock.

Lane, D.A. (1974) *The Analysis of Complex Cases*, London: ILEA.

Lane, D.A. (1975) *The Educational Guidance Centre – A New Approach to Children's Problems*, London: Kings Fund Centres.

Lane, D.A. (1978) *Impossible Child*, vols 1 and 2, London: ILEA.

Lane, D.A. (1990) *The Impossible Child*, Stoke-on-Trent: Trentham Books.

Lane, D.A. and Miller, A. (eds) (1992) *Silent Conspiracies*, Stoke-on-Trent: Trentham Books.

Levitt, E.E. (1957) The results of psychotherapy with children: an evaluation, *Journal of Consulting Psychology* 21: 189–96.

Levitt, E.E. (1963) Psychotherapy with children: a further evaluation, *Behaviour Research and Therapy* 60: 326–9.

Lush, D., Boston, M. and Grainger, E. (1991) Evaluation of psychoanalytic psychotherapy with adoptive or in care children, *Psychoanalytic Psychotherapy* Autumn.

Miller, A. and Burden, R. (1992) Intervention or prevention?, in D.A. Lane and Miller A. (eds) *Silent Conspiracies*, Stoke-on-Trent: Trentham Books.

Miller, L., Ruslin, M. and Shuttleworth, J. (1989) *Closely Observed Infants*, London: Duckworth.

Morris, R.J. and Kratochwill, T.R. (1983) *The Practice of Child Therapy*, Oxford: Pergamon Press.

Murphy, G., Callias, M. and Carr, J. (1985) Increasing simple toy play in the profoundly mentally handicapped child, *Journal of Autism and Developmental Disorders* 15: 357–88.

Murphy, G., Carr, J. and Callias, M. (1986) Increasing simple toy play in the profoundly mentally handicapped child, *Journal of Autism and Development Disorders* 16: 45–58.

Nichol, A.R., Smith, J., Kay, B., Hall, D., Barlow, J. and Williams, B. (1988) A focused casework approach to the treatment of child abuse: a controlled comparison, *Journal of Child Psychology and Psychiatry* 29: 703–11.

Ollendick, T.H. (1986) Child and adolescent behaviour therapy, in S. Garfield and A. Bergin (eds) *Handbook of Psychiatry: Modern Approaches*, 2nd edn, Oxford: Blackwell Scientific.

Pellegrini, D.S. (1985) Training in social problem-solving, in M. Rutter and L. Hersov (eds) *Child and Adolescent Psychiatry: Modern Approaches*, 2nd edn, Oxford: Blackwell Scientific.

Phillips, G.T. and Smith, J.E. (1986) The behavioural treatment of faeces retention: an expanded case study, *Behavioural Psychiatry* 14: 124–36.

Rachman, S. (1962) Learning theory and child psychology: therapeutic possibilities, *Journal of Child Psychology and Psychiatry* 3: 149–68.

Rayner, E. (1991) *The Independent Mind in British Psychoanalysis*, London: Free Association Books.

Richman, N., Douglas, J., Hunt, H., Lansdown, R. and Levere, R. (1985) Behavioural methods in the treatment of sleep disorders – a pilot study, *Journal of Child Psychology and Psychiatry* 26: 581–90.

Robertson, J. and Robertson, J. (1967–75) Film series, *Young Children in Brief Separation*, Tavistock Institute of Human Relations, obtainable from Concord Films Council, Ipswich, Suffolk and NY University Film Institute.

Robertson, J. and Robertson, J. (1989) *Separation and the Very Young*, London: Free Association Books.

Ross, A.E. (1981) Of rigor and relevance, *Professional Psychology* 12: 318–27.

Russell, G.F.M., Szmukler, G.L., Dare, C. and Eisler, I. (1987) An evaluation of family therapy on anorexia nervosa and bulimia nervosa, *Archives of General Psychiatry* 44: 1,047–56.

Rutter, M. (1982) Psychological therapies in child psychiatry: issues and prospects, *Psychological Medicine* 12: 723–40.

Rutter, M. (1985) Psychological therapies in child psychiatry: issues and prospects, in M. Rutter and L. Hersov (eds) *Child and Adolescent Psychiatry; Modern Approaches*, 2nd edn, Oxford: Blackwell Scientific.

Rutter, M. and Hersov, L. (1976) *Child Psychiatry: Modern Approaches*, Oxford: Blackwell Scientific.

Rutter, M. and Hersov, L. (eds) (1985) *Child and Adolescent Psychiatry: Modern Approaches*, 2nd edn, Oxford: Blackwell Scientific.

Scherer, M. (1992) Ethical perspectives on therapy: who decides? in D.A. Lane and A. Miller (eds) *Silent Conspiracies*, Stoke-on-Trent: Trentham Books.

Scott, G. and Richards, M.P.M. (1990) Night waking in infants: effects of providing advice and support for parents, *Behavioural Psychotherapy* 15: 224–39.

Scott, M.J. and Stradling, S.G. (1987) Evaluation of a group programme for parents of problem children, *Behavioural Psychotherapy* 15: 224–39.

Segal, H. (1973) *Introduction to the Work of Melanie Klein*, London: Hogarth Press.

Seymour, F.W., Brock, P., During, M. and Poole, G. (1989) Reducing sleep disruptions in young children: evaluation of therapist-guided and written information approaches: a brief report, *Journal of Child Psychology and Psychiatry* 30: 367–83.

Shaffer, D. (1985) Enuresis, in M. Rutter and L. Hersov (eds) *Child and Adolescent Approaches*, 2nd edn, Oxford: Blackwell Scientific.

Shuttleworth, A. (1984) Finding a link: from thinking at to thinking with a child, *Journal of Child Psychotherapy* 10: 1.

Smith, J.E. and Rachman, S. (1984) Non-accidental injury to children; II: a controlled evaluation of a behavioural management programme, *Behaviour Research and Therapy* 22: 349–66.

Smith, J.E., Rachman, S. and Yule, B. (1984) Non-accidental injury to children; III: Methodological problems of evaluative treatment research, *Behaviour Research and Therapy* 22: 367–83.

Speed, B. (1984) Family therapy: an update, *Newsletter of the Association for Child Psychology and Psychiatry* 6(1): 2–14.

Spence, S. (1989) Social skills training, in S. Lindsay and G. Powell (eds) *An Introduction to Clinical Child Psychology*, Aldershot: Gower.

Taylor, A.J.W. (1989) *Disasters and Disaster Stress*, New York: AMS Press.

Taylor, E. (ed.) (1986a) *The Overactive Child: Clinics in Developmental Medicine no 97*, Spastics International Medicine Publications, Oxford: Blackwell Scientific.

Taylor, E. (1986b) The causes and development of hyperactive behaviour, in E.R. Taylor (ed.) *The Overactive Child: Clinics in Developmental Medicine no 97*, Spastics International Medical Publications, Oxford: Blackwell Scientific.

Taylor, E. (1988) Psychopharmacology in childhood, *Newsletter of the Association for Child Psychology and Psychiatry* 10(2): 3–6.

Taylor, E., Schachar, R., Thorley, G., Wieselberg, H.M., Everitt, B. and Rutter, M. (1987) Which boys respond to stimulant medication? A controlled trial of methylphenidate in boys with disruptive behaviour, *Psychological Medicine* 17: 121–43.

Taylor, M. (1991) How psychoanalytic thinking lost its way in the hands of men: a case for feminist psychotherapy, *British Journal of Guidance and Counselling* 19(1): 93–103.

Thomas, H.J. and Hardwick, P.J. (1989) An audit of a small child psychiatry clinic, *Newsletter of the Association for Child Psychology and Psychiatry* 11(1): 10–14.

Tizard, J. (1973) Maladjusted children and the Child Guidance Service, University of London, *London Educational Review* 2: 2.

Tizard, J., Schofield, W.N. and Hewison, J. (1982) Collaboration between teachers and parents in assisting children's reading, *British Journal of Educational Psychology* 52: 1–15.

Topping, K. (1983) *Educational Systems for Disruptive Adolescents*, Beckenham: Croom Helm.

Wahler, R.G. (1980) The insular mother: her problems in parent–child treatment, *Journal of Applied Behaviour Analysis* 13: 207–19.

Warnock Report (1985) *Department of Education and Science in Great Britain*, London: HMSO.

Whedall, K. (ed.) (1987) *The Behaviourist in the Classroom*, London: Allen & Unwin.

Widlake, P. (1992) Involving parents in the education of children with special educational needs, in D.A. Lane and A. Miller (eds) *Silent Cospiracies*, Stoke-on-Trent: Trentham Books.

Wilson, P. and Hersov, L. (1985) Individual and group psychotherapy, in M. Rutter and L. Hersov (eds) *Child and Adolescent Psychiatry: Modern Approaches*, Oxford: Blackwell Scientific.

Winnicott, D.W. (1965) *The Maturational Process and the Facilitating Environment*, London: Hogarth Press.

Wolpe, J. and Rachman, S. (1960) Psychoanalytic 'evidence': a critique based on

Freud's case of Little Hans, *Journal of Nervous and Mental Disease* 130: 135–48.

Yule, W. (1984) Child behaviour therapy in Britain: 1962–1982, *Newsletter of the Association of Child Psychology and Psychiatry* 6(1): 15–20.

Yule, W. (1990) Developmental considerations in child assessment, in T.H. Ollendick and M. Hersov (eds) *Handbook of Child and Adolescent Assessment*, New York: Pergamon Press.

Evaluation of interventions with children and adolescents

MARIA CALLIAS

The purpose of evaluating psychological therapies or interventions is to enable us to determine what treatment carried out by whom is most effective for a particular individual with a specific problem in a particular set of circumstances. Progress in developing and evaluating treatments for children has been relatively slow compared to that for adults (Johnson et al. 1986; Kazdin 1988; Rutter 1982; 1985a). The need for effective treatments exists. Epidemiological studies show that many more children have problems than receive services (Rutter et al. 1970; Rutter 1989). A plethora of treatments are in use, but most have not been evaluated (Kazdin 1988). Moreover, some children's problems get better without specialist treatment, but we do not always know what contributes to such 'spontaneous' improvement. Thus despite progress, we are still a long way from being able to make reliable judgements about what to do for particular children. The need to escape from inertia and an acceptance of the status quo has been emphasized by Rutter (1982; 1985) and Kazdin (1988), who have both thoroughly reviewed current issues in evaluating treatments for children's problems. The aims of this chapter are to review evaluative strategies by examining conceptual and methodological issues in an attempt to bridge the gap between research intervention studies and clinical practice.

Issues in evaluating therapy pertain to all aspects of conceptualizing the therapeutic process and evaluation. All psychological treatments involve several facets: the patient and his or her problem, the therapist and his or her personal style and techniques, the passage of time (Kiesler 1971), the psychosocial context of therapy (Kolvin et al. 1981) and the goals. With children, other features are important too. The child's own developmental level and characteristics of the family and social context need to be considered in relation to understanding the problems, as well as processes of intervention, and goals. A further facet of the therapy is whether the therapist has direct contact with the child or only indirect contact by working in a triadic therapeutic model, that is, the therapist works with parents or teachers to effect changes in the child. The specific methodological practices that make for high quality research are not universally agreed upon (Kazdin 1988). Some issues pertaining to aims and goals, the process of therapy, and the assessment of outcomes will be considered before examining the two main research designs currently employed in evaluation. The chapter will conclude with some pertinent current issues in the design of evaluation studies.

Aims and goals

Aims of evaluative research

The three main substantive aims of evaluative research are first, to compare different treatments to find out whether some treatments are obviously superior to others; second, in so far as treatments are equally effective on a group basis, to find guidelines for deciding which clients do better with which form of therapy; and third, to discover the psychological processes by which various therapies produce effects. Most research has addressed the first issue of the general efficacy of treatment with very little attention to the other two (Rutter 1982).

Goals of treatment

The important treatment goals identified by Rutter (1985) have received differential emphasis in different therapeutic approaches. First, *symptom reduction* as an appropriate and necessary main goal of treatment has always been central to some treatments and is becoming more widely accepted. But there is no general agreement about whether this is a sufficient goal, or on the relative importance attributed to diverse aspects of intrapersonal and interpersonal functioning, maladaptive behaviours and psychological complaints. Approaches also differ on the issue of whether the reduction of such symptoms or behaviours is the direct, immediate goal or one that would be reached ultimately via other, intermediate goals such as improved family functioning (Rosen and Proctor 1981).

The second goal of promoting *normal development* seems self-evident for children with general or specific developmental delays in cognition and language (Callias and Carr 1975; Howlin and Rutter 1987). The relevance of a developmental perspective on socio-emotional functioning has always been a feature of dynamic therapies (Rutter 1985a) and is being recognized in behavioural approaches to children's relationship difficulties (Furman 1980) and the assessment and treatment of other problems including post-traumatic stress disorder (Yule 1990).

The third goal of *fostering autonomy and self-reliance* in order to cope with future problems is an explicit aim of some treatments such as social problem-solving approaches (Pelligrini 1985) and parent training (Callias 1987; Dangel and Polster 1984). As this goal has not been adequately evaluated it is unclear how far it is achieved (Rutter 1982; 1985a) even when it is explicitly intended.

The fourth goal of *generalization of improvements* from therapeutic settings to real-life contexts is no longer taken for granted. It is addressed from the point of view of how generalization can be effected and maintained as well as reducing the need for generalization by basing treatment in naturalistic contexts and by working with parents and teachers (Wahler et al. 1979). Finally, the closely related goal of how to achieve persistence of improvement over time is recognized in a greater emphasis on more adequate follow-up studies as well as techniques for maintaining changes.

Goals and the timing of outcome measures

Treatment outcomes can be conceptualized as immediate, interim and ultimate depending on the complexity of the process and aims of particular interventions (Rosen and Proctor 1981). This perspective puts goals in a temporal framework, recognizing that there may be a progression of steps towards the final goals of treatment which may be achieved either by the time treatment ends or only some time later. These issues are not usually addressed explicitly in treatment but are important for understanding the processes involved in therapy and evaluating outcome. The most common expectation is for treatment effects to be greatest immediately after therapy, and, if they do not remain stable, to decline thereafter. Follow-up studies of a range of disorders show more diverse long-term outcomes.

Treatment effects can persist over time as in the behavioural treatment of school refusal (Blagg and Yule 1984) or the behavioural problems of treated autistic children (Howlin and Rutter 1987). However, early gains over a control group may disappear by follow-up. Sometimes this is not because of a later loss of treatment gains but because the control group catches up over time; for example, autistic children's accelerations in developmental skills such as language were maintained but did not continue (Howlin and Rutter 1987). There may also be sleeper effects with greater improvements evident at follow-up than immediately after treatment as in Kolvin et al.'s (1981) study in schools and in the teacher–child interaction project (Berger et al. 1987).

The timing of outcome measures is clearly important. In addition to immediately post-treatment measures, later effects need to be assessed. This is becoming more accepted. The issue of how much later follow-ups should be done needs attention. Usually this is a few months after treatment ceases but occasionally one to two years later. Practicality seems to dictate the timing. Other issues are also relevant and depend on the way interventions are conceptualized and are expected to act.

A further major issue is to understand why these diverse outcomes occur. Long-term outcomes may depend not only on the nature of the problem and characteristics of children and families but also on treatment parameters such as the context of treatment, and techniques of intervention. Spontaneous generalization of treatment in special settings is no longer generally expected (Rutter 1985a). Specific techniques of treatment may affect extent of generalization and maintenance. For example, studies comparing behavioural, cognitive and combination approaches to the treatment of performance anxiety in adults suggest that behavioural interventions have early effects but that maintenance is considerably enhanced by cognitive interventions (Kendrick et al. 1982). Similarly, treatment approaches that are most effective in the long term may differ from those that are effective in the short term. For example, enuresis can be stopped by medication in the short term but usually recurs after medication stops (Shaffer 1985), while the bell and pad has long-term effects for most children including for those children who relapse and are treated again in the same way

(Dische et al. 1983). Differing effects over time will be more likely to be revealed by studies employing multiple outcome measures (eg Kolvin et al. 1981).

There is a need to identify factors affecting long-term outcome. The nature of the disorder and knowledge of its natural course, characteristics of the child and of the family all seem important in addition to the nature of the intervention. It appears too that treatments which enable the child, parents and teachers to develop their own skills and confidence rather than to continue to rely heavily on therapists or therapy are more likely to have positive longer-term effects.

The process of therapy

Conceptualizing treatment

A major issue in evaluative research is the way treatments are defined and described. Treatment methods are usually described in terms of the broad theoretical approach which serves as a shorthand for all facets. Problems with the global conceptual labels used are, first, that each label encompasses a wide variety of strategies and techniques, and second, that although differences may be stressed, diverse theoretical schools may actually share key features. For example, the rubric 'behavioural approaches' encompasses the use of specific techniques, such as reinforcement of desired behaviour or contingent time-out from positive reinforcement, complex flexible intervention strategies based on a comprehensive functional analysis of problems (Herbert 1987) and complex treatment packages such as social cognitive problem solving on its own (Kazdin et al. 1987a) or in parallel with parent training (Kazdin et al. 1987b). Second, despite different theoretical origins, many current therapies share important commonalities such as a focus on applying specific, focused techniques to overt current behaviour. Such underlying commonalities and mechanisms may account for the observed efficacy of apparently very diverse specific techniques (Rutter 1985a). A common pathway underlying this diversity may be the extent to which treatments establish and enhance self-efficacy – itself a key force in maintaining motivation and persistence in the face of obstacles (Bandura 1989).

Consequently, more thought needs to be given to the methodological aspects of specifying treatments (Kazdin 1988). Both the conceptual basis and the procedures of treatment need to be specified and fully described. Such information is essential for judgements to be made, first, about the extent to which a particular treatment is representative of a designated theoretical approach, and second, about the extent of similarity or difference between the interventions of different studies. Moreover, the question of how representative the research treatment is of good clinical practice needs to be addressed when considering issues of generalization.

Treatments can be described along several parameters which cut across the main ways of summarizing them. These include theoretical orientation such as behavioural, cognitive, psychoanalytic; whether treatment is predetermined or standard for all clients or whether treatment is individually planned on the basis of the information gathered in a functional analysis of the individual child's problems and strengths; who is seen – individual child, parents, family, or teachers; whether treatment is carried out individually or in groups; whether intervention is directly with the child or indirectly via parents or others; complexity of intervention; the setting of treatment, extent of 'homework' between sessions; whether the treatment duration and number of sessions are predetermined or variable; the attention given to different aspects of treatment such as agreeing goals and strategies for change and maintenance of treatment effects; what the focus is – behaviour, cognitions, emotions – and whether the problems are being addressed directly or indirectly; what level of analysis and goal setting is being addressed – intrapersonal or interpersonal; focus on specific or generalized difficulties; whether the aim is to treat, support or educate; the explicit or implicit attributions of responsibility for cause and for the solution of problems which underpin the model of helping and coping (Brickman et al. 1982). In addition, psychotherapeutic interventions need to be placed in the wider range of approaches to psychological problems, including medication and diet. Clearer descriptions of such attributes of intervention will facilitate conceptualization, communication and comparisons of effectiveness.

Treatment implementation

In addition to specification, the integrity with which an approach is implemented needs to be monitored and maintained. After all, a treatment approach can hardly be regarded as properly evaluated if it is not properly implemented. This is a major undertaking but essential, especially when what is being evaluated is a flexible treatment strategy. Written manuals describing strategies, using trained therapists, ongoing supervision and monitoring of the ongoing therapeutic process are all relevant (Kazdin 1988).

Specificity and duration of treatments

Some evidence shows briefer interventions using focused techniques to be better than long-term open-ended, less defined approaches; for example, for treating marital and parent–child relationship difficulties (Reid and Shyne 1969) and school refusal (construing in-patient milieu therapy and home tuition as less immediately focused on return to school) (Blagg and Yule 1984). Moreover, within time-limited approaches, direct contact approaches like group treatments, nurture groups and behavioural management were more effective than indirect parent counselling–teacher counselling with maladjusted school children (Kolvin et al. 1981) and direct contact with therapist brought speedier results than advice in manuals only for young children's sleeping difficulties (Seymour et al. 1989). Thus focused goals and specific strategies and techniques tend to be more effective than less direct, more diffuse treatments; they tend to be used in short-term therapy.

The issue of whether short-term treatments are always best needs some attention. It is likely that optimal treatment duration will differ according to the nature and complexity of the problem, with widespread problems and conditions with poor prognoses such as autism, conduct disorders, and hyperactivity requiring focused but longer-term interventions. For example, with autism, treatment contact with families even in research projects tends to be long and to encompass a number of problems and developmental issues (Howlin and Rutter 1987; Lovaas 1987). With severe conduct disorder, which also has a poor prognosis, Kazdin (1987) suggests that a change of goal may be required from the expectation that the problems can be eliminated to one where the intervention needs to be based on a 'chronic condition' model, that is management needs to be thought of as a long-term ongoing process, rather than a relatively brief curative intervention.

Selecting treatments

An aspect that has not received much empirical attention is how the focus of treatment is selected and how treatment methods are matched to goals. In most treatment research, the treatments tend to be standard and uniform; the same treatments are given to children who share a diagnosis in order to evaluate the overall effectiveness of treating aspects of functioning considered to be related to the problem; for example, social cognitive skills and parenting packages for treating conduct disorder (Kazdin et al. 1987a; 1987b); alternatively, a range of different specified treatments are compared with children showing a heterogenous range of neurotic and conduct disorders (Kolvin et al. 1981). Usually, treatment is demonstrated to be better than no treatment and sometimes differences in effectiveness are found between treatments (Kolvin et al. 1981). Such treatments fail to be effective with a substantial minority of the treated groups and there is no way of knowing why.

The diversity of children's problems and the circumstances in which they occur, such as whether they are part of normal development, reactions to events at home, aspects of developmental disorders, consequences of abuse or trauma, or misattributions of parents or others, plays a part in selection of treatment and expectations for change. Basic focused theory and research on child dysfunction and development, such as Patterson's programmatic studies and models for understanding conduct disorder (Patterson 1982; Patterson et al. 1989), are necessary for understanding the processes involved and thus for informing and developing intervention strategies (Kazdin 1988). Yet how these issues affect decisions about focus of treatment and choice of approach remains an issue.

Stages of treatment

A further issue is how the range of techniques and therapist interpersonal skills are relevant to different steps in the therapeutic process. Intervention is probably not best conceptualized as a single undifferentiated entity; the techniques and skills relevant to different parts of the process are likely to differ. Intervention has several phases which have not received equal research attention. These are establishing the need for intervention and engaging the family who need to perceive that the treatment may be able to alleviate their problems and distress; preventing drop-out, that is maintaining co-operation (both attendance and active involvement in therapy) for the duration of treatment;

therapy to alleviate current problems and distress; attending to the issues of generalization and maintenance specifically; and lastly, terminating contact satisfactorily.

Engagement in treatment is an issue that has not received sufficient attention. Refusal rates for treatment trials vary but are sometimes rather high (eg Taylor et al. 1987). It would seem important to know why families decline. Reasons may vary from trivial to fundamental differences in the way families and therapists construe the problems and what can be done about them (Firestone and Witt 1982). With children, the issue of engagement and co-operation are especially salient when treating families where children are at serious risk but parents themselves have not sought treatment; for example, with children who have been physically abused (Smith et al. 1984). Explicit discussion about the treatment contract and expectations may help to clarify expectations and thus enhance (Holmes and Urie 1975) as may basing treatment in more naturalistic community settings such as mother and toddler groups (Peterman 1981).

The issue of *generalization and maintenance* have usually been addressed by moving the place of treatment to the natural setting and changing the focus from direct child contact to triadic models of intervention. There is, however, also a place for considering building into treatments the features that enhance maintenance; these include booster sessions, tapering off and spending a few sessions towards the end of therapy focusing specifically on enabling clients to perceive change and maintenance as something within their control by focusing on future stresses, attributional style and coping strengths (Imber et al. 1982). Although research has not addressed this issue explicitly, comparisons of treatment components within the cognitive-behavioural tradition suggest that a behavioural focus may be more or equally effective to cognitive methods immediately after treatment, but that cognitive or combined behavioural-cognitive techniques resulted in better long-term success, for example with performance anxiety (Kendrick et al. 1982). Booster sessions of treatment are often effective in coping with relapse after a standard duration of treatment, for example, bell and pad treatment for enuresis (Dische et al. 1983).

Treatment or management

Finally there is a need to distinguish between treatment and management (Kazdin 1988). Treatment is concerned with alleviating or altering symptoms of the condition whereas management is broader in scope; it encompasses a range of interventions and is directed towards broader aspects of adjustment and functioning. Although these concepts blur and overlap into one another, a management strategy may encompass one or more treatments and the aims may differ; for example, treatment may be directed towards modifying particular problems of an autistic child within a broader management strategy that recognizes that the condition itself is not 'curable'. Moreover, a careful and systematic treatment intervention may play an important role in management decisions. For example, although the aim of treatment is to improve the parenting of abusing families so that child care is appropriate, treatment failure may be a more reliable way of judging potential for improving parenting skills than alternatives and can contribute meaningfully to important, far-reaching management decisions about the child's future (Smith et al. 1984).

Therapist characteristics

The qualities of a therapist that are associated with treatment outcome have received much less attention in therapy with children than with adults. Interpersonal qualities in therapy are associated with outcome, but the results of different studies do not identify consistent features. The qualities of genuineness, empathy and warmth (Rogers 1952; Truax and Carkhuff 1967) and short, specific and clear communications, together with specific techniques, have been shown to contribute to successful outcome in family therapy for delinquent adolescents (Alexander et al. 1976). But in treating children in a school setting, extraversion, treatment assertiveness and openness were associated with positive outcomes, whereas unexpectedly, qualities of empathy, warmth, genuineness, charm and good relationships were not (Kolvin et al. 1981). As well as these interpersonal qualities, other qualities such as total style of organizing and engaging in intervention including actively enlisting community resources can be important as a retrospective descriptive analysis of two therapists who achieved very different long-term outcomes for conduct disordered boys attending a clinic suggests (Ricks 1974). Interestingly, these therapists were equally successful with less disturbed boys, but 'supershrink' who was more active in treatment and in finding community resources was more successful with the more difficult subgroup.

With the increase in bibliotherapy – the provision of help and advice in written form – some studies have compared the role of therapist-mediated intervention with minimal therapist contact but similar written technical advice; for example, studies on sleep difficulties with infants and young children (Scott and Richards 1990; Seymour et al. 1989). When differences are found, these favour contact with a therapist (Seymour et al. 1989). More generally, manuals used on their own seem more effective for helping with specific problems and with the development of certain skills than for dealing with more complex or widespread difficulties (Callias 1985; McMahon and Forehand 1980). Clearly the therapist contributes to the therapeutic process.

The more extensive adult literature on the role of therapist qualities suggests that interpersonal behaviour and skills shown in therapeutic sessions are more consistently associated with outcome than are demographic characteristics such as age, sex, ethnicity (Beutler et al. 1986). When the latter are associated with outcome, it seems likely to be because of the mediating effects of interpersonal behaviour and attitudes of the therapist (Beutler et al. 1986). Process analysis of therapists' behaviour in early treatment sessions has shown that a range of specific technical and interpersonal errors are highly associated with poor outcome (Sachs 1983).

Taken together, these findings suggest that therapist qualities are important in therapy; interpersonal style, sensitivity and an active role in structuring treatment as well as the appropriate use of techniques seem important. Firmer evidence is needed before we can be sure of the precise qualities that enhance effectiveness and whether these differ with setting, age of children and who is seen in therapy. Research focusing on interpersonal skills within sessions as well as how therapists implement broader strategies and techniques would be more useful than investigations of therapist characteristics and behaviour that do not necessarily have a direct bearing on the therapy sessions.

Child characteristics

Although by far the most attention has been directed to the role of the treatment itself, one consistent feature of outcome studies is the variability within groups. Group differences may favour treatment by average scores or proportion of persons who improve, but even with well-defined clinical groups there are individual differences in responsiveness.

Early studies and interventions paid scant attention to describing individual characteristics that might be associated with differential outcome. There is a need to delineate the nature of the problem as well as characteristics that may be related to prognosis such as severity, intensity, frequency, scope and persistence (Kazdin 1983). Moreover, despite the recognition that diagnostic category does not mean uniformity in that individuals sharing the same diagnosis may differ on a number of other salient characteristics (Kiesler 1971; Rutter 1985a), the need for diagnosis in terms of widely used International Classification of Disorders (ICD) or the Diagnostic and Statistical Manual (DSM), is being recognized more widely as a means of comparison across studies and giving some idea of prognosis. The issue of appropriate levels of problem definition has been central to the development of both behavioural and family therapies, which have set out with contrasting methods of analysis to what had been perceived, perhaps simplistically, as 'the medical model' of diagnosis (Kanfer and Saslow 1969; Gurman et al. 1986). As Kazdin discusses, the issue is more complex and there are a range of interventions depending on the nature of the condition and the state of knowledge. Some psychological problems may be alleviated but the treatment of many, including serious conduct disorder, may need to be conceptualized differently, more in terms of continuing intervention to keep it under control rather than cure, much as the management of diabetes in the present state of knowledge (Kazdin 1987).

Potential moderating variables such as developmental level may moderate the effects of intervention (Achenbach 1986). For example, the prognosis of autism, a pervasive developmental disorder, is strongly associated with overall cognitive ability and language development (Lockyer and Rutter 1970). Intensive intervention accelerated the language usage of autistic boys relative to a control group immediately after treatment but, by follow-up eighteen months later, the control group had caught up (Howlin and Rutter 1987). In an even more intensive and longer lasting intervention with pre-school autistic children, the greatest gains were made by the more intellectually able children who were more likely to attend ordinary classrooms than both similarly treated less intellectually able children and similar children treated in less intensive programmes (Lovaas 1987). On the other hand there is some suggestive evidence that cognitive or developmental level is not related to the effectiveness of individually planned problem-focused behavioural treatments for the behavioural and emotional problems of developmentally handicapped children, such as more able autistic boys (Howlin and Rutter, 1987) or mentally handicapped children (Callias and Carr 1975).

The role of age, cognitive abilities and gender on treatment effects have been studied occasionally. In their school-based intervention study, Kolvin et al. (1981) did not find age to be a factor in treatment outcome or to be related to the types of interventions that were effective. However, there were some sex differences; girls did better than boys on many outcome measures and always on measures of conduct disorder. When boys did better than girls, this was on neurotic behaviour. These findings were interpreted as meaning that conduct problems were less deeply ingrained in girls than boys, and neurotic problems are less deeply rooted in boys. Gender and age are associated with different clinical problems, or vulnerabilities (Rutter 1989) and their role as potential moderating factors of treatment effectiveness needs further attention (Kazdin 1988).

Family and social characteristics

The broader social context is especially important with children and adolescents because of their dependence on their family; children with similar presenting problems may have widely divergent prognosis depending on family and school circumstances. There is a need to examine the characteristics of parents and families more systematically in relation to treatment outcome. Both parent training and family therapy recognize the relevance of families in therapy, but the role of family structure and style of interaction are seldom examined in relation to outcome. The role of social isolation of single-parent families in limiting the effective use of skills learned in behavioural parent training has been recognized (Wahler 1980). The way parents construe their children's problems (Wahler and Dumas 1984) and aspects of family functioning are being addressed as issues in parent training (Patterson and Fleischman 1979; Embry 1984) and often become the prime focus of therapy; for example, in family interventions altering the communication patterns of families with delinquent children from defensive and vague to more open and clearer communication (Alexander et al. 1976) and in other approaches to treatment of conduct disordered children (Patterson 1982; Kazdin 1987).

A more explicit focus on assessing child and family characteristics in treatment studies may help to clarify the role of such factors in treatment outcome. For example, most treatments seem successful with a proportion of children and families, but we do not know whether different treatments are effective with similar or different families, or whether all treatments are more successful with less stressed families, indicating that more attention needs to be directed to developing effective interventions for more troubled families.

Assessment measures

There are two main requirements for methodologically sound research: first, valid and reliable measures of problems and other relevant variables for measuring change; and second, suitable research designs to demonstrate experimental control over possible alternative explanations so that valid conclusions can be reached about the role of the intervention in bringing about change.

Measures of a child's problem

Assessment of a child's problem takes one of two main forms; either norm-referenced measures on which children are compared with peers and problem children score within deviant ranges (eg Rutter et al. 1970) or criterion-referenced measures, which provide some form of scaling of a particular problem leading to the setting of targets for therapy, for example, the extent of approach to a phobic object. The latter approach tends to be used in single case study or series designs and also for assessing progress during treatment. Groups comparisons tend to use some form of standardized instruments. Increasingly, multifaceted measures are being advocated with the aim of providing information from different perspectives and on different facets of the child, especially because of the low correspondence between data from different sources, probably reflecting situation and person specificity (Achenbach et al. 1987). Parents and teachers and sometimes therapists are the main informants. Children's self-report is seldom used on its own; not because they cannot report symptoms but because they often underestimate their dysfunction (Kazdin et al. 1983).

An important issue in interpreting results is that different measures do not necessarily give consistent results about the effects of treatment; moreover, results on these measures may differ at different points in time (Kolvin et al. 1981). Timing of follow-up is important and different patterns of change from post-treatment to follow-up may occur. Such changes are influenced not only by the nature of the treatments, but also by the character of the symptoms and dysfunction; knowledge of the course of the disorder is relevant too.

A major issue is deciding what is relevant to assess with children: reducing symptoms and increasing prosocial functioning are not necessarily two sides of the same coin. For example, reducing a child's aggressive behaviour to peers is not necessarily the same as increasing prosocial and more acceptable social interaction. To find out whether both problems need to be addressed, assessments of both are needed but seldom carried out.

Methods of reporting change due to treatment has shifted from a satisfaction with presenting changes in terms of group mean scores to more directly clinically meaningful presentations of the data, such as number of persons or families improving, the extent of improvement (Jacobson 1985; Kazdin et al. 1987a; 1987b; Blagg and Yule 1984) and whether this change is clinically meaningful. With children, developmental issues need to be taken into account in interpreting change. One solution is to compare post-treatment scores of treated problem children with the norms for non-problem children (Kazdin et al. 1987a; 1987b). While the desired goal may be to achieve age norms, in fact, the nature of the condition may set limitations. Nevertheless, careful assessment and comparison with different groups may well help to clarify these issues.

Satisfaction with treatment as an outcome measure

The assessment of client perceptions of change and of satisfaction with treatment are less direct but important measures of treatment. The issue of judgement of effectiveness is an aspect of agreement between different measures and perspectives. The extent of acceptance of the treatment and the feeling of being helped are important too. However, it needs to be recognized that sometimes interventions are perceived positively even when treatment gains are not dramatic or mixed (eg Scott and Richards 1990; Howlin and Rutter 1987). Clearly, families value intervention and support when coping with both transient and long-term difficulties even when interventions are not curative. This raises questions about the nature of service provision, particularly when present treatments are not 'cures'.

Cost-effectiveness

Finally, the administrative aspects of treatment costs in terms of professional time, training, facilities and support need to be assessed. Sometimes, very effective treatments are cheaper than many existing practices (Blagg and Yule 1984) but often they are costlier because of the chronicity of problems, the expense of developing new treatment strategies for many intractable problems, and because service provision is often sparse outside of research projects (Howlin and Rutter 1987; Callias and Carr 1975; Callias et al. 1987). Investment in research is essential for developing effective treatments and service provision.

Issues in research design

Issues in evaluative research encompass those relevant to adults as well as those specific to children such as the role of development and the social context.

Most research has addressed the question of whether a particular treatment is more effective than others, or than a control condition in ameliorating children's problems. A few studies have compared a number of different approaches to a range of heterogeneous problems of a large number of children (Kolvin et al. 1981), but most studies have been more modest in scale and have compared the experimental intervention with no-treatment waiting list controls (Frosh and Callias 1980) or a generally accepted treatment or routine clinical practice (Blagg and Yule 1984; Smith and Rachman 1984; Howlin and Rutter 1987). Posed in these competitive terms between rival schools of thought or between variants within an approach, the answer is usually that the experimental intervention is superior at least immediately after treatment and on some measures of outcome. Thereafter, gains may be maintained in comparison with no intervention controls (Kolvin et al. 1981) or alternative services (Blagg and Yule 1984) or treatment advantages differences attenuate. The question of how confidently such results can be applied generally to similar children and problems is difficult to answer because of variability of responsiveness to treatment even within diagnostically well defined groups, sample selection including refusal rate which can be high (Smith and Rachman 1984; Taylor et al. 1987) and subsequent drop-out rates for a variety of reasons.

Moreover, most treatments involve a complex set of strategies and skills on the part of the therapist. Sometimes treatments within an orientation are uniform and specified, though they may be complex (Kazdin et al. 1987a; 1987b); but increasingly, the details of treatment will be individually tailored to the needs of an individual child and family even though the group share the same diagnosis and the approach is similar (Blagg and Yule 1984; Howlin et al. 1987). In such approaches, experimental control, that is ensuring that change is correctly attributed to the treatment rather than due to other factors, is demonstrated by single case methodology (Yule and Hemsley 1977; Morley 1989) and patient series (Owens et al. 1989). Thus in these latter approaches, experimental control is demonstrated within an idiographic rather than a nomothetic tradition; the focus being on assessing the individual child's problem and then selecting treatment strategies to modify these difficulties rather than applying a uniform intervention to a randomly selected group of children with the same problem. Such an approach comes closer to the ideal clinical practice. Blends of individually oriented and group designs are possible.

Subject selection and randomization

In group designs, the most accepted way of controlling for systematic bias from sources other than the treatments being compared is to assign large numbers of children and families randomly to different treatment conditions to minimize the effect of extraneous factors (Pocock 1983). In practice, this design presents difficulties. First, there is the problem of recruiting large numbers of subjects to the study, especially if the problem to be treated is rare. Second, on ethical grounds, participants need to be informed of the treatment trial and may not choose to participate in a trial in which they will be randomly allocated to treatments, especially if they have definite opinions about the form of treatment that they will accept or co-operate with. In order to overcome the problems of recruitment into clinical trials, research designs incorporating patient choice of treatment are being developed within the framework of randomized designs (Zelen 1990). Such designs are considered appropriate when there is genuinely no preferred treatment for the condition. When a decision has been taken to enter the patient into the trial, the patient is randomly allocated to one condition and then asked for informed consent for that treatment. If consent is refused, an alternative treatment is chosen. While this approach gives some choice (to accept or reject the randomly assigned treatment) it does not allow for choice after discussing all options.

Finally, most psychological treatments require active participation by the client and, while randomization is intended to control for motivation and other confounding factors, simple randomized control trials may not always be most suitable for evaluating participative interventions because equal distribution of these factors may not necessarily be achieved (Brewin and Bradley 1989). Where there are no clear indications for regarding one treatment as superior to another, it may be preferable to allow patients to participate in making the decision, especially if they have strong preferences or concerns about the consequences of treatment (Owens et al. 1989). For example, when there were no medical indications for preferring one of two forms of surgery for breast cancer, women who were allowed to exercise choice were found to have better psychological adaptation to their disease and treatment, regardless of the specific surgery undergone, than women with similar problems but no choice of treatment in the past (Owens et al. 1986). Such studies do not prove that choice is related to outcome, but enable some quasi-experimental control in situations where ethical and practical considerations preclude true experimentation. Evaluating the effectiveness of alternative treatments under optimal conditions of motivation is a legitimate alternative to random allocation although it is unrelated to the traditional question of establishing which is the best treatment per se. But as active participation is essential for most psychotherapeutic interventions, maximizing motivation may be an important ingredient for success.

Ethical and scientific considerations require alternative designs to random allocation as high refusal rates, especially if they are biased towards one treatment condition, lead to uninterpretable results in random allocation designs. There is a need to move away from the belief that only random assignment designs are 'scientific', to recognizing that some but not all questions are best addressed by such designs and that other designs such as quasi-experimental, single case and series of cases may yield more interpretable results, especially if more careful attention is paid to describing and assessing the problems not only in terms of diagnosis but also in terms of other child and family characteristics that seem to be associated with variability of outcome.

Adequate control conditions

One of the most important concerns of evaluative research has been to demonstrate efficacy of a specific treatment over and above the passage of time, or the general effects of contact with therapists. The passage of time effect is controlled for by a no-contact control group. The long-term effects of no treatment have only rarely been studied because usually this group is a waiting list control group that will be offered treatment after some period of time. Ethically, it is difficult to justify no intervention for parents and children unless there are genuinely no grounds for expecting positive change as was the case when Kolvin et al. (1981) conducted their study in schools. A confounding factor with no treatment controls is that there is usually no information about the extent to which effective treatment has been sought elsewhere (Lambert et al. 1986). Such initiatives are often linked to improvements which reduce the difference between treated and untreated groups of small sample size (Smith et al. 1984).

The concept of controlling for the general effects of therapeutic contact, that is placebo effects, when evaluating the contribution of specific therapeutic strategies and techniques, has been adopted from medical research into drug effects. In such research, the need to distinguish the active drug effects from the psychological effects has led to the development of 'double blind' trials where both patient and therapist are kept in the dark as to whether the active drug or an inert substance is being given (Pocock 1983). While this strategy is very appropriate for testing pharmacological agents, the placebo control in psychological interventions poses both practical and conceptual problems and has undergone several changes over time (Lambert et al. 1986). In practice it is impossible to keep the therapist and the patient unaware of the treatment, or to provide plausible 'inert' treatments. Consequently, a therapy deriving from a different theoretical perspective has often been used as a placebo control (Critelli and Newmann 1984), raising an additional question about the fidelity of that treatment especially when practised by therapists who do not perceive it as a potent treatment.

It is also increasingly recognized that it may be inappropriate to control some of the psychological processes of change in psychological treatments which are fundamentally interpersonal experiences encompassing perceptions, cognitions and attributions (Kazdin 1988). Placebo issues have undergone several conceptual transformations. They were reformulated as the non-specific effects of treatment common to all interventions in contrast to the specific effects of a particular treatment approach (Kazdin 1986). This rather vague term for the interpersonal, and other aspects of treatment assumed to be common to all treatments has been regarded as misleading because the factors it encompasses are neither inert nor trivial nor non-specific. The term Common Factors has been proposed as a more suitable generic term for these potent ingredients of treatment which include engendering hope, attention, support, modelling and encouraging efforts (Lambert et al. 1986). A major advantage of this conceptual shift is that these factors can be conceptualized and studied in the same way as the other factors regarded as specific therapeutic agents. Moreover, as 'common factors' refer to interpersonal skills, motivational and attributional factors in the therapist and client, issues relevant to therapist and client characteristics are pertinent to them. Such factors may be inherent dimensions of all therapy, but they too are specifiable and may vary both within a particular treatment approach as well as between approaches. Studying their contribution rather than controlling them out as confounding factors, or disregarding them on the assumption that they are uniform across treatments, may be a more fruitful approach to understanding the process of therapeutic change.

However, a distinction should be made between these common factors and some placebo conditions in research studies. Although placebos are conceptualized as conditions composed of these common factors, empirical evidence shows that the components of placebo controls are often not common with, but very different from the components of designated therapies being studied (Horvath 1988). The usefulness of placebo controls in treatment research is being questioned; instead research questions could be directed towards elucidating which are the effective elements in treatment, by comparing alternative forms and modalities (Parloff 1986).

Thus choice of design for a particular study, and the nature of the controls, depends on the question being addressed, on the existing knowledge base, on ethical and practical considerations, as well as the acceptability of interventions and the commitment of participants. Generalizability of the results of any one study may be more modest than the grand questions such as 'Does psychotherapy work?' or 'Which therapy works best?' would imply. It may be more productive to base conceptual models and research designs on the assumption that generalizability needs to be tested empirically by replication with both similar and different groups of subjects, and by varying treatments in a series of studies, rather than simply by extrapolation to other groups.

The developmental context of children's problems

After long neglect from all theoretical perspectives except psychoanalytic therapy, the role of development in therapy for children is becoming a salient issue (Rutter 1985a; Achenbach 1986; Yule 1990). Development is relevant from the perspective of understanding the nature of problems and prognosis, choice of therapeutic strategy and evaluation of change.

The child's problems need to be understood in a developmental context (Rutter 1985a). First, children's needs and sensitivities vary with age, as does vulnerability to different types of disorders; for example, depression and anorexia nervosa may be uncommon in early childhood but become significant clinical problems in adolescence. Second, the clinical significance of specific behaviours changes with development and age. Some behaviours, such as bedwetting, would not be regarded as clinical problems requiring intervention unless they persisted beyond the age when most children cease to show such behaviour, while others such as lack of language or speech would be problems if development failed to occur when expected. Third, pervasive and specific delays in development affect prognosis and the nature of the intervention. Children with developmental disorders need interventions to foster the development of skills as well as ameliorate or reduce emotional and behavioural problems. Moreover, some behavioural problems such as tantrums, may occur because children lack more appropriate means of communicating their needs and thus require different therapeutic goals and strategies from children whose problems behaviours have a different basis.

Fourth, an increasingly developmental perspective to the psychological disorders of children, is evident in the emergence of developmental psychopathology (Sroufe and Rutter 1984; Achenbach 1986). Longitudinal research mapping the developmental course of disorders has the potential for providing a means of assessing severity and persistence of problems and therapeutic efficacy (Rutter 1988).

Implicitly or explicitly, the decision about whether and how to intervene depends on expectations about the role of maturation and naturally occurring experiences in righting difficulties. A better understanding of the processes involved in determining whether problems persist or resolve without therapy would enable better decision-making.

Developmental issues have seldom been explicitly addressed in selecting techniques and strategies of intervention. However, even in behavioural approaches based on general principles of learning, the particular techniques, strategies and focus of interventions chosen implicitly take account of developmental considerations (Yule 1990). Other issues that require further empirical attention are first, how therapists take into consideration the young child's ability to conceptualize and deal with emotions and distressing experiences (Achenbach 1986; Yule 1990), and second, the role of family and school in fostering more adaptive development.

Finally, a developmental perspective provides a backdrop for interpreting the efficacy of new treatments in reducing difficulties and enhancing the quality of life over conventional approaches as well as the extent to which problem children become more like their untroubled peers.

In highlighting the value of a developmental perspective to understanding the nature of children's difficulties and their treatment, it is important to recognize that there is no such thing as one developmental perspective. Much of developmental psychology examines age-related changes with little attention to the individual differences which are important in clinical practice. The course of both normal and dysfunctional development are poorly understood and many problems wax and wane over time (Rutter 1985a).

Theories of development, both descriptive and explanatory, are subject to controversy and debate (Lerner and Kauffman 1985; Kendler 1986). Issues such as the role of context for understanding children's development and the nature of causal models find echoes in the intervention literature. For example, the concept of reciprocal causality has stirred debate in family therapy about the validity of assessing change within the traditional linear cause-effect model of intervention, as well as questions about whether change can be assessed objectively (Gurman et al. 1986). Nevertheless, evaluation of outcome in family therapy remains within the linear model although the debate has been useful in distinguishing between, on the one hand, measures of process within therapy sessions and, on the other hand, outcome measures external to the therapy, which, if repeated at intervals rather than taken only once, provide a different measure of the process of change. This latter use of repeated measures parallels the monitoring of change in single case designs within the behavioural tradition (Morley 1989). Linking intervention with development raises questions about the role of therapy as one planned influence designed to altering the course of development positively.

Narrative reviews and meta-analyses

A further issue is how the growing literature on treatment efficacy should be drawn together and interpreted (Rutter 1985a; Kazdin 1986; 1988). This has been tackled in two main ways: narrative reviews and meta-analyses. In narrative reviews, the reviewer gathers together, describes and qualitatively judges and evaluates the merits of studies in order to draw conclusions about the efficacy of psychological treatments. The second approach, meta-analysis, is a quantitative procedure whereby the outcome data from all published studies are quantified and weighted according to a set of explicit rules for taking account of the methodological characteristics of studies and then statistically analysed to provide measures of the size of the therapeutic effect. In essence, a meta-analysis is a statistical analysis of studies, taking account of their methodological characteristics.

Historically, the earliest narrative reviews on the general effectiveness of psychotherapy with children led to the conclusion that therapy had no measurable effects because about the same proportions (approximately two-thirds) of both treated and untreated children improved (Levitt 1957; 1963). These reviews of methodologically weak studies sparked off a train of controversy about the interpretation of these studies paralleling in nature if not in magnitude that following Eysenck's (1952) first review on the efficacy of psychotherapy with adults (Kazdin 1988).

Meta-analysis was introduced as a way of overcoming the criticisms that narrative reviews are heavily influenced by the unknown implicit judgements and biases at each step of the process, from the initial criteria for including methodologically sound studies to the final general conclusions. Yet meta-analyses of the literature on adult treatments have also generated controversy which has centred mainly on the appropriateness of methods of quantification and on the claims of greater objectivity and power (see Kazdin 1986; 1988). As the conclusions of different meta-analyses of essentially the same pool of studies diverge depending on the methods used, it is evident that subjective judgements determine choice of rules for weighting and quantifying the treatment effects of methodologically diverse studies, even though these rules are made explicit. At a conceptual level, many meta-analyses are difficult to interpret because they are based on pooling the data of studies of very different treatments and varied methodology. The conceptual problem also affects many narrative reviews addressing the question of the general efficacy of therapy but, because studies are described, the problem is more transparent to the reader. Meta-analyses may yield more meaningful summaries and estimates of the overall effectiveness of subgroups of studies which share salient features, such as aims, problems and methods of assessment and treatment.

Overall, the main positive effect of these controversies has been to challenge initial conclusions and to raise important issues of methodology and conceptualization both for outcome studies and reviews. First, it is clear that well-planned and well-executed studies will yield more meaningful results than further analyses and reviews of poor studies (Rutter 1985a; Kazdin 1988). Second, it will be more fruitful to address more specific questions. As Kazdin succinctly puts it, to ask 'Does psychotherapy works?' is analogous to asking 'Does medicine or surgery work?', a question which today seems ridiculous (Kazdin 1988). Recent better designed studies show more positive effects for more precisely defined treatments (Kolvin et al. 1981). Similarly, more meaningful findings emerge to questions posed as comparisons between more specific interventions, or for treatments applied to particular problems or groups of children. Such evidence suggests that some treatments are more effective than others; for example, for school refusal (Blagg and Yule 1984), truants (Berg 1985; Berg et al. 1978), enuresis (Shaffer 1985), and neurotic and conduct disorders (Kolvin et al. 1981).

Recent narrative reviews and meta-analyses have reflected this focus on greater specificity in two main ways (Kazdin 1988). First, focused reviews have concentrated on individual treatment techniques or clusters of conceptually related procedures, such as behavioural (Ollendick 1986), cognitive-behavioural therapies (Kendall 1984), self-monitoring (Dush et al. 1989) interpersonal cognitive problem-solving (Pellegrini and Urbain 1985), individual therapy (Barrett et al. 1978), group (Abramowitz 1976; Julian and Kilmann 1979) and parent training (O'Dell 1974; Clements 1985). The issue here is still on the overall merits of different treatments. In the second approach, reviews have focused on the clinical problems and key issue of how effective one or several treatment approaches are with problems such as, school refusal (Burke and Silverman 1987), delinquency (Sheldrick 1985) or child abuse (Smith et al. 1984).

Particular treatments have been used selectively with certain problems or have been more generally applied. Likewise, the number and diversity of treatments implemented with any particular problem has varied. The problem of deciding on how specific or general to be in conceptualizing therapies and clinical problems when summarizing studies affects all types of reviews. It is especially relevant when the research findings on particular, often atypical exemplars of a general approach are considered as applicable to the whole range of procedures under that rubric (Kazdin 1988).

Recent meta-analyses of research on therapeutic approaches with children have examined findings for several different broad approaches as well as generally (Casey and Berman 1985; Weisz et al. 1987). These systematic literature searches confirm that most treatments have some effect but that the effects tend to be greater for behavioural and cognitive behavioural therapies than for client-centred and dynamic approaches. Other parameters of treatment, such as individual or group approaches, play therapy or non-play therapy, child or parent focused, and many therapist characteristics do not affect efficacy of treatment. Child characteristics such as nature of problem and age are related to efficacy, but sex is not. Carefully applying the same criteria to all studies highlights the nature of the field and draws attention to some of the problems about making comparisons. Some degree of caution is needed before accepting broad generalizations because of the paucity of studies examining non-behavioural treatments, because different techniques are associated with different specific kinds of problems and outcome measures, because treatments are rarely evaluated with serious clinical problems and because of the variable information given when reporting results (Kazdin 1988).

In summary, narrative and quantitative reviews have different strengths and limitations. Confidence in accepting the conclusions of reviews is constrained by the quality of the studies reported, and the ability of reviewers to weigh the evidence appropriately and to draw valid inferences.

Research and the practice of therapy

Treatment studies differ along several dimensions in the extent to which they resemble the clinical situation. Some of these parameters are the nature of the target problem, the population and the way it is recruited, client expectations, experience of the therapist, how treatment is selected, treatment setting and variation of treatment (Kazdin 1986). Despite progress in closing the gap, the observation made a decade ago, that an overview of the literature leads to the conclusion that there is an inverse relationship between scientific rigour and clinical relevance (Ross 1981), is still true of psychological therapies with children today. Elegant designs, perfect sampling, valid highly objective measures and sophisticated data analyses are less characteristic of research into difficult therapeutic problems, often because the crisis nature of the problem thwarts such efforts (eg Smith and Rachman 1984). Moreover, the goals of clinicians and families differ from those of researchers in that they are usually more concerned with achieving the desired outcome by whatever reasonable means than with sticking to specified research procedures to demonstrate the efficacy of specific techniques or to show with greater certainty that a particular intervention rather than other factors was responsible for the change. Reasonable flexibility is the essence of problem-solving approaches based on functional analyses of the presenting problems (Herbert 1987) which lead to strategies for deciding how to proceed in each case. Guidelines for assessing and intervening over the complex problems of children diagnosed as autistic (Rutter 1985b) or hyperactive (Schachar and Taylor 1986) combine such individual analysis with suggestions for intervention based on drawing together the findings of research studies.

The issue of how the complex problems encountered in clinical practice should be addressed raises many important questions. For example, should problems be addressed sequentially or in parallel? Should one approach be used or several? How should they be combined into a coherent strategy? How should therapists of different backgrounds share skills? An emerging interest in grappling with the problem of matching therapeutic strategies to intervene with the more complex problems of children and families and also to address the conceptual and methodological issues of demonstrating efficacy is reflected in some recent single case studies (eg Hogg et al. 1986; Evans 1989; Phillips and Smith 1986). Strategies developed in this way can be tested further in a series of cases followed by comparisons with alternative approaches or control groups in studies using quasi-experimental designs to provide reasonable demonstrations of effectiveness of clinical practice. Conversely, supplementing group methods with clinical case studies in order to try to understand deviant individuals who failed to respond to standard interventions as expected can also help in elucidating some complex cases (Ross 1981).

Assessment and monitoring of clinical practice is another important way of finding out whether treatments offered in everyday working conditions are effective. This is a different level of investigation from research development of treatments for problems but an essential one for bridging the research–practice divide. Computers and other modern technological developments will make such systems possible given adequate resources (Berger 1989). However, gathering sufficiently valid and reliable data is a major issue which depends on the development of concepts and suitable measures as well as data management systems.

Values and ethical issues

Ethical issues cannot be avoided in developing effective therapies or in clinical intervention. Values enter into all scientific endeavours and some are especially relevant to psychological studies because of the characteristics of people

(Howard 1985; Scarr 1985). Issues directly pertinent to the conduct of research on treatment include informed consent for participation in clinical trials and possible conflict with client preferences for treatment; decisions not to offer treatments that therapists consider effective (whether these are existing practices or new developments) to needy families; the use of no-treatment control group with serious clinical problems; and the adequate duration of such no-treatment control conditions. Most of these issues relate to potential conflicts between the rights of individuals and the need for sound methodology for drawing valid conclusions. Clearly, how the research aspects are resolved within any particular study depends on the current state of knowledge with informed consent always being paramount. Where refusals and drop-out rates are high, design issues need to be reconsidered.

Future directions

The theme of development underlies the issues relevant to the evaluation of psychological therapies. The process has been one of increasing differentiation and refinement of questions, specification of therapies, and their appropriate application. The issues in evaluating treatments for children's problems are still complex but are being addressed more explicitly. In both planning evaluative studies and appraising the outcomes of such studies, questions need to pay increasing attention to several domains: characteristics of the sample, the competence of the therapists, conceptualization of intervention strategy and techniques, methods of assessing change and the design of the study (see Kazdin 1988). The controversies on each of these aspects are likely to be resolved only by clearer specification and empirical tests. Such developments require changes in many professional beliefs and half-truths about both the nature of research and therapy, such as 'research is too difficult', 'therapy is an art' and 'everyone is an individual' (Kazdin 1988). An increasing set towards evaluation in training as well as coverage of a broader range of therapeutic issues is likely to move the main focus from competitive rivalry between schools of therapy to identifying the key aspects of the most effective ways of treating and managing the diverse psychological problems of children and families.

References

Abramowitz, C.V. (1976) The effectiveness of group psychotherapy with children, *Archives of General Psychiatry* 33: 320–36.
Achenbach, T.M. (1986) The developmental study of psychopathology: implications for psychotherapy and behavior change, in S.L. Garfield and A.E. Bergin (eds) *Handbook of Psychotherapy and Behavior Change*, 3rd edn, New York: Wiley.
Achenbach, T.M., McConaughty, S.H. and Howell, C.T. (1987) Child/adolescent behavioral and emotional problems: implications for cross-informant correlations for situation specificity, *Psychological Bulletin* 101: 213–32.
Alexander, J.F., Barton, C., Schiavo, R.S. and Parsons, B.V. (1976) Systems-behavioral intervention with families of delinquents: therapist characteristics, family behavior,

and outcome, *Journal of Consulting and Clinical Psychology* 44: 656–64.

Bandura, A. (1989) Human agency in social cognitive theory, *American Psychologist* 44: 1,175–84.

Barrett, C.L., Hampe, I.E. and Miller, L.C. (1978) Research on child psychotherapy, in S.L. Garfield and A.E. Bergin (eds) *Handbook of Psychotherapy and Behavior Change: An Empirical Analysis*, 2nd edn, New York: Wiley.

Berg, I. (1985) The management of truancy, *Journal of Child Psychology and Psychiatry* 26: 325–31.

Berg, I., Consterdine, M., Hullin, R., McGuire, R. and Tyrer, S. (1978) The effects of two randomly allocated court procedures on truancy, *British Journal of Criminology* 18: 232–44.

Berger, M. (ed.) (1989) *Clinical Services: Monitoring, Evaluation and Micro-Computers*, Association for Child Psychology and Psychiatry: Occasional Papers no. 1.

Berger, M., Yule, W. and Wigley, V. (1987) The teacher–child interaction project (TCIP): implementing behavioural programmes with troublesome individual children in the primary school, in K. Wheldall (ed.) *The Behaviourist in the Classroom*, London: Allen & Unwin.

Beutler, L.W., Crago, M. and Arizmendi, T.G. (1986) Therapist variables in psychotherapy process and outcome, in S. Garfield and A. Bergin (eds) *Handbook of Psychotherapy and Behavior Change*, 3rd edn, New York: Wiley.

Blagg, N.R. and Yule, W. (1984) The behavioural treatment of school refusal: a comparative study, *Behaviour Research and Therapy* 22: 119–27.

Brewin, C.R. and Bradley, C. (1989) Patient preferences and randomized clinical trials, *British Medical Journal* 299: 313–15.

Brickman, P., Rabinowitz, V.C., Karuza, J., Coates, D., Cohn, E. and Kidder, L. (1982) Models of helping and coping, *American Psychologist* 37: 369–84.

Burke, A.E. and Silverman, W.K. (1987) The prescriptive treatment of school refusal, *Clinical Psychology Review* 7: 353–62.

Callias, M. (1985) Group treatments, in M. Rutter and L. Hersov (eds) *Child and Adolescent Psychiatry*, 2nd edn, Oxford: Blackwell Scientific.

Callias, M. (1987) Teaching parents, teachers and nurses, in W. Yule and J. Carr (eds) *Behaviour Modification for People with Mental Handicaps*, 2nd edn, London: Croom Helm.

Callias, M. and Carr, J. (1975) Behaviour modification programmes in a community setting, in C.C. Kiernan and F.P. Woodford (eds) *Behaviour Modification with the Severely Retarded*, Elsevier, N. Holland: Associated Scientific Publishers.

Callias, M., Frosh, S. and Michie, S. (1987) Social skills training of young children in a clinical setting, *Behavioural Psychotherapy* 15: 367–80.

Casey, R.J. and Berman, J.S. (1985) The outcome of psychotherapy with children, *Psychological Bulletin* 98: 388–400.

Clements, J. (1985) Update: training parents of mentally handicapped children, *Newsletter of the Association for Child Psychology and Psychiatry* 7(4): 2–9.

Critelli, J.W. and Newmann, K.F. (1984) The placebo: conceptual analysis of a construct in transition, *American Psychologist* 39: 32–9.

Dangel, R.F. and Polster, R.A. (eds) (1984) *Parent Training: Foundations of Research and Practice*, New York: Guilford.

Dische, S., Yule, W., Corbett, J. and Hand, D. (1983) Childhood nocturnal enuresis: factors associated with outcome of treatment with an enuresis alarm, *Developmental and Medical Child Neurology* 25: 67–81.

Dush, D.M., Hirt, M.L. and Schroeder, H.E. (1989) Self-statement modification in the treatment of child behavior disorders: a meta-analysis, *Psychological Bulletin* 106: 97–106.

Embry, L.H. (1984) What to do? Matching client characteristics and intervention through a prescriptive taxonomic key, in R.F. Dangel and R.A. Polster (eds) *Parent Training:*

Foundations of Research and Practice, New York: Guilford.

Evans, I.M. (1989) A multidimensional model for conceptualizing the design of child behavior therapy, *Behavioural Psychotherapy* 17: 237–51.

Eysenck, H.J. (1952) The effects of psychotherapy: an evaluation, *Journal of Consulting Psychology* 16: 319–29.

Firestone, P. and Witt, J.E. (1982) Characteristics of families completing and prematurely discontinuing a behavioral parent-training program, *Journal of Pediatric Psychology* 7: 209–22.

Frosh, S. and Callias, M. (1980) Social skills training in an infant school setting, *Behavioural Psychotherapy* 8: 69–79.

Furman, W. (1980) Promoting social development: developmental implications for treatment, in B.B. Lahey and A.E. Kazdin (eds) *Advances in Clinical Child Psychology*, vol. 3, New York: Plenum Press.

Gurman, A.S., Kniskern, D.P. and Pinsof, W.M. (1986) Research on the process and outcome of marital and family therapy, in S.L. Garfield and A.E. Bergin (eds) *Handbook of Psychotherapy and Behavior Change*, 3rd edn, New York: Wiley.

Herbert, M. (1987) *Behavioural Treatment of Children with Problems: A Practice Manual*, 2nd edn, London: Academic Press.

Hogg, C., Callias, M. and Pellegrini, D. (1986) Treatment of a 7 year-old hyperactive boy with educational problems, *Behavioural Psychotherapy* 14: 145–61.

Holmes, D.S. and Urie, R.G. (1975) Effects of preparing children for psychotherapy, *Journal of Consulting and Clinical Psychology* 43: 311–18.

Horvath, P. (1988) Placebos and common factors in two decades of psychotherapy research, *Psychological Bulletin* 104: 214–25.

Howard, G.S. (1985) The role of values in the science of psychology, *American Psychologist* 40: 255–65.

Howlin, P. and Rutter, M. with Berger, M., Hemsley, R., Hersov, L. and Yule, W. (1987) *Treatment of Autistic Children*, Chichester: Wiley.

Imber, S.D., Pilkonis, P.A., Harway, N.I., Klein, R.H. and Rubinsky, P.A. (1982) Maintenance of change in the psychotherapies, *Journal of Psychiatric Treatment and Evaluation* 4: 1–5.

Jacobson, N.S. (1985) Family therapy outcome research: potential pitfalls and prospects, *Journal of Marital and Family Therapy* 11: 149–58.

Johnson, J.H., Rasbury, W.C. and Siegel, L.J. (1986) *Approaches to Child Treatment: Introduction to Theory, Research, and Practice*, Oxford: Pergamon Press.

Julian III, A. and Kilmann, P.R. (1979) Group treatment of juvenile delinquents: a review of the outcome literature, *International Journal of Group Psychotherapy* 29(1): 3–37.

Kanfer, F.M. and Saslow, G. (1969) Behavioural diagnosis, in C.M. Franks (ed.) *Behavior Therapy: Appraisal and Status*, New York: McGraw Hill.

Kazdin, A. (1983) Psychiatric diagnosis, dimensions of dysfunction, and child behavior therapy, *Behavior Therapy* 14: 73–99.

Kazdin, A.E. (1986) The evaluation of psychotherapy: research design and methodology, in S.L. Garfield and A.E. Bergin (eds) *Handbook of Psycho-therapy and Behavior Change*, 3rd edn, New York: Wiley.

Kazdin, A.E. (1987) Treatment of antisocial behavior in children: current status and future directions, *Psychological Bulletin* 102: 189–203.

Kazdin, A.E. (1988) *Child Psychotherapy: Developing and Identifying Effective Treatments*, Oxford: Pergamon Press.

Kazdin, A.E. (1990) Childhood depression, *Journal of Child Psychology and Psychiatry* 31: 121–60.

Kazdin, A.E., Esveldt-Dawson, K., Unis, A.S. and Rancurello, M.D. (1983) Child and parent evaluations of depression and aggression in psychiatric inpatient children, *Journal of Abnormal Child Psychology* 11: 401–13.

Kazdin, A.E., Esveldt-Dawson, K., French, N.H. and Unis, A.S. (1987a) Problem-solving skills training and relationship therapy in the treatment of antisocial child behavior, *Journal of Consulting and Clinical Psychotherapy* 55: 76–85.

Kazdin, A.E., Esveldt-Dawson, K., French, N.H. and Unis, A.S. (1987b) Effects of parent management training and problem-solving skills training combined in the treatment of antisocial child behavior, *Journal of American Academy of Child and Adolescent Psychiatry* 26: 416–24.

Kendall, P.C. (1984) Cognitive-behavioral self-control therapy for children, *Journal of Child Psychology and Psychiatry* 25: 173–89.

Kendler, T.S. (1986) World views and the concept of development: a reply to Lerner and Kauffman, *Developmental Review* 6: 80–95.

Kendrick, M.J., Craig, K.D., Lawson, D.M. and Davidson, P.O. (1982) Cognitive and behavioural therapy for musical-performance anxiety, *Journal of Consulting and Clinical Psychology* 50: 353–62.

Kiesler, D.J. (1971) Experimental designs in psychotherapy research, in A.E. Bergin and S.L. Garfield (eds) *Handbook of Psychotherapy Research and Behavior Change*, 1st edn, New York: Wiley.

Kolvin, I., Garside, R.F., Nicol, A.R., Macmillan, A., Wolstenholme, F. and Leitch, I.M. (1981) *Help Starts Here: The Maladjusted Child in the Ordinary School*, London: Tavistock.

Lambert, M.J., Shapiro, D.A. and Bergin, A.E. (1986) The effectiveness of psychotherapy, in S.L. Garfield and A.E. Bergin (eds) *Handbook of Psychotherapy and Behavior Change*, 3rd edn, New York: Wiley.

Lerner, R.M. and Kauffman, M.B. (1985) The concept of development in contextualism, *Developmental Review* 5: 309–33.

Levitt, E.E. (1957) The results of psychotherapy with children: an evaluation, *Journal of Consulting Psychology* 21: 189–96.

Levitt, E.E. (1963) Psychotherapy with children: a further evaluation, *Behaviour Research and Therapy* 60: 326–9.

Lockyer, R.L. and Rutter, M. (1970) A five to fifteen year follow-up study of infantile psychosis, IV: Patterns of cognitive ability, *British Journal of Social and Clinical Psychology* 9: 152–63.

Lovaas, O.I. (1987) Behavioral treatment and normal educational/intellectual functioning in young autistic children, *Journal of Consulting and Clinical Psychology* 55: 3–9.

McMahon, R.J. and Forehand, R. (1980) Self-help behavior therapies in parent training, in B.B. Lahey and A.E. Kazdin (eds) *Advances in Clinical Child Psychology*, vol. 3, New York: Plenum Press.

Morley, S.V. (1989) Single case research, in G. Parry and F.N. Watts (eds) *Behavioural and Mental Health Research: A Handbook of Skills and Methods*, Hove and London: Lawrence Erlbaum.

O'Dell, S. (1974) Training parents in behavior modification: a review, *Psychological Bulletin* 81: 418–33.

Ollendick, T.H. (1986) Child and adolescent behavior therapy, in S. Garfield and A. Bergin (eds) *Handbook of Psychotherapy and Behavior Change*, 3rd edn, New York: Wiley.

Owens, R.G., Ashcroft, J.B., Leinster, S. and Slade, P.D. (1986) Psychological effects of the offer of breast reconstruction in mastectomy patients, in M. Watson and S. Greer (eds) *Psychosocial Issues in Malignant Disease*, Vol. 8, New York: Plenum Press.

Owens, R.G., Slade, P.D. and Fielding, D.M. (1989) Patient series and quasi-experimental design, in G. Parry and F.N. Watts (eds) *Behavioural and Mental Health Research: A Handbook of Skills and Methods*, Hove and London: Lawrence Erlbaum.

Parloff, M.B. (1986) Placebo controls in psychotherapy research: a sine qua non or a placebo for research problems?, *Journal of Consulting and Clinical Psychology* 54: 79–87.

Patterson, G.R. (1982) *Coercive Family Process*, Eugene, Oregon: Castalia Publications.

Patterson, G.R. and Fleischman, M.J. (1979) Maintenance of treatment effects: some considerations concerning family systems and follow-up data, *Behavior Therapy* 10: 168–85.

Patterson, G.R., De Baryshe, B.D. and Ramsey, E. (1989) A developmental perspective in antisocial behavior, *American Psychologist* 44(2): 329–35.

Pellegrini, D.S. and Urbain, E.S. (1985) An evaluation of interpersonal cognitive problem-solving training with children, *Journal of Child Psychology and Psychiatry* 26: 17–41.

Peterman, P.J. (1981) Parenting and environmental considerations, *American Journal of Orthopsychiatry* 51: 351–5.

Phillips, G.T. and Smith, J.E. (1986) The behavioural treatment of faeces retention: an expanded case study, *Behavioural Psychotherapy* 14: 124–36.

Pocock, S.J. (1983) *Clinical Trials: A Practical Approach*, Chichester: Wiley.

Reid, W.J. and Shyne, A.W. (1969) *Brief and Extended Casework*, New York: Columbia University Press.

Ricks, D.F. (1974) Supershrink: methods of a therapist judged successful on the basis of adult outcomes of adolescent patients, in D.E. Ricks, M. Roff and A. Thomas (eds) *Life History Research in Psychopathology*, Minneapolis, Minn.: University of Minnesota Press.

Rogers, C.R. (1952) *Client-Control Therapy*, Boston, Mass: Houghton Mifflin.

Rosen, A. and Proctor, E.K. (1981) Distinctions between treatment outcomes and their implications for treatment evaluation, *Journal of Consulting and Clinical Psychology* 49: 418–25.

Ross, A.E. (1981) Of rigor and relevance, *Professional Psychology* 12: 318–27.

Rutter, M. (1982) Psychological therapies in child psychiatry: issues and prospects, *Psychological Medicine* 12: 723–40.

Rutter, M. (1985a) Psychological therapies in child psychiatry: issues and prospects, in M. Rutter and L. Hersov (eds) *Child and Adolescent Psychiatry: Modern Approaches*, 2nd edn, Oxford: Blackwell Scientific.

Rutter, M. (1985b) The treatment of autistic children, *Journal of Child Psychology and Psychiatry* 26: 193–214.

Rutter, M. (ed.) (1988) *Studies of Psychosocial Risk: The Power of Longitudinal Data*, Cambridge: Cambridge University Press.

Rutter, M. (1989) Isle of Wight revisited: twenty-five years of child psychiatric epidemiology, *Journal of the American Academy of Child and Adolescent Psychiatry* 28: 633–53.

Rutter, M., Tizard, J. and Whitmore, K. (1970) *Education, Health and Behaviour*, London: Longman.

Sachs, J.S. (1983) Negative factors in brief psychotherapy: an empirical assessment, *Journal of Consulting and Clinical Psychology* 51: 564–87.

Scarr, S. (1985) Constructing psychology: making facts and fables for our times, *American Psychologist* 40: 499–512.

Schachar, R.J. and Taylor, E. (1986) Clinical assessment and management strategies, in E.A. Taylor (ed.) *The Overactive Child*, Clinics in Developmental Medicine no. 97, Spastics International Medical Publications, Oxford: Blackwell Scientific.

Scott, G. and Richards, M.P.M. (1990) Night waking in infants: effects of providing advice and support for parents, *Journal of Child Psychology and Psychiatry* 31: 551–67.

Seymour, F.W., Brock, P., During, M. and Poole, G. (1989) Reducing sleep disruptions in young children: evaluation of therapist-guided and written information approaches: a brief report, *Journal of Child Psychology and Psychiatry* 30: 913–18.

Shaffer, D. (1985) Enuresis, in M. Rutter and L. Hersov (eds) *Child and Adolescent Psychiatry*, 2nd edn, Oxford: Blackwell.

Sheldrick, C. (1985) Treatment of delinquents, in M. Rutter and L. Hersov, (eds) *Child and Adolescent Psychiatry*, 2nd edn, Oxford: Blackwell.

Smith, J.E. (1984) Non-accidental injury to children: I. A review of behavioural interventions, *Behaviour Research and Therapy* 22: 331–47.

Smith, J.E. and Rachman, S.J. (1984) Non-accidental injury to children: II. A controlled evaluation of a behavioural management programme, *Behaviour Research and Therapy* 22: 349–66.

Smith, J.E., Rachman, S.J. and Yule, W. (1984) Non-accidental injury to children: III. Methodological problems of evaluative treatment research, *Behaviour Research and Therapy* 22: 367–83.

Sroufe, L.A. and Rutter, M. (1984) The domain of developmental psychopathology, *Child Development* 55: 17–29.

Taylor, E., Schachar, R., Thorley, G., Wieselberg, H.M., Everitt, B. and Rutter, M. (1987) Which boys respond to stimulant medication? A controlled trial of methylphenidate in boys with disruptive behaviour, *Psychological Medicine* 17: 121–43.

Truax, C.B. and Carkhuff, R.R. (1967) *Toward Effective Counselling and Psychotherapy: Training and Practice*, Chicago: Aldine Press.

Wahler, R.G. (1980) The insular mother: her problems in parent–child treatment, *Journal of Applied Behavior Analysis* 13: 207–19.

Wahler, R.G. and Dumas, J.E. (1984) Changing the observational coding styles of insular and non-insular mothers, in R.F. Dangel and R.A. Polster (eds) *Parent Training: Foundations of Research and Practice*, New York: Guilford.

Wahler, R.G., Berland, R.M. and Coe, T.D. (1979) Generalization processes in child behaviour change, in B.B. Lahey and A.E. Kazdin (eds) *Advances in Clinical Child Psychology*, Vol. 2, New York: Plenum.

Weisz, J.R., Weiss, B., Alicke, M.D. and Klotz, M.L. (1987) Effectiveness of psychotherapy with children and adolescents: a meta analysis for clinicians, *Journal of Consulting and Clinical Psychology* 55: 542–9.

Yule, W. (1990) Developmental considerations in child assessment, in T.H. Ollendick and M. Hersen (eds) *Handbook of Child and Adolescent Assessment*, New York: Pergamon Press.

Yule, W. and Hemsley, D. (1977) Single case methodology in medical psychology, in S. Rachman (ed.) *Contributions to Medical Psychology*, Vol. 1, Oxford: Pergamon Press.

Zelen, M. (1990) Randomized consent designs for clinical trials: an update, *Statistics in Medicine* 9: 645–56.

PART II

Practice

3

An interactive approach to language and communication for non-speaking children*

PHIL CHRISTIE, ELIZABETH NEWSON,
JOHN NEWSON AND WENDY PREVEZER

This approach is grounded in a view of child development which emphasizes the importance of communication in the life of the ordinary infant, particularly during the first year of life and certainly before she produces her first understandable word. It is based on the observation that spoken language only begins once the child can already communicate many of her feelings, thoughts and intentions effectively by non-verbal means, although at first this may be possible only with people who know her well and in situations with which she and they are already reasonably familiar.

From the moment the newborn baby first opens his eyes to gaze at the face and listen to the voice of another interested human being, he displays a remarkable repertoire of action patterns, combined with a variety of expressive facial gestures, which are of such a compelling quality that they will, in effect, ensure that any reasonably sympathetic caregiver will interpret this activity as a valid attempt at communication. The process of imputing meaning to the infant's natural behaviour clearly begins from the moment a mother first looks into her baby's eyes and greets him. Babies seem to come already equipped with a whole collection of convincing expressions which are readily interpreted by adults as having meanings such as puzzlement, anxiety, interest, excitement, relief, boredom, distress, and so on; during the first few months mothers willingly rely on such cues when they try to respond to their baby's mood.

From systematic study of these early encounters between mothers and babies, it can be shown that their interactions take the form of dialogues which have a distinct turn-taking character: each partner first acts and then attends to the actions of the other in an alternating sequence of reciprocally prompted vocalizations and gestures. The expressive gestures of one partner seem to call forth

---

* Part of this chapter appeared in much briefer form as 'Some practical guidelines for the teaching of language to non-speaking children', in A. Hales (ed.) (1978) *The Children of Skylark Ward*, Cambridge University Press.

an answer from the other and, in this sense, it appears that babies are proficient in being able to hold 'conversations' with other responsive people, even though for many months they obviously will not contribute anything remotely resembling proper words.

From the beginning of life, babies emit signals which include all kinds of apparent gestures, postural changes, hand and arm movements, head and eye pointings, mouth movements, and so on. It is the *temporal* patterning and inter-weaving of all these reactions in reciprocally adjusted sequences which underlie what we call social empathy between human beings; it is this rapport which in turn creates shared understandings. Even when spoken language is impossible, people – whether infant or adult – have inbuilt endowments which enable them to enter into dialogues and hence to evolve shared personal codes of communi-cation; and this is what every normal baby does with his mother during the first twelve months.

Of course the spoken language which most children go on to acquire involves much more than this. The way in which language proper is learned remains puzzling. Even so, there does seem to be a consensus about the fundamental importance of non-verbal communication as the first scaffolding to support the use of words; practical guidelines for language therapy must therefore start from the assumption that one needs to build up a substantial repertoire of shared understandings with a child before looking for the use of words as such. With normal children this is hardly a problem, because a whole corpus of shared understandings will already have developed before the child himself attempts to add isolated words to an already functioning non-verbal dialogue within which he habitually operates. These general guidelines are aimed at situations where, for whatever reason, this transition to verbal language fails to occur naturally; we shall go on to show their application for a particularly difficult group, children with autism.

Although one of the first questions asked about children whose speech is not developing is 'Is she deaf?', deaf children are in the minority among language-impaired children. Language can be vulnerable to disability of any kind. Kay Mogford (1973), looking at a sample of children referred for any reason to a toy library for handicapped children, estimated that more than 85 per cent had speech and language problems. She developed an interview schedule for use with mothers, which enables a base-line to be established for communication skills in those cases where the child is functioning below the level at which formal testing procedures (eg Derbyshire Language Scheme or Reynell) are possible. The virtue of this instrument is that it relies on a mixture of different sorts of evidence including direct observation, maternal report and demonstrations of what the child does when interaction is attempted by an adult (Mogford 1973); a more recent and comprehensive checklist is that of Dewart and Summers (1988).

In practice, then, there will be many children for whom it seems pointless to ask 'What is his mean length of utterance?', 'How many words does he use?' or even 'How many words does he understand?'; it is more relevant to ask 'How does he make his needs and wishes known?' and 'How can you persuade him to cooperate with you?' A large proportion of these children also have severe attention difficulties, so that the initial problem must be to engender some kind of rapport with the child in order to help him at least to share with another person common experiences, objects or points of reference. Whether one's intention is assessment or remediation (more often a progressive combination of the two), little can be accomplished until rapport is achieved. Our first need is, therefore, to unravel the mysterious process known as establishing rapport.

The nature of rapport

We have to assume that, at an earlier age, the child was prevented by some disability from taking full advantage of the communication practice offered by his parents. It is now therefore necessary (our argument goes) not only to prolong the period of active pre-verbal dialogue, but also to reaffirm the basic social messages of early interaction with deliberate clarity and intensity.

To begin with, it is worth reminding ourselves that the first intentional communications which infants develop depend upon their being in a very familiar setting, doing things they have often done before in much the same way, and collaborating with people they are used to. For most babies it is the routines of caregiving such as feeding, changing or bathing which provide the most fruitful occasions for the dialogue format.

Feeding a baby with a spoon is a good example: anyone who has done this regularly will know that it is not just a matter of shovelling the food into an open mouth. There is an element of negotiation involved. One has to be sure that the child has accepted and swallowed one mouthful and is interested in the next before offering it to her. The dialogue thus consists of offers and acceptances, refusals and re-negotiations. As with other giving-and-taking routines, the adult signals that the food is ready and the infant signals whether or not she is willing to receive the next mouthful. The way the infant looks, swallows, opens her mouth, purses her lips or turns her head away provides the feeder with important signals to indicate what response to make next: if these signals are ignored, the whole feeding routine may be disrupted. Because feeding is a very repetitive experience, it tends to develop into a ritual which involves a definite and recognizable pattern of events. Each adult–child pair will evolve their own characteristic ways of signalling what to expect next, and their own code of what actions are recognized as permissible and which upset the partnership; each knows how to play a part in an interaction which has become habitual. Feeding is just one example of parent–baby routines which have a ritual quality. Such routines provide a framework within which shared understanding can develop and to which language can in time become attached.

Language is normally first encountered by the infant as a kind of background music to familiar action sequences in which he is caught up and fully involved as a participant. At this stage words and phrases (not understood as such) have the same function as the dramatic 'oo's', 'ah's' and 'mm's' with which mothers also communicate to their babies. That is, they serve as 'markers' or punctuation within the dialogue: they act as triggering and pacing signals for the gestures and changes in facial expression that are included in the sequence of familiar actions and responses. In practice, language will continue to have some function as an *intonational commentary highlighting significant events*, at least in face-to-face interaction, even when words are fully understood: and this is an important carrier of meaning.

It has been shown, for instance, that during face-to-face conversation between adults there is an interactional synchrony between the sounds and gestures emitted by the speaker and the sympathetic responsive gestures of the attentive listener; it is also claimed that babies under 3 months automatically move their limbs and time their facial gestures in harmony with the pattern of sounds with which adults address them (Condon and Sander 1974). Furthermore it is now being claimed that profoundly deaf children may be assisted in learning to speak by being given auditory feedback through an artificial cochlear implant, which conveys the *intonational* pattern of spoken speech even when the words themselves are so indistinct as not to be heard as words except by lip-reading. All these facts point to the importance of what may be called the social timing of natural conversation (which is seriously impaired in autistic children (Newson 1978; 1987)). The intonational commentary not only provides information about when to change from listening to responding and what sort of response is expected, but also indicates which parts of the communication sequence have special significance or mark noteworthy events in some external happening on which both partners are focused. The intonation pattern also marks when events are building to a climax and when an event sequence has come to an end; and it does this in such a way as to help the listener to anticipate what is coming next in terms of a new event starting.

The course of language development in individual children may, of course, be highly idiosyncratic. Some children get hooked on the naming game, and build up a large vocabulary of single words which are used as labels for distinct objects, but this is not necessarily the case. Long ago M.M. Lewis (1963) noted that one of the first words used by his child was a contraction of 'Pretty', a very abstract descriptive category. Some children produce utterances mainly to comment upon surprising environmental events like appearance, disappearance or novelty; others use words mainly to solicit adult co-operation. One child known to us, for instance, used the word 'Mummy' as a mere label for some months before discovering that the same word could serve a better function as a powerful demand that his mother should do something for him. Because of these and other individual variations we need to recognize that, once the child has developed his dialogue skills, there are probably many different routes by which he may attain the ultimate goal of linguistic competence. An over-simple stage theory of language development may not provide the best model in devising therapeutic strategies for every child.

The nature of imitation

Imitation clearly plays an important role in learning to communicate, but this does not imply that children normally learn language simply by copying the words they hear from adults: we can see the sterility of this in autistic children's echolalia. Attempts to teach children by drilling them in words or sentences out of any meaningful context are not very helpful, and may actually be inimical to real interpersonal communication. The 'parrotting' of words, if used at appropriate moments, may be one step on the road to helping a child to state his needs baldly, but it does not have much to do with shared understanding or dialogue.

However, imitation is important in pre-verbal development because it enables the child to appreciate and try out many subtle gestures which underlie communication. But the phenomenon of imitation remains both puzzling and intriguing. Consider, for example, how mothers try to teach their pre-verbal infants to blow their noses, suck through a straw or make tongue-clicking noises when they recognize a horse. Undoubtedly some children do learn to do such things as a result of demonstration by an adult; quite how they know what to do merely from seeing another person performing defies rational explanation. In some instances it seems that mothers may have waited until the child performed the act spontaneously, and then capitalized on this by applauding and urging the child to repeat the performance; one study has shown that imitation frequently begins by the mother copying some spontaneous act of the child (Pawlby 1977). This does not explain all imitation in infants: one is tempted to conclude that the mere sight of certain gestures in adults tends to induce a similar sympathetic response in the child's own musculature. Piaget comments on the effect of seeing an object opening and closing, causing the child's own hand or mouth to open and close in sympathy (Piaget 1951). This can also be observed in parents feeding their children by spoon, when their own mouth may open just before the expected response in the child *even when they are sitting behind him*, or in the teeth-clenching that may accompany hand gripping movements. With the pre-verbal infant we can hardly assume a role for complex cognitive processes; the implication may be that human beings share some kind of inbuilt capacity for what might be called sympathetic motor contagion, which precedes conscious imitation and is as yet very inadequately researched. The capacity to watch an action performed by another, and to sense its *similarity* to an action which could potentially be performed by oneself, could thus underpin eventual creative and selective learning-by-observation of acts perceived as successful.

Facilitating meaning

Language is most easily learned as an accompaniment to gestures and actions, where the meaning is virtually self-explanatory. When one says 'Ups-a-daisy' after a child has fallen over and is trying to get up; or when a child breaks off his activity in response to a noise and looks enquiringly at his mother, who 'answers', 'It's just a door banging': then it is probably the tone of the words rather than the words themselves that affect the child. Nevertheless, he reads the reassuring intent from the way the words are said, and this is a significant part of their meaning. Both tone of voice and accompanying facial expressions tend to induce appropriate reactions by a process of emotional contagion. Thus words said at a significant moment in a particular setting to coincide with other significant events, including changes in the mother's face, are pregnant with meaning for the child and easy for him to understand and respond to.

It can hardly be stressed too often that in the normal course of development the *understanding* of language precedes the active production of speech. This suggests caution in the use of techniques which are primarily designed to elicit active speech sounds from the child. In fact, one might go so far as to say that these are appropriate in contexts only where any utterance the child makes will have an immediate reference which is self-explanatory to the child; that is, it will refer to what she herself is doing, or to some event she is actively attending to. In other words, speech-eliciting techniques should not intrude to the extent that the child's utterances no longer fit into a natural two-way communication flow. The only exception to this rule might be where speech is already being used appropriately but is too quiet, indistinct or garbled for the child to be making herself effectively understood. In such circumstances there may be a case for intensive sessions designed to increase the volume or clarity of utterance; or, in rare cases where the child is completely mute, to encourage the *mechanical habit* of utterance. Generally speaking, however, utterance needs to be embedded in the context of a meaningful two-way exchange, which makes sense to the child because the words are supported by gestural and expressive communication signals. (Obviously for assessment purposes it may be necessary to suspend context temporarily in order to test verbal comprehension.) Children acquire language most easily and spontaneously when they are confident in their ability to make their own needs and wishes known to other people, if necessary without words.

It is too easy to stifle a child's natural or emerging need to communicate by insisting that he does this in some arbitrarily approved manner, rather than by responding to anything the child might be trying to convey. Behavioural stimulation programmes which concentrate mainly on the form and correctness of the child's input, rather than on its content, may serve to inhibit the spontaneous and meaningful use of words. There has been a tendency for behavioural programmes to strip down the learning situation to its bare essentials on the grounds that this should make matters less confusing for the child. This may be useful for many situations, but language has different characteristics. In practice children often seem to acquire language best in 'over-determined' situations where many different sorts of cues are available, and where there is an element of choice as to which cues the child will, in practice, utilize. We should be ready to seize upon any instance of genuine communication which the child shows he can make use of, whether or not these are theoretically prescribed.

If, as we believe, the evolution of shared understandings is essential to the development of functional and flexible language, it is inappropriate to view language acquisition as a process of transmitting a commodity called knowledge from an adult instructor to a child pupil. Shared understandings are the product of joint and reciprocal involvement between two people. New understandings can emerge only on the basis of genuine reciprocity between two individuals, each of whom is allowed to take turns: that is, to take the initiative in acting to sustain the dialogue. Neither partner is in complete control of the understandings which will emerge, but each participant quickly begins to share with her partner a whole history of successful past attempts to arrive at such understandings. External observers must understand that this history may not be evident at any given point, whatever the sophistication of their observational recording methods.

Communication between individuals is sustained only to the extent that it is intrinsically self-rewarding. Arriving at new shared understandings is rewarding in itself; the introduction of extrinsic rewards does not automatically result in an improvement in real two-way communication, partly because these can distract from communication's aim. Strategies based on extrinsic rewards for specific acts of behaviour may eventually work *against* the evolution of those experiences of sharing that lay the groundwork for spontaneous language development. However, extrinsic rewards may *sometimes*, with *some* children, be useful initially to establish the basic prerequisites for communication to take place – level of attention, for instance, when the child needs to stop and look in a particular direction where something interesting is to happen. Rewards are no substitute for the actual interest of events.

In the ordinary child, the social interaction which precedes the apparently effortless evolving of language is frequently game-like and humorous. Well-worn rituals emerge which, once they are firmly entrenched, develop further as a focus for surprise or anticlimax when normal expectations are violated. At this stage, anticipatory teasing play can be initiated by either partner, which introduces a lively, joking element into dialogue, and gives the child a vested interest in elaborating these two-person games so that they change before they have a chance to become predictable and boring. However, a minimum requirement for this kind of productive play is that the adult should put himself wholeheartedly at the disposal of the child in a one-to-one relationship.

The familiar rituals which children most obviously enjoy almost always incorporate patterns of sound and movement which are synchronized rhythmically, have a distinctive prosodic beat and are encapsulated within some overall melodic contour. The child's willing attention is clearly captivated as he becomes caught up and carried along in patterns of reciprocal interaction which both actively and intimately involve him. The rhythmic, repetitive format that is characteristic of the songs, dances, nursery rhymes and anticipatory lap games which so obviously appeal to babies seems to make these especially memorable; the child readily appreciates when he is being invited to participate and what he has to do. He will rapidly learn to anticipate the part he might play and what will happen next. Even very young babies have this capacity for mutual rhythmic involvement, so that musical activities are naturally engaging. It is also easy to manipulate the mood of a baby by altering pace, rhythm and pitch so as to deliberately induce states varying between calm contentment and vigorous excitement.

All of these considerations from normal developmental psychology can contribute richly to the ways in which we devise a pre-language programme for any non-speaking child; they are perhaps of especial significance when we are working with children who have little interest in or knowledge of social dialogue patterns, who have impaired social timing, whose paucity of verbal development is matched by paucity of facial expression and of natural gesture, and who, in sum, are multiply handicapped in every communication mode: children suffering from autism.

Interactive approaches to education and therapy in autism

The interactive approach to autistic children, and in particular the use of music as a framework for this approach, has been developed at Sutherland House School for Autistic Children in Nottingham. It has come about as the result of a unique collaboration between a school and an academic research unit. The research-based understandings were derived from two research programmes: one headed by John Newson and concerned with the way normal language development is built upon the shared understandings and reciprocal exchanges of baby and caregiver (Newson 1974; 1979); the other headed by Elizabeth Newson and concerned with the nature of autism and the ways in which its triad of impairments (global language impairment, including that of social timing; impairment of social empathy; rigidity of thought processes) are destructive to such development and require specific interventional methods. The school-based understandings derived from two successive Principals, both developmental psychologists whose postgraduate training was at Nottingham, the second (Phil Christie) having a sustained interest in music therapy (Christie and Wimpory 1986); from a staff which has developed an adventurous and imaginative outlook to match their expertise; and from the pioneering work of Isabel Jones, who was the first music specialist at Sutherland House.

As the curriculum of the school has evolved, we have become acutely aware of the limitations of traditional approaches to teaching autistic children which have centred upon structured teaching and behavioural techniques. While this style of teaching has been enormously effective in helping the autistic child acquire functional skills and in developing more appropriate ways of behaving, it has had much less impact in facilitating flexible and appropriate communication. Earlier diagnosis of autistic children in the area led to involvement with an increasing number of under-5s; this challenged us to consider more appropriate ways of working on pre-verbal dialogue skills, using 'intersubjective' methods alongside behavioural techniques. The frequent observation by autistic children's parents, that they felt most 'in tune' with their children during rough-and-tumble play, supported our exploration of interactive methods facilitated by music.

Basic principles and description

Children with autism have a particular need for prolonged and intensive periods of individual teaching with a restricted range of familiar adults. Whatever the curriculum content, little can be achieved without rapport between adult and child. In fact the fundamental impairments of autism, regardless of the intellectual ability of a particular child, mean that the establishment and development of social rapport has to be seen as one of the central aims. This determines both staffing levels and the way that the children's education is organized. A classroom ratio of one adult to every two children, with the addition of a separately staffed central playroom, allows each child to receive a full hour's individual work with the same member of staff each day. At certain times, most notably in the musical interaction sessions described below, the individual staff members' endeavours are supported by additional therapists.

The development of individual music sessions, particularly with younger children, has given staff a way of focusing on the establishment of rapport between child and familiar adult; this has been the catalyst for extending interactive approaches into all areas of the school's work. The essential orientation of this approach has been to reproduce the conditions and circumstances which, as we have seen, effectively promote language development in the normal infant. Children with autism to varying degrees are unable to enter into this process of rapport and dialogue in a natural way. This is not due to any lack of opportunity or experience, but because their basic innate impairments sabotage the critical processes of development which are involved (Newson 1978; 1987). The sessions to be described set out to reproduce this essential element of the infant's experience at a time when the impaired child may be more ready to benefit from it. They deliberately enhance the experience by using music in an attempt to compensate for the child's difficulties and to facilitate his access to the process.

The musical interaction takes place in a small comfortable room, set away from the main part of the school, where distractions are kept to a minimum. It is furnished with some small chairs, a sofa, floor cushions and a digital piano, which allows the therapist to see the child over the top while playing. A selection of simple percussion and other instruments is available and used for particular purposes with certain children, but these are not central to the approach.

The majority of the children have an individual hour-long session each week, although some in the early stages may have shorter but more frequent sessions. The child is accompanied to the music room by the teacher or nursery nurse who works individually with that child elsewhere; in some instances one of the child's parents might join, or take the place of, the individual worker. The therapist currently carrying out this work is a speech therapist (Wendy Prevezer) who has musical skills and is employed as a music/language therapist.

The most important difference between the work developed at Sutherland House and what might be described as 'traditional music therapy' concerns the therapeutic relationship. In traditional music therapy the emphasis is on the relationship between child and therapist which is developed through the expression by the child of an 'inner mood music' (Nordoff 1988). As Isabel Jones early pointed out, this might be highly satisfying to the therapist, but seemed a wasteful self-indulgence on the part of someone seeing a child with autism only once a week. Socially impaired children need *meaningful* relationships: in the musical interaction approach at Sutherland House, the emphasis is on the building of a relationship between the child and a significant other – his individual worker or a parent. The music is used to facilitate that dialogue; the musician bases her contribution on a sensitive interpretation of the interaction taking place, and on her prior knowledge of both child and adult gained from observation and discussion at other times and in other settings.

While sessions will vary at the will of both child and adult, the central consideration is to give the child repeated and exaggerated experience of a pre-verbal dialogue in the hope that this will help the child realize the enjoyment in shared experience. It is the role of the therapist to help the child to 'tune in' to his partner and the adult to tune in to the child's social world. In general, the interaction is initiated and maintained by means similar to those observed between mothers and babies. For example, the child's spontaneous behaviour, whatever its purpose, can be assigned communicative intent by one or both of the adults. Actions or sounds may be imitated and extended. Pauses are left in the flow of action and music, and these often seem to compel the child to 'fill in' the space with a look, a sound or an action.

The therapeutic triad

Before going on to describe and illustrate some of the specific techniques that have evolved, it is worth touching on one or two particular considerations that are relevant to the rather unusual situation of two adults working simultaneously with one child.

The therapist, to a large extent, has to see herself as being outside the interaction. The role of the therapist is very much one of a facilitator: enabling the interaction to occur between others, but bringing with her a knowledge of what has been successful with other children and staff. This requires a high degree of both self-discipline and generosity on the part of the therapist. For the establishment it means that there has to be some recognition of a degree of 'unmet need'; in practical terms, the therapist must be provided with other opportunities for direct contact with children.

In addition to the 'tuning in' between adult and child, consideration also has to be given to a tuning in between the therapist and other adult. They need an opportunity for discussion before and after the session, so that explicit exchanges at the time can be kept to a minimum. Both adults will bring to the session their knowledge of the child and of techniques that they have used before. It must be recognized that there are essential differences between the process of musical dialogue and the 'objective' approach which will underpin many other areas of the curriculum. Negotiation and compromise are required to reach an agreed approach for any particular child.

Any approach which sees its fundamental aim as being that of establishing rapport between the child and his significant others must, inevitably, consider ways of including parents. This aspect of the work began with a few of the children's mothers taking over the role of staff member with their own child. The dynamics of this more intimately based therapeutic triad have to be given even greater thought. The parent, as opposed to a staff member, will have detailed knowledge of her own particular child but will not, clearly, have worked with others in a similar way. It is often helpful for her to observe musical sessions with other children first, and also to be supported directly by the staff member when she first starts to work with her own child. The potential for reactivation of earlier feelings of rejection or failure in trying to build up this intensely personal relationship is very great. Time also needs to be spent ensuring that parents focus on the importance of their child enjoying shared experience, rather than on any failure to 'perform' in a musical sense; the 'educational' expectations that parents have of schools can impede this focus.

Practical strategies in musical interaction

The strategies described in what follows have been developed intuitively during music sessions, as ways of helping individual children to experience the natural 'give and take' of pre-verbal interaction. While listed here in discrete sections, in practice of course they often occur simultaneously, or overlap within one session.

'Tuning in' to the child

Assuming that the child with autism is *unable* to take part in early social dialogue (rather than simply unwilling), it makes sense to begin with what he *is* able to do: for adults to tune in to his own social world, before expecting him to tune in to theirs.

The starting-point for working in this way is for the adults concerned to be prepared to put aside some of their own inhibitions, as well as their preconceptions about what constitutes 'teaching'. The child's actions and sounds are accepted as valid in the context of the interaction, and this acceptance is communicated to him by both non-verbal and verbal means. The limits of acceptability for individual children must be discussed and negotiated by the adults, according to what is known about each child in other contexts. The limits are likely to be different from those in other situations. For example, it is generally acceptable for a child to climb on the furniture in the music room, so long as this does not directly conflict with a specific behavioural objective in the classroom or at home.

In practice, tuning-in happens in three main ways, which may vary in degree of structure from low to comparatively high.

Imitation and extension

The adults imitate or join in with the child's spontaneous sounds and movements, treating them as if they were intentional attempts at communication. At the beginning of *Extract 1* (see p. 81), after a 'commentary' song from the adults about hiding and finding a pen, Paul, a very slow-learning child with very severe autism, runs off towards the door making a 'ba ba ba' sound (lines 6–12). As soon as Carol imitates this sound, he turns, makes eye-contact, and comes back towards her. He soon starts making sounds intentionally for Carol to imitate, and five minutes later, in *Extract 2*, he has even begun to imitate some of her own spontaneous sounds (lines 0–6). Meanwhile, the piano improvisation gives continuity to the whole episode, filling in pauses and reinforcing sounds, words and movements, both rhythmically and melodically.

The piano improvisation is usually based on a pentatonic scale, at a pitch in keeping with the vocal sounds. The therapist at the piano interprets the spoken or sung sounds using very simple melodic patterns. For example, many two-syllable utterances are set to the simple two-note falling figure (the cuckoo tune) 'which is so natural to children that the two-year-old uses it to call his mother' (Sidaway, undated).

'Running commentary'
The adults extemporize a song about whatever the child is doing. In *Extract 3*, both adults anticipate Paul's jump (line 0) and sing *'Jump*ing, Paul is *jump*ing', so that the syllable 'jump' coincides with his landing. With other children, the 'running commentary' may be much more sophisticated – for example, to the tune of 'For he's a jolly good fellow': 'Now he's . . . sitting on the table, sitting on the table, looking out of the window – and giving a little smile', etc. The child is given the message that what he is doing is valued, and that the adults are 'with' him in the sense used by Pinney and colleagues, who propose that a child has a 'special time' when an adult donates to him a defined period of 'total non-directive and non-judgmental attention' (Pinney et al. 1985).

Using the child's spontaneous actions within the framework of a song
This differs from the 'commentary' in that a simple structured song is introduced. It has short verses, with definite 'slots' for the child's ideas. In theory, expectations would be higher, but in practice the adults again often treat any spontaneous movement as if it had communicative intent. For example, some minutes before *Extract 1*, Paul touched his chin. Carol said 'tickling your chin', and the therapist extemporized a suitable tune, which was sung as the tickling action was imitated and extended. Towards the end of this verse, Paul formed one hand into a fist, so Carol imitated and asked 'What are you doing?' . . . 'going to knock?' . . . 'shall we knock on here?' and the next verse was sung about knocking. At a more advanced stage of communicative competence, a child may perform an action intentionally, to have it included in the song, and eventually he may be able to suggest actions verbally.

Use of dramatic pauses before emphasized key words

This second general strategy is used very frequently in music sessions, most characteristically within familiar songs. However, in the early stages it may be necessary to devise short repetitive routines (such as 'Here we go . . . *up*!' or 'I'm coming to . . . *swing* you round!') which, like many features of the 'tuning in' activities, are commonly seen in the natural play between parents and very young infants.

Once the song or routine is familiar, a dramatic pause is made before the emphasized 'key' word ('up' or 'swing' in the above examples). The child's spontaneous sign of anticipation – a glance, a movement, a sound or a word – is interpreted by the adult as a *signal* that the child wants to continue. Eventually, the signal is used, as such, intentionally by the child – very much in line with the stages described by Coupe and Jolliffe (1988). In this way, autistic children can be helped with one of their core difficulties: that of 'social timing'. They learn when to take their turn on the interaction.

The metric rhythm of simple songs and rhymes, more than the free but word-linked rhythms of ordinary speech, means that a sudden pause can be a very effective way of drawing a child into the interaction: most seem to feel compelled to give some response, however basic. Parents of young children often use nursery rhymes in this way, pausing before emphasizing key words (eg 'wall' and 'fall' in Humpty Dumpty) for the child to fill in. Working with a young autistic child, the adults have to be prepared not only to wait longer for a response, but also to accept *any* sign of anticipation as the child's 'turn', gradually increasing their expectations over weeks or months. In the music sessions where two adults are working very closely together with each child, they may actually discuss beforehand when they intend to pause within each activity, so that a sudden silence from the piano contributes to the suspense. Once they have worked together in this way for some time, the adults are usually able to interpret very quickly each other's non-verbal cues, such as slowing down, getting louder, gasping, and so on.

Three further video extracts of Paul's music sessions show how his sense of social timing has developed over a period of about eighteen months from the first videoed session. In the first two, the dramatic pause is made before the word 'boo'. In *Extract 4* Paul seems to understand the basis of the 'peek-a-boo' game, as he covers and uncovers his eyes (lines 6–12), but he is not yet able to time his responses to coincide with the 'slots' left for him. It is interesting to note that during some *spontaneous* sound-making in the earlier session, Paul had used the word 'boo' appropriately, but he is not able to do so in this structured situation.

In *Extract 5* Paul is now working with a different adult, Karen. His social timing in a slightly different 'peek-a-boo' song is extremely good. He is now able to put 'key' words into many songs, and to make verbal choices.

These two basic strategies, tuning in and using dramatic pauses, can be adapted to any level or situation. They appear to help autistic children to develop some of the pre-verbal conversation skills which are vital for communication. With more able children than Paul, the work proceeds much faster and reaches a much higher level of sophistication. Above all the children come to enjoy *sharing* experiences with a significant adult, and to appreciate the sheer pleasure of interaction. At the very least they are motivated to be more responsive at a pre-verbal level and to discover themselves as communicative people. At best, they are enabled to develop true linguistic competence: words and phrases, as they arrive, can be settled into a framework for dialogue flow which has been made ready for them, and the child begins to take on the 'personal powers' afforded by language.

Conclusion

The understandings developed through using a musical and interactional approach have come to inform and influence the way staff work in all areas of the curriculum. In general terms, the experience has led to an appreciation that in all teaching situations the *process* must be considered alongside the *product*, and that in many cases the process will be the foremost consideration. For example, when working with a young child on an inset board, the process of her making communicative eye-contact with her teacher before receiving each piece may well be more significant for a child with autism than her mastering of the inset puzzle.

A more specific instance arises in the teaching of pointing, particularly (but not exclusively) with the young pre-verbal child. Developmentally the distance-pointing gesture appears towards the end of the first year and is perhaps the most significant sign of gestural communication (Savage 1985). In the case of young children with autism, this gesture is delayed, impaired or altogether absent. A pattern of pointing is now deliberately taught to these children, which is based on the development of pointing in normal infants; its perceived importance as a taught skill derives from observation of the explosion in functional communicative competence that occurs in normal infants once pointing is achieved. The pattern starts with a 'touch point', the child's hand being physically shaped to touch with his index finger whatever he is approaching or referring to. The next stage is distance pointing, again shaping his hand if necessary and rewarding him with attainment of or reference to the object. The third stage is a distance-point accompanied by a glance towards the adult (eye contact), and in the fourth stage vocalization (or even verbalization) is added. Throughout, the aim is for the child to recognize that the significant element in a pointing sequence (ie a request for or reference to an object) is that he and the adult have *shared understanding*.

Musical interaction techniques are not, then, an isolated part of the curriculum: the principles underlying the approach can be used in many classroom and home situations in interactional play. Rough-and-tumble sequences, lap play and singing games can be extended and elaborated. The personal interactive mode even spills over into table-top tasks, to their enrichment. What is important is that we widen our preconceptions about what constitutes teaching, appreciate the significance of the pre-verbal stage of communication development, and persevere in finding ways to engage the child; and that, throughout, we base our interventions at a level at which the child can feel comfortable, and take him gently forward from there.

Notes on the video extracts

These short extracts are taken from three separate music sessions with the same child. Extracts 1–3 are from his first videoed session in October 1987; Extract 4 is from June 1988; Extracts 5 and 6, with a different adult, are from March 1989.

The people in the video extracts

Paul the child, who entered the nursery class in September 1987.
Carol Paul's teacher, who interacts directly with Paul.
Karen the nursery nurse, who took over Paul's work and music sessions from September 1988.
Wendy the therapist, seated at the piano, supporting and facilitating the musical interaction between Paul and the other adult.

The approximate timescale is recorded down the left-hand column, at intervals of 6 seconds. These figures are referred to as line numbers in the text.

Extract 1 – October 1987
Approximately 20 minutes into session

Time (sec.)	Paul – vocal	Carol – vocal	vocal – Wendy – piano		Notes – behavioural
0		Paul's got the pen (sung)	Paul's got the pen (sung)	Playing the song, 'Paul's got the pen'	Paul takes the pen from Carol, after it has been hidden and found – this game has held his attention for 10 minutes. He twiddles the pen near his face and gazes at the camera.
6				'Filling in' music, based on accompaniment of the song	
	ba ba ba ba ba	ba ba ba ba			Paul runs away from Carol towards the door as he speaks. He turns as she joins in with his sound, and moves back towards her.
12				Changes to improvisation	Paul leans on the settee and looks at Carol.
18		ba ba (whispered)			
24	brrrrr	ba (whispered) brrrr brrrr brrr			Paul turns away as he says 'brrrr', climbs over the arm of the settee, then turns to face Carol.
30					
36					Paul stands on the settee, watching Carol.
42	Oh choo (quietly spoken)	Oh choo choo choo (chanted)	Oh choo (sung)	Piano chords are used to reinforce chanting	
48	Oh wo (much more forceful)	Oh cho (chanted)	Oh Oh (sung)		Paul jumps off the settee towards Carol as he calls 'Oh wo!'

Extract 2 – October 1987
Approximately 5 minutes later than Extract 1

Time (sec.)	Paul – vocal	Carol – vocal	vocal – Wendy – piano	Notes – behavioural
0		Bim Bam	Improvisation 'filling in' with quiet bass figures	Paul is walking towards Carol, who is sitting on the floor, hiding behind a cushion. 'Bim bam' was used spontaneously by Paul the previous week.
6	Bim bam bim	bim bam bim bam bim	bam bim bam bim bam bam bam Chords used to reinforce syllables	Paul puts his head around the side of the cushion to make eye-contact with Carol as he speaks.
12	ba			
18		ba ba	ba Reinforces own singing of 'ba' with loud chord	Carol moves cushion aside to make eye-contact with Paul.

Extract 3 – October 1987
Approximately 2 minutes later than Extract 2

Time (sec.)	Paul – vocal	Carol – vocal	vocal	Wendy – piano	Notes – behavioural
0		Jumping (sung)	Jumping (sung)	Within the piano improvisation, very simple repetitive melodic figures are used, to coincide with the words and actions	Paul bends his knees – Carol and Wendy anticipate his jump and sing the word 'jumping' as he lands. Carol is leaning on a cushion on the floor.
		Paul is jumping	Paul is jumping		Carol stands up and jumps, facing Paul; on the first syllable of 'jumping', Paul raises his arms and watches Carol.
6		Jumping	Jumping		Carol jumps twice, matching the syllables of 'jumping'.
12	Jump	Jumping	Jumping		Paul walks forward, stamping his left foot as he says 'jump', laughing.
	Jump	Jumping	Jumping		Carol jumps again, and Paul watches. Paul steps forward again as he speaks.
18 24		Step step step step step step step (chanted)	Stepping		Carol steps in an exaggerated way as she speaks, and moves to stand beside Paul.

Extract 4 – June 1988
Approximately 2 minutes into session

Time (sec.)	Paul – vocal	Carol – vocal	vocal	Wendy – piano	Notes – behavioural
0		(sung)	(sung)	Playing familiar tune, in short verses	The previous verse, 'Paul can hide like this', was sung when he covered his face with his hands. Paul is sitting facing Carol on her lap. Carol now covers her eyes.
			Then say	Pause	
		Boo Like this	Boo Like this	Playing again with words	Paul looks up and takes one hand away from his own eyes as Carol parts her hands and sings 'boo'.
6		Then say	Then say	Pause	Carol covers her eyes with her arms as Paul watches.
		Boo Like this	Boo Like this	As before	Carol takes her arms away to make eye-contact.
		Then say	Then say	Pause	Paul covers his eyes with his hands just before Carol does hers. During the silent pause, Paul uncovers his eyes and looks at Carol. She uncovers hers and waits for a vocal response.
12		Boo (whispered) Like this	Like this	As before	Carol covers her eyes as Paul watches.
		Then say	Then say	Pause (6 seconds)	Carol and Wendy pause for longer, hoping for a vocal response. Paul watches silently.
18		Boo	Boo		Carol uncovers her eyes and makes eye-contact.

Extract 5 – March 1989
Approximately 10 minutes into session

Time (sec.)	Paul – vocal	Karen – vocal	vocal	Wendy – piano	Notes – behavioural
0		(sung)	(sung)	Using the tune of 'Skip to my Lou'	Paul is sitting on Karen's lap on the floor. Several verses have been sung for different actions. Karen initiates the peek-a-boo game by putting her hands up between her own eyes and Paul's.
		Peek a boo	Peek a / Peek a boo		Paul leans forward and puts his own hands on Karen's. He leans back and smiles as she parts her hands on 'boo' and makes eye-contact.
6		Peek a / Peek a	Peek a / Peek a		Paul leans forward again to hide his eyes.
12	Boo	Boo	Boo	Pause / Piano continues	Paul's vocal response is quick, and so the song continues almost immediately. Karen parts her hands to make eye-contact on 'boo'.
18		Peek a / Peek a	Peek a / Peek a	Pause	Paul leans forward again. He anticipates the 'boo' by leaning back and tapping Karen's hands.
24	Boo	Boo	Boo	As before	Paul smiles and makes eye-contact.
30	Boo	Peek a	Peek a	Pause / As before	Eyes are covered again.
36	Boo	Boo like this	Boo like this		Paul sits back and smiles as he says 'boo'. Keeps smiling and makes eye-contact as Karen parts her hands. He looks away, then makes eye-contact again as he says 'boo'. This extra 'boo' is taken as a request for the song to be repeated.

Extract 6 – March 1989
Approximately 10 minutes later than Extract 5

Throughout this extract Paul uses much sustained eye-contact, and smiles frequently. He looks away from Karen briefly, and then back again in a natural and appropriate way.

Time (sec.)	Paul – vocal	Karen – vocal	vocal–Wendy–piano	Notes – behavioural
0		Tummy. It's your tummy. Tummy. Tickle tummy (spoken)	'Filling in' music, based on accompaniment figure of previous song.	Paul is sitting on a small chair: Karen kneels on the floor facing him. She has been tickling his knees, and is now tickling his tummy lightly, holding his jumper up slightly with the other hand.
6	Tickle . . . ha Tickle . . . ha	Let's do the 'tickle tickle' song (spoken)	Changes to suggested song, now playing this tune as words are sung.	
12		Karen and Wendy sing together Tickle tickle, tickle tickle tickle Tickle Paul's tummy Sit up (whispered)		Karen continues tickling lightly.
18		Tickle tickle, tickle tickle tickle, Tickle Paul's . . . tummy	Music slows down a little with a very short pause before 'tummy'.	Karen lifts Paul up again to a sitting position: he had slid down on his chair. This time she makes a tickling action in the air, only making contact on the work 'tummy'.

Extract 6 – Cont.

Time (sec.)	Paul – vocal	Karen – vocal	vocal–Wendy–piano	Notes – behavioural
24		Tickle tickle, tickle tickle tickle Tickle Paul's		Karen's 'tickling' hand moves up towards Paul's face, tickling his nose as soon as he says the word 'nose'. Then she moves her hand up to his head. He looks from her eyes to her arm and back again, then says 'neck' very decisively, so Karen tickles his neck. Then the 'tickling' hand 'hovers' near his tummy, tickling only when he says 'tum'.
30	Nose Tickle-a-ma	Nose . . . and tickle tickle, tickle tickle, Tickle Paul's	Definite pause for Paul to name 'nose', then music continues.	
36	*Neck*	Neck That's a new one! (spoken)	Pause in music, continues as soon as Paul says 'neck'	
42		Tickle tickle, tickle tickle tickle, Tickle Paul's	Pause	
48	tum Tickle . . . tum	tum . . . Tickle, tickle, tickle tickle tickle, Tickle Paul's tum	Music continues as soon as he says 'tum'. This last time, there is no pause, as he has already said 'tum' during the singing.	
54	(ETC)			This time Paul holds his jumper himself, and speaks during the singing. Karen tickles his tummy as the word 'tum' is sung.

References

Condon, W.S. and Sander, L.W. (1974) Neonate movement is synchronized with adult speech, *Science* 183: 90–101.

Coupe, J. and Jolliffe, J. (1988) An early communication curriculum: implications for practice, in J. Coupe and W. Goldbart, *Communication Before Speech*, London: Croom Helm.

Christie, P. and Wimpory, D. (1986) Recent research into the development of communicative competence and its implications for the teaching of autistic children, *Communication* 20(1): 4–7.

Dewart, H. and Summers, S. (1988) *The Pragmatics Profile of Early Communication Skills*, Slough: NFER-Nelson.

Lewis, M.M. (1963) *Language, Thought and Personality in Infancy and Childhood*, London: Harrap.

Mogford, K. (1973) *Communication Schedule*, Child Development Research Unit, University of Nottingham.

Newson, E. (1978) Making sense of autism, Inge Wakehurst Papers, London: National Autistic Society.

Newson, E. (1987) Education, treatment and handling of autistic children, *Children in Society* 1(1): 34–50.

Newson, J. (1974) Towards a theory of infant understanding, *Bulletin of the British Psychological Society* 27: 251–7.

Newson, J. (1979) The growth of shared understandings between infant and caregiver, in M. Bullowa (ed.) *Before Speech*, Cambridge University Press.

Nordoff, P. (1988) Quoted in R. Sandall, 'Getting out of the groove', *Sunday Times*, 20 March 1988.

Pawlby, S.J. (1977) Imitative interaction, in H.R. Schaffer (ed.) *Studies in Mother–Infant Interaction*, New York: Academic Press.

Piaget, J. (1951) *Play, Dreams and Imitation in Childhood*, New York: Norton.

Pinney, R., Carr-Gomm, P. and Robinson, M. (1985) *Special Times* (booklet), Children's Hours Trust, 28 Wallace House, London N7 8TL.

Savage, C. (1985) The point of pointing, BA dissertation, University of Nottingham.

Sidaway, P. (undated) The work of the Orff Society (information sheet), 31 Roedean Crescent, London SW15 5JX.

Stephenson, S. (1988) An exploration of an approach using music to develop pre-verbal interaction skills in autistic children, BSc dissertation, Manchester Polytechnic.

4

The barefoot play therapist: adapting skills for a time of need

ELIZABETH NEWSON

The literature that has been handed down by the great names of play therapy can be off-putting for the ordinary common-or-garden developmental or clinical psychologist ready to get her hands dirty but lacking the confidence bestowed by a 'proper' therapy training. In my own case, I had started reading Klein, Winnicott, Axline and many more in my undergraduate days, and had become increasingly doubtful about some of what was going on behind these accounts. For a start, the stories seemed too neat and the children too articulate: could the mute Dibs, after only a short time in therapy, really have uttered the poetic words 'I am a builder of cities'? The fees presumably paid to the therapist often seemed to be reflected by the middle-class luxury problems of some of the children: Winnicott had written a whole book about 'the Piggle' who suffered from sibling rivalry, but didn't we all, and wasn't growing-up about resolving that without recourse to therapists? And was I alone in being taken aback by Klein's certainty of interpretation, unswervingly shared with children of 7 and younger? Remembering (as I do) my own critical 7-year-old self, I wondered how she could assure the child that what he had chosen from the little toys was actually his father's penis with which he was trying to stir up the bad things in his mother's insides, without quailing at the thought, 'But suppose I am *wrong*?' My overall conclusion was to be appalled at the opportunities for a prolonged ego-trip at the expense of the child which play therapy undoubtedly offers the therapist; I dismissed play therapy as something I could not with honesty believe in, and turned with relief to children with the more obvious, if intractable, problems of mental and physical disability.

However, our referral system at Nottingham is open, and some of our most useful work has been elaborated in response to referrals for which at the time we doubted our own competence, but where nobody else was offering help. Children were being referred whose problems were anything but middle-class luxury ones: children who had been the victims of cruelty and neglect; some who had lived in five or six different households by the time they were 5 and who now were all too aware of themselves as 'hard to place'; children who had witnessed violence and death among the adults in charge of them; children who were facing the reality of death themselves because of terminal conditions such as muscular dystrophy, or life-threatening illnesses such as leukaemia or serious heart disease. All of these children were coping (or not coping) with life scenarios which any of us as competent adults would have experienced as problems of paralysing magnitude if they had happened to us; most of them, however, also had in common that they could not articulate their anxieties, for a number of different reasons. For most, their intellectual level was not high, so that they would have been regarded as children with 'moderate learning difficulties' even without other problems; many had had very little personal day-by-day communication with adults because of their impoverished social environments; for some, speech delay was the outcome of living in a series of households during the period of speech development. The most sympathetic of adults, therefore, could not easily have been used as a listening ear or sounding board by these children; more seriously, it seemed likely that they were incapable of articulating their predicaments even in their own thoughts. And for some, of course, the material of their thoughts was too painful anyway to have been bearable for their surrounding adults, particularly where children were in life-threatening situations.

So there was no doubt that the children needed help for problems that anyone could recognize as undoubtedly serious. But help of what kind? Sometimes, if a social worker was the referring agent, it was suggested that 'play therapy would be the thing'; for several years we resisted, with 'we can't do play therapy, and anyway we don't believe in it'. There was nobody local to whom children could be referred on for this kind of intervention. Finally, we had to accept that we did not know what else to do with these children; at that point we decided that we would have to create a model of play therapy that we *could* believe in. The result has evolved over time in response to the series of children we have attracted: still very much as described above, but now joined by those who have been sexually abused.

Needless to say, we did not have to start entirely from scratch, and we have probably borrowed more than we know from those who have preceded us. Some of our debts are in terms of a stance or point of view: for instance, Strayhorn's notion of the 'competent child' and George Kelly's 'No-one needs to be the victim of his biography' seemed not too optimistic as a starting-point (though perhaps less helpful to a terminally-ill child). Carl Rogers and his disciples in child work, Moustakas and Axline, gave us useful ideas for the structures and frameworks of procedure, though we adapted them for our own needs. In particular, however, their notion of being able to trust the client's competence to work constructively for himself or herself, even where the client is an apparently incompetent child, confirmed our own wish to reduce the therapist's status to facilitator rather than central director of operations: the self-discipline imposed by my own original vicarious anxiety on Melanie Klein's behalf, 'But suppose I am *wrong*?', can be seen at many points in the workings of the Nottingham model of play therapy. But our main debt must be to Margaret Lowenfeld (1979), whose 'World' technique we adapted with relatively few changes, and whose generous note that others might use the technique in ways different from her own encouraged us to try. Our fear of being wrong was also calmed by her statement that 'It is essential for the proper understanding of the nature and use of this technique that no interpretation be given by the therapist to the child'. I shall come back to this later.

The Nottingham model of play therapy

At this point the reader needs a description of the basic package developed at Nottingham. This package will normally be the starting-point for any child, but adaptations and variations may be made in response to the needs of particular children as they come to light during the process; as child and therapist become comfortable with the alternative language of play, they will learn to use it in more creative and specific ways.

The one-hour therapy session is divided into two parts, which may be of unequal lengths at the will of the child, but which both take place each week in the same order. The first activity is to make a 'World', using Lowenfeld-devised equipment with slight adaptations. The second part is a role-played drama session played out by child, therapist and as many additional 'actors' as the child wishes in the form of large dolls and animals. The two parts take place in this order because making a World is essentially contemplative and quiet, with the child standing in one place and working with concentrated attention, while the Drama can be very boisterous and noisy or involve the explicit expression of intense emotions, following which the child may need a short period of rest and relaxation but will not easily adapt to a thoughtful and attentive mood for a while.

The two-part nature of the session does more than offer the child two different activities: it also allows him to work from two different perspectives. In Make a World he plays God, creating a world beneath hands and eyes in the sand-tray. He may choose or not, as he wishes, to have himself represented in this world; if he does put himself into it, it is at one remove in that he chooses a doll or animal of whom to say 'This is me', or simply indicates a location ('I'm in that bus'). In Drama, the child becomes bodily part of the action (or inaction) and enters into membership of the scenes he chooses: if he also chooses to stand aside from them, this too is physically explicit. In both activities the child has responsibility for what is played out, but the change of perspective from one to the other adds richness and depth to both.

The two parts of the session are indeed intended to feel very different to the child, and this is deliberately marked by having two separate rooms for the two activities, each appropriate in scale for its purpose: World-making takes place in a small room just big enough to contain the equipment and the two participants comfortably, while Drama needs a large room with plenty of space to run and climb. Both rooms can be observed via one-way screens for supervision purposes, and the child is of course aware of the nature of these screens. He also knows that no 'others' in his life will be allowed to observe, and that if he wishes to draw the curtain across he may do so, in which case the supervisor will be excluded also: this has in fact happened on only one occasion with one child (on first being told that he could do so, and perhaps he wanted to test that this was indeed acceptable).

Make a World procedure

The sand-tray we use was made for us in polished aluminium to Lowenfeld's measurements (75 cm × 50 cm × 7 cm), which have proved well suited to the activity. However, she used her tray on tables of different heights according to the child's size, while ours is set into a former paper storage chest at waist height for a 7–8 year old, and very small children kneel on a chair or stand on a low stool; there seems no problem for older children or adults. The chest allows additional storage on shelves under the sand-tray; a more important advantage is that the insetting of the tray provides a 6 cm border to the main field of activity, and this is much used by the children as a roadway and as a boundary both explicit and implicit. For instance Cliff, an extraordinarily chaotic child, made mountains whose contours came down to the outer edge, which resulted in sand running off in showers; months later he checked that it was 'OK' to drop sand on the floor and, once reassured of this ('It's your world'), took time to assert the inner boundary to his landscape. (This significant use of the border, unavailable to Lowenfeld, has made me interested in the effects of different kinds of trays on the material produced: what would be the result of using a circular tray, for instance?)

The polished surface of the metal is useful for providing a semblance of water for rivers and seas when the sand is scooped away. Lowenfeld provided water at hand; we used to do so, but found that some children made a sea of mud which rendered the tray unusable for the next child. The chief use for water is to make the sand mouldable into hills and valleys at will, and we now have a very coarse and heavy silver sand which moulds well if kept only a little damp, and contains tiny stones which the children like and use.

At right-angles to the tray, so that the child stands comfortably within the angle, is a cabinet which contains the hundreds of objects and creatures that might be in a 'World'. Lowenfeld used drawers; we use a school cabinet holding removable plastic storage trays, with every second tray removed so that the child can see at a glance what category of things is in each tray. (The fourteen trays are also labelled with their categories, but very few of our children can read confidently.) The categories are for the convenience of the child, so that she can find what she wants with ease. They include: *Ordinary people* (little dolls representing people of all ages, including Asian and African families); *Strange people* (robots, Star Wars and similar characters, ghosts, gods, devils, etc.); *Fighting people and things* (soldiers of many kinds, cowboys and Indians (who normally carry weapons), armoured cars and tanks, bowmen, guns and cannon etc); *Domestic animals* (farm animals and pets); *Wild animals* (including some insects and amphibians which are of too large a scale, so that they have qualities of monsters; and also prehistoric animals); *Furniture* (on a doll's house scale, including lavatory, etc.); *Things for the house* (plates of food of all kinds, vases and pots of flowers, ornaments, kitchen gadgets, crockery and cutlery, clocks, baskets, lamps, TV, Christmas tree and almost anything else one might think of that 'makes a house a home'); *Street things* (pavements, lampposts, street signs, including traffic lights); *Hedges, trees, walls and fences*; *Road and rivers* (sections in green, brown or grey card); *Ordinary vehicles* (cars, lorries, motor-bikes, many kinds of service vehicles including crisis vehicles – fire engine, ambulance, police car); *Trains, boats and planes* (including helicopters and police/fighting items); *Buildings* (churches, houses, windmills, architectural features – these are obviously small and out of scale, but the children seem not to mind); *Hospital things and people* (beds, screens, wheelchairs, operating tables, bedside cabinets, doctors, nurses, patients). In addition there are trays kept on the shelves under the sand-tray which hold a large assortment of ambiguous material such as Plasticine, glitterwax, beads, pipe-cleaners, small bricks of different kinds, laths and coloured sticks of varied colours and lengths, so that a child who can't find what she wants can usually fashion something to suggest it.

On her first visit, the equipment is introduced to the child as 'a special game called Make a World'. She is shown each of the trays in turn, so that she knows what is at her disposal; if she tries to start to play after seeing the toy objects in the first two or three trays, this is resisted with 'Let me just show you all the things we've got first'. She is then invited to 'Make a World in the sand-tray – any kind of world you like, whatever comes into your head'. Oddly, only one child has ever asked 'What's a world?' Lowenfeld gives quite complex instructions for explaining to the child the purpose of World-making, to do with 'Picture Thinking' and how this may 'make a bridge between two worlds – that of the child and that of the adults' (Lowenfeld 1979), but our children find this too abstract, and confusing in its reference to bridges and the worlds of children and adults as well as the World that is to be made in the sand-tray.

The great majority of children start work immediately. If there is any reluctance it can be met in an ad hoc way; for instance, if the child is very shy he may be helped by the therapist saying 'Shall I start it off? You tell me what you want me to put in. Where shall I put it?' and so on. Reluctance is in no way correlated with the use the child may later come to make of World-making. Cliff was full of reasons why he should not 'play this game', starting with 'the sand might get in my eyes' (countered by the fact that his glasses would protect his eyes) and ending with 'I might get bored, I do get bored very easily you know'. This was a useful indication of Cliff's self-image, reflecting many other people's images of him; we assured him that we did not think he would be bored, and in a year of play therapy his Worlds became increasingly complex, subtle, integrated and thought out. Cliff is one of many children who clearly think about their Worlds between sessions, often arriving with an eager 'I know what I'm going to do this week'. Most of the children we work with are doing badly in school (Cliff is in a special school), and came to us, like Cliff, with a reputation of 'poor concentration, low attention-span'; we have been the more impressed by the high level of concentration they show, usually for about half-an-hour, when making their Worlds.

The therapist simply watches the making of the World in an accepting way, without interruption. Some children talk about what they are doing throughout; a few talk about something different. The therapist receives these communications but does not comment more than is necessary for courtesy. Some children remain silent and absorbed, in which case the therapist must have the discipline to respect the silence – difficult for some at first! At some point the child will seem to have come to a halt, and may in fact say that he's finished; if not, the therapist may ask 'Have you finished?', but should be ready to accept if the child says 'yes' but then changes his mind and continues for a few more minutes. At this point it is important not to comment on the World in an evaluative way, including approval. Beginning therapists have a tendency to try to show positive acceptance with 'That's a very good World' or 'That's nice', conveying the implication that there are some Worlds that might be made that would *not* be 'good' or 'nice'; often a full and busy World is equated by adults with 'good', which would make it difficult for the child at some later stage to express emptiness, desolation or chaos, as he may well want to do.

So the therapist must express acceptance and interest without false enthusiasm; and she may now ask the child, 'Can you tell me something about what's going on in your World?' For some children this is too general a question, and she may at first need to be more specific: 'What's happening here?' (pointing to one part of the action), 'What's this person doing?' and so on. We find it particularly fruitful to follow up these present-tense questions with a shift to the future perspective: 'What's going to happen next? Who's going to do something first? And then what will happen?' and so on. This will often be taken by the child as an invitation to move the pieces a little more, which is quite acceptable; it has the advantage of making more sense of the meaning the child is both putting into and taking out of his World.

It will be seen that, although we may wish to draw or photograph the child's final World for the record, this will be only a static *aide-mémoire* to what is essentially a mobile and dynamic creation, and it is important to record the changes that take place; for instance, the final world might seem empty and unpeopled, but beneath the sand we might know there to be a population overcome by some natural or man-made disaster. We have found no difficulty in recording the world by drawing or photography, and the children seem supported by the fact that we value their Worlds enough to record them permanently 'to help me remember your World'. It is also possible to record via computer graphics (some pioneering work has been done in this field by Margarita Wood), which at its most sophisticated allows one to survey the World from many different angles. Valuable for research purposes, this is hardly needed for the ordinary therapist; all that is required is to be able to look again at leisure at what the child has produced, and this can also be helpful for children themselves, who sometimes later ask to 'look through' their Worlds as if to gain a perspective on their thoughts.

Is the child herself represented in her World? Obviously we would like to know, but it is rare for children to indicate this the first time they make a World. Because we feel that children have enough to adapt to when they start therapy, we resist asking the question 'Are you in this World?' for the first two sessions. At the end of the making of the third World, we do ask; a few children say no or look surprised, but it is most usual that the child answers in a matter-of-fact way: 'Yes, this is me' or 'Yes – I'm in that house', for example. This poses an intriguing question: did the child know all the time that she was there, or is she simply hospitable to such a suggestion and very quick to take it up? Once the question has been asked, the child is likely regularly and spontaneously to identify herself in her World, so presumably this is a notion with which most children can feel comfortable.

Figure 4.1   Make a World: Kathy aged 6 years – her second 'world' (Photo: S. Tristram)

World symbols

This brings us to the whole question of symbolism. Because of the poor linguistic and social development of most of the children we see, we would not have expected a high level of symbolic play generally, and in fact the majority of them are said not to be interested in 'pretend' activities. Yet we have been impressed by the ability of these low-achieving children to set out their predicaments in the sand in a highly symbolic way, to an extent which, however unwilling we are to make interpretations, is difficult to ignore. Lowenfeld (1979) points out that analysts of different schools will see very different meanings in the same material, and indeed we would not ourselves be at all comfortable in imposing the heavy convolutions of meaning which the children's configurations would be made to support by, for instance, Jungian, Kleinian or Adlerian analysts. However, provided we are disciplined enough not to assert our interpretations willy-nilly to the child, it seems reasonable to receive positively what is offered to us as bystanders, and to allow the material to assume meaningful patterns for our own understanding without resisting whatever seems manifest.

Let me give just a few examples at this stage to illustrate children's use of symbolism. In Figure 4.1 we see a very early World by Kathy, aged 6. Little was known about this child's history; she had been found abandoned as a toddler in a derelict house, and had earlier wandered the roads of Ireland with her mother. Now in care, she attended infants school where it had been suggested that a school for children with moderate learning difficulties might be more appropriate for her. Kathy has chosen a procession entirely made up of wild animals to walk across the front of her World. In the most distant corner is a church, which Kathy describes as 'a long way away'. On the far right is a containing wall carefully built as a curve, with one brick (described as a 'door') standing open; inside, two very young children sit on chairs. Erikson would say that the curved structure would be built only by a female (Erikson 1958) and that it is highly protective in character, symbolizing encircling arms; but we see that its protectiveness is vitiated by the open door, just as the ability of the church to protect is weakened by its location 'a long way away'. What is to prevent the wild animals turning aside in their progress and coming to eat the children? There are two hindrances to this, but each is ineffective: the animals might be slowed by the temptation of the delicious food laid out on the table; and they might be delayed by negotiating the barrier presented by the row of houses. This barrier is particularly interesting because the usual way of making a row of houses is as a terrace, each house presenting two windows and a door to the front and joined without gaps: Kathy has deliberately organized them in a less conventional way and, in doing so, has made them ineffective as a barrier. We have to regard non-conventional structures as having more significance than conventional ones, simply because the child makes a more deliberate effort in their construction; similarly, the curved walls have to be seen as significant both because they are atypical of the usual squared 'house' or 'room' structure and because it requires more careful effort to set the bricks in this way. So we have a World which is consistently permeated with risk and danger.

Nesta, aged 8, was suffering from a tumour above the eye, which grew weekly bigger, stretching the skin of her temple over a lump the size of a tennis ball and eventually obscuring her eye. Her Worlds contained repeated images of things bursting from containment with consequent danger. One had a bull in a field as its centrepiece, with a warning notice, and adults watched for a while but then went away (the hospital was concerned that her parents were reducing their visiting). Another World showed two adults walking towards a church, and Nesta said that they were going to pray for their daughter, because she was 'going to have a baby'; in this same World was a park with 'very good little children' who 'go there without their mother' and who were helped across the road by a lollipop lady (in a white coat), who would 'tell them when it's time to go home'.

Ben, too, was terminally ill at 8 years, and his Worlds also showed repeated themes: this time of initial security and safety, into which would intrude some element of danger or emergency. There was usually ambiguity about this danger, especially in that the causes were a mystery. Precautions were always being taken, but these would be either inappropriate or ineffective; there was a sustained theme of authority figures being incapable either of preventing the danger or of dealing with it. In one World there was a policeman 'calling to tell people there's an emergency' and the ambulance, police car and fire-engine (with Ben driving it) were there in a row, but the gate in front of them was closed and there was a STOP sign to prevent them going further. In another World there was an accident with a child lying in the road; an ambulance was 'going to come' but remained in an enclosure, a policeman was talking to the child's father whose 'car has broken down', and a fire-engine on its way was impeded by a load of furniture which it was 'going to empty into the rubbish dump behind'. In a further World, which contained lion cubs 'fighting' and an elk, zebra, cheetah and tiger 'trying to get out', a baboon was 'shouting' but, like the warning policeman, was being ignored by all other inhabitants.

Children's symbolism may be still more direct. A slow-learning child expecting open-heart surgery set up a funeral procession in her very first World, with her parents sitting at home having tea but 'very sad'; she herself was not identified, but her parents were. Linda, a still illiterate child who had been in and out of care for most of her twelve years, following neglect and abuse, set out a long drive with a gate and Keep Out notice at one end and a house at the other, the scene very recognizable as the children's home where she lived; on one side of the drive were wild animals and on the other side farm animals. A man with a bucket was set in between, and this 'slow-learning' girl verbalized his difficulty in 'looking after fierce animals' but went on 'You've got to feed them, even when they're fierce'; her preoccupation with the reconciliation of good and bad overflowed also into her repeated role-play as a lady with two husbands, one nice, one nasty. A bright 6-year-old facing death, whose stricken family was proud of 'making a joke of a lot of what happens', divided the tray into four totally walled-off sections and placed a hospital ward in one, a 'happy family' scene in a second, an unoccupied bathroom in a third, and left the fourth quite empty – a statement shocking in its stark absence of integration, even to someone looking at it without any knowledge of the circumstances of its maker.

In all of this, we offer the child a means of setting out his situation for his own contemplation. Obviously we cannot assume that the scenes he portrays represent his own predicaments in any precise or detailed way; but what we *can* assume is that they have relevance for him, since he has chosen to make them in this way. We can now look at the 'Drama' part of the session and it will become clearer how these different techniques work so well in conjunction.

Dramatic role-play

On the first occasion of the role-play the child, who has just completed his first 'World', sits for a moment with the therapist while she explains what will happen in the playroom. He is told that all the play in the playroom will be under his control; that he's 'The Boss' and she is there to help him in whatever he wants to play. They then both move into the playroom, and she sits on the floor, leaving him to explore.

The room is large, and is furnished with squashy armchairs, a low table, benches and children's chairs, and rugs and cushions. The most important items of equipment are a large play-house and a climbing frame. The play-house includes domestic equipment including teaset, pots and pans and a cooker, and, especially necessary, a frying pan containing 'joke' fried eggs and bacon, and shelves of many other kinds of plastic food and real tinned food; its window has a broad sill with a cash register, and it can therefore become a shop at will. The climbing frame is very large and has a platform halfway up; it is important because it can be so many things for the child: a prison, spaceship, mountain, castle, upstairs bedroom, throne, escape hatch and so on, really without limit. There is an accessible dressing-up chest and a line of pegs, from which the most used items are handbags, doctor's bag (with real stethoscope, etc.), handcuffs, wigs and hats: wigs offer a quick sex change, hats an identity in terms of police officer, cowboy, uniformed officer, smart or less smart lady, nurse and so on. There are telephones with working bells in all parts of the playroom, and a 'sand-tray' with dried peas instead of sand, which seems to do service for many fantasy activities – making beer, cooking zoo animal food and sorting stolen jewellery are three examples. There is also some kind of vehicle usable by children of different sizes: we are currently using a somewhat stylized tractor (by Little Tikes) which is both robust and anonymous enough to be accepted as whatever vehicle is momentarily required by the scenario.

It would be difficult to create much of a drama with only two actors, so many other figures are at hand. We use large dolls, both male and female; sexually explicit ones are available, but we do not regard disclosure work as compatible in time with play therapy. We have a real hutch with a family of plush rabbits in different colours and sizes (who are usually victims, but have on occasion been 'man-eating' or 'hunter' rabbits for several children); a variety of large soft animals such as giraffe, bear and tiger, with large-scale glove puppets of many kinds including parrots and other birds; and, especially important, a life-size alsatian. This last is repeatedly brought into the drama play by children: probably because he is a high-profile but ambiguous figure, not only good for cuddling and nestling into, or as a protective character, but also capable of savaging others. So he might be used by the child to attack the adult or the rabbits (this also offering opportunities for the child to take a rescuing role), but the child might equally choose to become the dog's victim and experience rescue or death himself. We have found this creature so useful in stimulating and extending drama that, when our first model was stolen (how? by whom?), we hastily raised the money to buy a replacement.

Roles and rules

There seem to be three major aspects of the therapist's responsibility in relation to drama work. The first is to provide an *environment* hospitable to role-play. This means that the playroom should not contain a great variety of toys that are in themselves attractive to sit and play with, because these would distract the child from role-play; rather, all toys should be chosen as merely offering support for roles. For instance, there are many amazingly realistic cash registers on the toy market, but we chose the simplest because we do not want to distract the child from the shopkeeper role into just playing with the cash registers; similarly, we need a means of making music, but we use the very basic Fisher Price nursery record player (really only a musical box) rather than a tape recorder and supply of tapes.

The second necessity lies in the therapist's behaviour, which makes it possible for the child to take roles and pursue them by being quickly and sensitively responsive in a supportive role of one's own. If the child says 'I'm the mummy and you're the baby', the adult must *immediately* get down on the floor, thumb in mouth: beginning therapists can find themselves inhibited in this, and may ask questions such as 'Am I a girl or a boy?', 'Am I happy or sad?' as a kind of delaying tactic. This slows up the action to the point that it feels like wading through treacle, and the child justifiably becomes bored. One or two quiet questions can be useful, but action must come first. The child may, of course, take up a role without indicating what the adult is to be: then the adult must slip into whatever role feels intuitively right in relation to the child's, perhaps asking as an aside, after a few minutes, 'Am I being the person you want?' When the adult's response is sensitively done, children quickly learn to take the initiative in correcting the adult's role-taking to support their own needs.

The third requirement is a matter of *structure*: the child is freed to direct both the plot and the players, partly by the responsiveness already mentioned, but equally by being given playroom rules of behaviour *which govern both participants*. It may seem paradoxical to describe the child as freed by rules, but in fact children remain fettered by their notions of adult–child control until they are offered playroom rules within which both can feel free. When we tell the child that she is in charge of what happens in the playroom, this on its own cannot give the child freedom because she knows that no adult will actually allow her to break windows and lights, tear her own hair out, flood the room or poke sticks into the therapist's eyes. The truth of this promise therefore immediately invites aggressive testing, particularly where children's experience of adult–child relationships so far has been of the testing and controlling kind. True freedom for these children, and equally for chaotic and impetuous children, lies in an impersonal containment ('belonging' to the playroom) which applies to all participants alike, as surely as the containing structure of the playroom's four walls.

For this reason, the rules are stated either impersonally or in terms of 'we':

- no hurting – only pretend hurting
- no breaking – only pretend breaking
- when it's time to go home, we have to go home, and we can't take anything with us.

The combination of *role-play* and a *rule structure as safe as the playroom walls* has a liberating effect of an extraordinary kind, which I shall describe shortly; first, we need to consider the management of the child's first experience of dramatic role-play.

The child has been told that he is the Boss (see p. 97), and the therapist is sitting on the floor watching him explore. The floor is chosen because all children have long experience of adults sitting in chairs and supervising them, and we want explicitly to abandon this position. At this point the rules have not yet been mentioned to the child; because children find it difficult to integrate the notion of being 'Boss' with the notion of rules if they first encounter them together, but have no difficulty at all if there is a separation in time.

Typically the child will make a couple of circuits of the room, picking up objects and sometimes commenting; almost always she will eventually be drawn into the play-house by the oddness of the fried egg and bacon in the frying pan, which is why I have described this equipment as 'especially necessary'. In exploring the objects in the play-house, she is likely either to start 'cooking' or to try out the cash register. At this point, the therapist may lift the nearest telephone and start the bell ringing, an invitation that few children can refuse. If the child does answer the phone in the play-house, the therapist tries to get into the action in whatever way seems appropriate to what the child is already doing. He might say 'Can I come and have tea at your house?' or 'I need a few things, can I come to your shop?' Most children will accept positively; if the child says, as has been known, 'No, I'm too busy clearing up', or 'No, we're closed', or simply doesn't answer the phone, the therapist must wait passively for at least five minutes and try again. If again refused, he may develop a role, probably in relation to the dog or a doll, in which he can complain to them about the difficulties of shops being closed or people not answering the phone; one of these ruses will invariably be effective in drawing some sort of invitation from the child.

Once the therapist has received permission to join the child, he loses no time in finding a role. He will grab, for instance, the dog, a bag and perhaps a hat (hats being the quickest way of becoming someone other than yourself), and knock on the play-house door or start to do business as a customer at the counter. From now on, the therapist is concerned to sustain a role or series of roles in quick response to the child, and to enable the child herself to enter any roles she wishes, by giving her many opportunities and choices. This is a learned skill: beginning therapists, in their effort to allow the child the initiative, often miss opportunities in the first session. Since it is essential that role-play be experienced on both sides on the first occasion, live supervision is important, to allow the supervisor to intervene with suggestions (the one and only time anyone will ever interrupt a session). For instance, the child might not have entered the house in the first place: perhaps she is riding round the room on the vehicle. The therapist could take a policeman's hat and beg a lift to chase a burglar; or take a lady's hat, nudge the dog under the wheels and call for a doctor to come and treat her injured animal, pointing out in an undertone where the doctor's bag is (another piece of equipment that few children can resist). If the child is playing ball, the therapist might become a sports commentator, or another child in the park, or a grumpy park-keeper.

The chief aim of the first session, apart from getting to know each other, is to achieve role-play and, if possible, to state the rules; rules can, if necessary, be left until the next time, but therapy will be greatly delayed by not establishing role-play. The rules are most conveniently stated the first time they seem on the point of having been broken. The therapist comes right out of any role she may be in, stops whatever action is in progress, and says to the child very clearly, 'I'm sorry – I forgot to tell you. There are three playroom rules that we have to keep when we're in the playroom. Listen and I'll tell you what they are. No hurting . . .' etc. Although it is not quite true that the therapist 'forgot', this way of explaining is so effective in enabling children to understand that it does seem worth the subterfuge. Thereafter, if a child does break a rule, it will be enough to stop, revert to one's true self momentarily, and remind the child 'Remember the rule, Paul', and possibly to restate the appropriate rule. We are very impressed with the ability of irresponsible children to take responsibility for rules by this means; to see the usually aggressive and violent Paul stopping a mock fight for a moment to ask gently in his own voice 'Am I hurting you?'

can be moving in the expression of his determination to take control of himself, at least in this protected context.

I have emphasized the importance of establishing role-play because it is rules and roles in conjunction that seem to make up the therapeutic experience. Why should this be?

First, the conjunction allows the couple to ignore the imbalance of the adult–child relationship. In other situations, the adult is almost always experienced by the child as either in control or vehemently trying to reassert control. Within the playroom walls, and therefore rules, there is no longer any issue of 'naughty or good', or 'what can I get away with?' (the thought which is paramount for so many of these children). Whatever is to happen today in the playroom will not happen between Paul and the therapist, but *between the characters Paul has chosen*. If everything is pretend (though given relevance by being chosen or modified by the child), then anything is acceptable: this is why we cannot just say 'no hurting . . . no breaking', because there must still be action within the safe context; the action that is relevant to this child's life may well be above all about breaking and hurting.

It is particularly important to get rid of the question 'What can I get away with?' because this puts children in the undignified posture of wheedling. The last rule especially takes care of the pleading 'Just five more minutes' and '*Please* can I have this little balloon', which kind adults find hard to resist, but which puts them in the position of a controller to be got around. The adult need invoke no sanctions or personal authority; it is obvious to the child that 'playroom rules' are an automatic part of the privilege (as he regards it, having chosen a contract to be here) of playing in the playroom. Playroom and rules are an indivisible package. He knows that he will be given five minutes warning before time is up (which some children use to complete a chosen scenario, and therefore must not be forgotten); he also knows that once he leaves the playroom he cannot re-enter until the next session. Thus 'being in the playroom' becomes something special to be cherished.

The sanctuary offered by roles and rules allows the child to act out any theme she chooses; to switch roles or exchange them; and to explore areas such as cruelty, protection, authority, rejection and death, all of which might be too dangerous or painful to explore in real-world contexts with real-world people. In particular, we have found that children who have been or are still the victims of others (or of fate) may feel a need to explore and contemplate the victim role. The context of dramatic role-play allows this to happen: that is, the child may make the decision to move into such a role and to designate a controlling and even cruel role to the adult. If the child is also to experience 'being the boss' and making the overriding decisions for the couple, it would be impossible for her to experience powerlessness concurrently *except* in role, which is why the establishment of role-play is a priority for the therapist. Similarly, it would be difficult for the therapist to allow the child's victimization by himself if both were in their own persons.

Futhermore, role-play allows the therapist to protest *in role* against the actions of the child's persona. A child may, in role as a father, a policeman or a gangster, engage in an orgy of killing or maiming. It is appropriate that the therapist in another role – whether perhaps as bereaved friend, mother or dog-owner – should show grief and anger. Retribution is not the most useful response (fetching police, killing in turn, etc.); grief is more likely to make the child think. Children sometimes kill and quickly say 'He's alive again'; it can be helpful to remind the child of the finality of death by *in role* denying that this can be. These responses, again, are only possible in role if the child's overall control is not to be violated.

An additional advantage of role-play within the structure that I have described is that it makes play therapy far more usable by the 'helping professionals' who are already involved with their client children in other ways: social workers, care staff, nurses, hospital play workers, educational or clinical child psychologists and so on; this is what gives it the quality of 'barefoot play therapy', in that it can form part of the helping strategies offered to children in those geographical areas where a 'proper' (ie fully trained) play therapist has never been seen within living memory. When I and my postgraduate students started to develop play therapy methods, we found ourselves so successful in helping children that other professionals asked us to share our methods with them, so that they could work with selected children: perhaps only one at a time from their caseload, but that one chosen as particularly resistant to their more normal methods. The first group to press for this was the social workers who had wanted us to do play therapy in the first place, and at first I was very doubtful: how could someone who already had a social-work role towards a child stand aside from that role to be a therapist? I thought of Linda, the 12 year old who weekly tried to reconcile her nice and nasty husbands, and whose therapist in the role of sympathetic lady-next-door had asked 'What *is* a social worker?': he had been told 'Oh, you know – one of those people that tells you where you've got to go and what you've got to do' – simplistic perhaps, but signifying a perception which had some pragmatic truth and was surely not consonant with therapy?

Nothing if not responsive to demand, we decided to try it out with a self-selected group of social workers. I had expected the group to be the young and adventurous; they turned out to be mainly middle-aged, jaded and disillusioned with traditional methods, but still adventurous in wanting a new way of reaching their least accessible child clients. All were successful in this aim, some remarkably so; their own perception was that they also learned much about themselves and the aspects of control that had informed their usual styles with children. Some of the most creative work between therapist and child has been done where these double roles have been successfully juggled, and I have therefore included examples from that project in the final section of this chapter.

The child's experience of therapy

In what ways do children actually use this kind of therapy? If this chapter were a book, a series of case studies would give perspective; more economically, we can illustrate with brief examples.

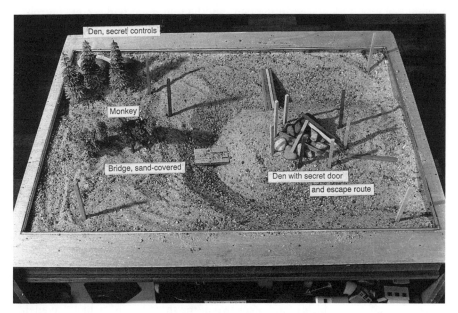

Figure 4.2 James aged 9 years – his ninth 'world'

Expressing issues of uncertainty, powerlessness and lack of involvement in decision-making

James, aged 9, had been in care for seven years; his most stable foster placement had broken down just before Christmas, and he would spend Christmas Day in a children's home. James thought (so did we!) that 'they might have waited till after Christmas'. The social worker/therapist describes his 'World' of 17 December (Figure 4.2).

> The sand was scooped to both sides of the tray to leave a semi-circular river. He placed two trees to one side and put a monkey on one of the trees. He then placed several wooden bars across the river like a bridge, and several in a heap on the other side. This took five minutes or so, and he declared 'I've finished, can we go in the other room?' I said perhaps he would like to tell me about his world. He said it was a deserted island, with no people on, only one monkey who lived by himself. I asked if the monkey enjoyed being alone; he said 'Yes, it's great, he enjoys himself, he has the whole place to himself and he can do what he likes'. Then, as I made a move to go, he stopped me and said 'No, wait, I haven't finished'. He got wooden sticks and began to place them upright in the sand, telling me there had been a war on the island and these were ruined buildings. He built another 'den' for the monkey with a secret door. He put 'look-out posts' on each corner. He then got more trees and bushes to hide the dens, and asked me to build a bridge across the water and cover it with sand. (It is perhaps of interest that the therapist was chosen to build this hidden bridge.) The

monkey was then placed in the den, and he told me it had secret controls in there and proceeded to show me what the monkey could do by operating these. The fir trees could be controlled to move away from the den at night, but always returned to the same place by morning. He could operate the bridge so that if invaders came they couldn't get across. James went into elaborate details of how the monkey could get into his den by one secret door and escape if necessary by another.

In the person of the 'poor monkey' we see a child explicitly under siege; any power he might have is reduced to defence. The theme of escape was continued in the following session (7 January), when James ran away as his therapist's car arrived at the children's home, and she accepted this gesture. A week later James came for therapy, but announced 'I'm going to muck around': which he did, wandering about, getting on and off the rocking horse and, once in the 'World' room, slouching in his chair, fingering the World items but saying 'No' when asked whether he was going to make a World. After ten minutes, his therapist asked whether the electronic car he had had for Christmas was like any of those in the cupboard. He said 'No – but OK, I *will* build a world'. He chose a police car and an ambulance, threw them on the sand and said '*That's* my world!'. The fact that the child is deliberately making a choice from about fifty civilian vehicles, and takes two of the three 'crisis' vehicles available, has to be seen as significant; the throwing, rather than the usual careful placing, must also be accepted as the gesture it is. James's was a long, difficult but increasingly positive story, in which we steadily built up the explicit relevance of the play-work for the decisions being made; at the end of the second year, he was successfully adopted.

Discovering new aspects of old relationships

Although therapists who have another role (such as social worker) must be careful to keep the two roles firmly separate, the fact that the person is *bodily* present in both roles makes some 'leakage' likely. This can be wholly beneficial.

Jack was 12, living in a community foster home, and daily truanting from his local comprehensive school. His social worker, Mary, chose him as the child on her caseload with whom she had achieved least communication or trust over two years. Each Monday Jack would take himself to school by 4 o'clock, and would be picked up at the gate by Mary as therapist; neither would mention the fact which both knew, that he had not been in school all day.

On his sixth drama session, Jack planted Mary on the climbing frame with the toy record-player, and quickly arrived as a policeman: 'Turn that damn thing off. I've a complaint about you . . . you've got to come with me to the police station . . . I've got to tie you up . . . I've got a warrant'. He tied her hands behind her with a skipping rope, as she protested bitterly:

Mary: Oh dear, I won't get down like this, not with my hands tied.
Jack: You'll have to manage it or I'll break your neck.

There followed increasing threats, pleading from Mary about prisoners' rights,

and denial of them by Jack: 'No questions asked. . . . Ten years' imprisonment
. . . All our police station does this!' The exchange (in which Mary later described
her own real feelings of anger, injustice and powerlessness) ended after about
twenty minutes of altercation by Mary being bundled, tightly tied, into the far
depths of the climbing frame and Jack walking out of the playroom, putting the
lights out as he went. I, as supervisor, found him drinking coffee in the waiting
area, and asked 'Where's Mary?' – 'In there', he gestured to the playroom.
Knowing she would have had a difficult struggle to extricate herself in the dark,
I suggested we should help her; but at that moment Mary emerged from the
playroom. For a second Jack's face was stricken and it was evident that he knew
he might have gone too far; a second later it cleared as Mary said cheerfully,
'Hey, haven't you got me a cup of coffee?' Her ability to leave her feelings
behind in the playroom, and so earn his trust, was rewarded a week later when
Jack asked for 'a talk' and proceeded to discuss his history and anxieties in a
way that she had never achieved with him in two years of social work.

Contemplating situations without accusation or blame

This experience can also be well illustrated by Jack. A few weeks later, Mary
in supervision described how, as social worker, she had visited Jack at home
to discuss the continuing truancy, and had said to him 'I wish, Jack, that you
would sometimes think what it's like to be me trying to get you to school –
because I often try to think what it's like to be you'.

I suggested that in drama that evening she might like to ask Jack if he would
like to try out a new game – being each other for half an hour. Mary wasn't
sure; she'd think about it and see how it felt at the time. That evening Jack's
World was entirely concerned with the difficulty of getting to school: there was
a school bus (containing Jack) waiting at the traffic lights which were turned to
red, two tanks also halting the bus, Mary following in her car which was 'broken',
another social worker in a car containing a bomb, a 'light getaway plane' and
a car with 'neighbours going on their holidays'. Subsequently Jack went into
the playroom and immediately divided it into two, putting Mary on one side
at a desk and himself on the other, also deskbound, where he stayed throughout.
He began 'There's your desk. You're my secretary'. After some conversation
by phone, it gradually transpired that he was a headmaster. He proceeded
spontaneously to discuss on the phone the case of a boy of 12 (represented as
a large doll) who wanted to go back to junior school – 'He says, well, I would
like to go to senior school, but he's finding it hard with the work you see . . . he
can't take it . . . he isn't frightened of doing it, it's just too complicated for
him. . . . See, if we get his mind back to the work what he did for the fourth
year, and try him out on it, and keep trying till he knows it, then we can just
join him on to the senior school and he won't be so difficult'. The conversation in this vein lasted more than twenty minutes; there is no way that one
can imagine it taking place in such a manner, on an objective 'professional'
level with the child taking the higher status, other than in role-play. Mary was
especially conscious of being liberated from her inevitable accusatory stance
(given that non-attendance at school is illegal), but one can assume that Jack

found the responsible and caring role of concerned headmaster equally enlightening.

Exploring issues of identity and contamination

Children whose parents are criminal, insane or cruel may be deeply concerned as to how far they themselves can preserve a separate identity and escape from contamination. A less common but more extreme form of this issue was the problem for Oliver, aged 7, whose twin brother was autistic. When Oliver was looking a little dreamy, he could easily be mistaken for his twin, and indeed often had been: an event which was painful and alarming to both Oliver and his mother. Oliver had begun to practise 'autistic' mannerisms in the mirror, which horrified his mother still more. On first coming to see us, he brought with him a drawing of two prehistoric animals, which he described as 'a triceratops and a stegosaurus fighting'. Encouraged to tell us more, he went on 'There's something special about them. This one *looks* like a triceratops, but he's actually a stegosaurus pretending to be a triceratops. And this one *looks* like a stegosaurus; but he's actually a triceratops pretending to be a stegosaurus'. This theme of 'How far can you go in pretending to be someone else . . . where will it end?' was to be central to Oliver's Worlds and role-play for a full year; people were magicked into each other in a dizzying way for the therapist, and the question always hung in the air: suppose you can't change back? It took a full year before Oliver was able to leave characters to develop their own identities, and we gave him a second year to be sure that he was, as he said, 'Properly safe'.

Conclusion

Perhaps the best way of summing up is to set out a statement of our intentions when we take on a child for the Nottingham play therapy package. Given that the child clearly needs help, we have only two very basic criteria: that she is capable of 'pretend' or symbolic play, and that she is not among the group of children who pathologically lack boundaries between reality and fantasy (Newson 1989). Within these criteria, our aims are:

1 At the very least, to give the child our total attention for an hour per week; he is guaranteed no interruption, short of life or death emergencies, and a commitment over time about which he makes the decisions. It is sobering to consider how few children can count on this amount of weekly undivided attention from one adult.
2 To offer the child experience of being master over a situation and over ourselves. The experience of mastery is rare for most of our children. The experience of *responsibility* within mastery may be still rarer, particularly with an adult who assumes that responsibility will be accepted and achieved without adult control.
3 To give the child a totally new experience which is *relevant* to her real world

but encapsulated and separate from the real world: that is, it takes place in a protective and privileged environment. There are no strings attached to the situation, and the concepts of 'well-behaved' or 'naughty' no longer apply. The novelty of the experience is deliberately intended to shock the child, since the experience of shock is likely to make her think, and hence help her reassess and reconstruct.

4 To offer the child an alternative language with which to conceptualize whatever is relevant for him or her. Whether in making Worlds or acting out situations and roles, the work the child does through the language of play is for his own benefit, not for the therapist; that is, the *essential* communication is with himself, not with the therapist. This is very different from the package which is offered by interpretative therapists, where there is always the tacit claim that the therapist is so expert in reading the child's play that she knows better than he what he means. We are looking for the child to create something in sand or playroom that *makes sense to the child*; if it makes sense to us too, that is a bonus. We listen to children with care and respect, hoping for insight on their thoughts; but we do not in fact need insight. It is enough that we should facilitate the work that the child needs to do, by giving him a language in which to do it. Barefoot play therapists should not aspire to high heels.

References

Axline, V. (1947) *Play Therapy*, Boston, Mass.: Houghton Mifflin.
Axline, V. (1990) *Dibs: In Search of Self*, rev. edn, Harmondsworth: Penguin.
Bowyer, R. (1970) *The Lowenfeld World Technique*, Oxford: Pergamon Press.
Erikson, E. (1958) Sex differences in play construction of twelve-year-old children, in J.M. Tanner and B. Inhelder (eds) *Discussions on Child Development*, Vol. 3, London: Tavistock.
Klein, M. (1964) *Contributions to Psychoanalysis 1921–1945*, London: McGraw Hill.
Lowenfeld, M. (1979) *The World Technique*, London: Allen & Unwin.
Lowenfeld, M. (1991) *Play in Childhood*, Classics in Developmental Medicine 6, London: MacKeith Press.
Moustakas, C. (1973) *Children in Play Therapy*, rev. edn, New York: Aronson.
Newson, E. (1989) *Pathological Demand Avoidance Syndrome: Mapping a New Entity in the Autistic Spectrum*, inaugural lecture, CDRU/University of Nottingham.
Rogers, C. (1959) A theory of therapy, personality and interpersonal relationships as developed in the client-centred framework, in S. Koch (ed.) *Psychology: A Study of a Science*, Vol. 3, New York: McGraw Hill.
Strayhorn, J. (1988) *The Competent Child: An Approach to Psychotherapy and Preventive Mental Health*, New York: Guilford Press.
Winnicott, D. (1971) *Therapeutic Consultations in Child Psychiatry*, London: Hogarth Press.
Winnicott, D. (1980) *The Piggle*, Harmondsworth: Penguin.

5

Abuse of children

DANYA GLASER

Introduction

Children are deemed to have been abused when they have suffered maltreatment of some sort, or when they undergo experiences which are detrimental to their development, regardless of whether the process is perceived by the child as pleasant or unpleasant. Abuse requires the existence of some form of prior relationship between the child or her family and the person or persons who abuse the child. Thus, abuse often becomes an integral part of a significant relationship between the child and an important person in the child's life. This abusive relationship is in its turn usually integrated into a wider network of family and other extended relationships. For a time, the child may grow to accept the abuse as an inevitable aspect of his or her life. This has been described by Finkelhor (1988) as 'overintegration' of the abusive experiences by the child into her life. Abuse may be intensely physically painful, or unpleasant. Some abused children are too young to be rationally aware of the wrong perpetrated upon them, others are tricked into believing that they have brought their misfortunes on themselves or that the abuse is part of normal, socially accepted adult behaviour.

Forms of abuse

All forms of abuse are to some extent psychologically damaging. In that sense, all abuse is emotional abuse. The basic trust and benevolence which would usually be assumed to have existed between the dependent child and the adult is breached. The emotional abuse may be expressed through acts of omission, when it is termed neglect or lack of protection, or when insufficient or inappropriate feeding leads to failure to thrive. It may be expressed through a wide variety of acts. These include varying forms and degrees of violence, poisoning, or induction of fictitious illness in the child which leads to the child being subjected to unpleasant and often harmful medical intervention (Munchausen by Proxy) (Rosenberg 1987). Sexual abuse is a more recently though now widely recognized form of emotional child abuse. Finally, the abuse may be expressed, unaccompanied by physical acts, through the attitude to and behaviour towards the child, including systematic denigration, blame, scapegoating and withholding or deprivation of warmth and affection.

The response to child abuse

It is understandable that in the face of such a catalogue of misfortunes, cruelty and deprivation of human rights accorded to abused children, society's response, mediated through its appointed professionals, is to seek protection for the children, at times accompanied by demands for this to be obtained at any cost. Failure to protect arouses censure and extreme disapproval towards the professionals (eg London Borough of Brent 1985). In this climate the therapeutic needs of the child may acquire a lower profile and be accorded a lower priority. Therapy, defined as a curative or healing process, is a challenging, arduous, prolonged and only poorly evaluated process, whose need may be recognized but for which resources are often not available. Furthermore, the extent to which a cure, as distinct from the formation of a 'good enough' scar can realistically be achieved, is questionable. Therapy is therefore understood here to refer to the professional interaction with the abused child, which is intended to promote the optimal psychological recovery and personal development possible. Therapy in childhood is concerned retrospectively with past events, their current meanings and consequences and with a prospective view which is intended to be preventive of future difficulties. Indeed, insight gained from therapeutic work with adults abused as children (Briere and Runtz 1988) has informed much of the preventive aspect of therapy with abused children.

In this chapter, an attempt is made to consider the emotional issues which abused children are likely to face and to define their consequent therapeutic needs. This is followed by a critical outline of the various treatment modalities available and a discussion of the relative indications for their use. Finally, there is a consideration of the importance of the context in which therapy proceeds and challenges and conflicts likely to face those who undertake this work.

Emotional issues

In considering the emotional impact and significance of traumatic experiences, account must be taken of several aspects. The **nature** of the experience itself, including its duration and intensity, will form significant determinants. Since abuse constitutes an expression of a **relationship**, much of the response of the abused child is related to feelings towards the abuser or abusers. Furthermore, the human context of this relationship and the perceived roles of other significant persons in the child's life at the time of the abuse will help to shape the emotional impact of the abuse and child's responses. The child's understanding of the experience, and the **meaning** attached to it, are related to the role which the child ascribes to his or her own participation in or precipitation of the abuse. Children, particularly in their earlier years, perceiving their universe from an egocentric and omnipotent perspective (Selman 1980), tend to attribute cause and therefore blame to themselves. In seeking an explanation for their experiences, and in the absence of an alternative one, abused children conclude that their own inherent badness must lie at the root of the negative treatment which they have experienced at the hands of their presumed benevolent caregivers.

Consequences of recognition of the abuse, including separations, blame and possible punishment for the abuser, offer further sources of turmoil for the abused child. The **cumulative effect**, of these feelings combine to determine to a very significant extent the child's view of herself and her **self-esteem**, her or his development and the nature of her future relationships.

The nature of the abuse

Some abusive acts inflict definable and memorable physical or mental injuries and will be clearly recalled by the child. Such abuse is likely to leave the child frightened and acutely distressed at the time of the abuse, and may lead to sequelae now described collectively as the Post-Traumatic Stress Disorder (Eth and Pynoos 1985). Here, the experience is repeatedly relived in some form, leads to a degree of emotional disengagement from current life and relationships and the reaction to this abusive trauma is accompanied by a variety of disturbances including guilt, difficulties with memory and concentration, and renewed fear when the child encounters situations reminiscent of the abusive situation. Abuse which leaves physical scars, marks or other tangible signs is likely to be more constantly remembered. A child who experiences multiple forms of abuse is more likely to be severely emotionally affected. Sexual abuse, which includes pseudo-religious, black magic or other bizarre practices and which involve multiple abusers, is more damaging (Briere 1988).

Sexually abused children often fear that their genitalia have been irreversibly damaged or that the abuse has led to structurally based and permanent sexual or reproductive impairment. Indeed, this may occasionally be the case, for example if the child is infected by a sexually transmitted disease. Boys who have been homosexually anally abused often come to believe that the abuse has turned them into homosexuals.

What requires further clarification is the relevance of these abuse-factors to treatment, since they are based on generalizations concerning child abuse, and may or may not apply to individuals.

The context of the abuse

Both clinical experience and several studies have pointed to the crucial nature of the relational context in which abuse is committed and experienced (eg Conte and Schuerman 1987). This includes the nature of the relationship between the abuser and the child, the abuser and the non-abusing caregiver and the non-abusing caregiver and the child. Broadly, the existence of some form of non-abusive and child-centred relationship for the child is seen as a protective factor, ameliorating to some degree the emotionally damaging effects of the abuse. Conversely, multiple abusers and non-belief in child's innocence compound the damage to the child. In this context, a close relationship between the non-abusing caregiver and the abuser may well not be in the child's best interests, even though such closeness may offer the only support available to the caregiver or mother during the period of abuse. When abuser and caregiver are one and the same person, the child is often in a perilous state. Furthermore, the closer, more dependent and based on trust is the relationship between the child and the abuser, the more confusing is the abuse for the child. This is, for instance, the case when sexual abuse is committed by the child's natural father (Harter et al. 1988).

In addition, children whose families experience significant difficulties apart from the abuse itself, are more likely to be detrimentally affected by the abuse. Abused children however continue to remain loyal to their abusive parents. Haynes-Seman (1987) describes observations of the self-reinforcing cycle of the relationship between an abused infant and his mother. The author goes on to describe a likely repetition of such 'morally masochistic' behaviour by abused children, based on their perceived need to employ this way of relating as the only means of attachment available to them.

In addition, children whose families experience significant difficulties apart from the abuse itself, are more likely to be detrimentally affected by the abuse.

Consequences of the identification of abuse

With society's increasing awareness and intolerance of all forms of child abuse has come intervention in this process. This relatively recent response has introduced new and highly significant events and experiences into the 'natural history' and lives of abused children. These events often profoundly affect the emotional states of already abused children and will affect the therapeutic process. The declared aim of intervention in child abuse is to lead to child protection with cessation of the abuse. The test of providing these already traumatized children with the least detrimental alternative may or may not be satisfied. Certainly the children do not always perceive their 'rescue' as such. For abuse to cease, several changes are required including the abuser's assumption of responsibility for the abuse, the ensuring of the presence or introduction of reliable, protecting adults and the beginning of a process of changing the underlying issues which have culminated in, and maintained the abusive relationship. This process of protection not infrequently includes separations from some significant persons in the child's life and constitute a profound and at times traumatic loss for the child. Unlike the situation during the abuse, when the assumption of blame or responsibility by the child may be regarded as an adaptive emotional response, enabling the child to feel a measure of control over her or his experiences (Conte 1985), abused children often feel resentful and victimized by the process of protection which they feel unable to comprehend or influence. Children understandably lack the ability and information to adopt a long-term view, and their tenuous sense of trust in adults' selfless benevolence towards them is often translated into mistrust of their 'rescuers.' The therapist may be perceived as one of these.

The child's state: feelings and behaviour

The resultant of such a complex set of variables, to which constitutional factors of the particular child must be added, precludes an easily definable state. Rather, an awareness of the likely conflicting and confusing emotions which abused children experience and struggle to accommodate, is of help. At the root of these lies the child's constant attempt to make sense and retain a degree of autonomy over her or his experiences and life, seeking at the same time to maintain attachments which will, for the dependent child, ensure emotional, and sometimes physical survival. For these reasons, both the manifest and unconscious feelings of abused children may not conform to adults' expectations. Anger and protest may be initially lacking, over compliance and 'frozen watchfulness' being expressed instead (Crittenden and DiLalla 1988). The sense of continued loyalty to and identification with natural parents, while at times seemingly inexplicable, is nevertheless almost universal. The child (and indeed the later adult) sense their own identity and personal survival as being inextricably bound with that of their parents, however neglectful, uncaring or abusive they have been. Abused children therefore often construct and maintain alternative and possibly elaborate explanations and beliefs about the nature and causes of the abuse which they have experienced. They may believe that the physical violence is deserved punishment, that the sexual abuse is an expression of a required relationship between a daughter and her father, or that the neglect and lack or protection from abuse or injury was an understandable expression of a mother's need to attend to her own survival. Although pain and fear often accompany abuse, the child's sense of guilt makes these more bearable.

It is in that sense that adopting a position of personal responsibility allows the child to survive emotionally. Emotional abuse is often explained by abusive carers as being the natural consequence of the child's disturbance. Another form of adaptation to prolonged abuse is the child's consciously held denial of the nature of the experience. This is actively maintained by the abuser's and sometimes carer's denial, and is particularly manifest in sexual abuse, termed by Summit (1983) as the 'Child Sexual Abuse Accommodation Syndrome'. The alternative explanation, proferred by adults not emotionally involved in the abusive relationship, that of viewing the child as the victim of the abuser's exploitation, abuse of the child for the gratification of the abuser's emotional needs and unconscious projections is unavailable to the abused child. Belief in that explanation would require a view of the child as unloved, worthless and unwanted and would implicate the child as being essentially and constitutionally bad. Such feelings threaten the child's very right to exist and are therefore resisted. An alternative 'strategy' which some abused children adopt is to assume control of their life by themselves creating situations in which their bad behaviour will precipitate negative responses from others.

Amid such confusion and incongruity between the child's view and that of others around her, behavioural disturbance of various and non-specific manifestation as well as learning difficulties are more easily understood. These further compound the resultant low self-esteem which so many abused children experience and express in different ways.

At the time of commencing therapy, all these factors need to be taken into account in attempting to understand the child's position, behaviour and emotional state. Whether the actual process of therapy offered in its various modalities is significantly different when involving abused children, is questionable. It is not not so much the 'how' but rather the 'what', 'when' and 'who', or the particular content and issues arising during therapy which will be profoundly influenced by the fact of abuse and the nature of the protective responses accorded to the child.

The aims of therapy

Therapy might be seen as a process intended to enable the abused child to begin giving up previously possibly adaptive defences (Mrazek and Mrazek 1987), which in the light of new experiences of safety and trust might now be maladaptive and redundant. Thus, a degree of denial of the pain or discomfort of the abuse, as well as the need to maintain the secret of the abuse often leave the child unable to talk about it. An aspect of therapy involves offering the child an opportunity to describe the past experiences and indeed to find an acceptable way of 'telling her story'. The ability to talk about past experiences more freely allows the trauma to recede into the past and renders the process of recollection a more elective one and more under the child's control. The isolation which many abused children feel, be it based on shame, guilt or fear will begin to be reversed.

Therapy furthermore aims at helping the child to gradually develop a new and different view of her/himself. Exploration of the child's fears and understanding of the abuse may be coupled with a progressive reinterpretation of the evolution of, and adults' responsibility for past experiences. There is no intention here of denying or minimizing the child's anger as well as possible continuing love and concern for the abuser, if a significant relationship exists. Providing the child is offered the reality experience of safe dependency, she may gradually be able to shed the assumption of responsibility for the abuse or believe in the appropriateness of disclosure. This new position, however, exposes the child to the most threatening feelings of powerlessness, and may explain why feelings of guilt often persist. Nevertheless, these explorations in therapy may enable the child to form future relationships free from the expectations of repetition of abuse and neglect.

Therapy also includes an element of promoting future protection for the child through the active exploration of ways in which the abused child may he maintaining his or her vulnerability to reabuse.

Therapeutic modalities

Therapy is mediated through play and talk in their broadest sense. It may be offered in different settings including individual, group or family. The therapeutic process requires careful co-ordination between the many professionals usually involved in these situations and several modalities may well be offered simultaneously. For example, group or individual therapy may continue alongside family work, although a child is less likely to be offered individual and group therapy simultaneously. Therapy may be structured or unstructured. It may entail active exploration by the therapist, include the giving of information and a degree of education and may proceed through role-play, drawing, using toys and play materials including anatomically correct dolls. It may, too, when appropriate include writing imaginary letters in which feelings can be expressed towards persons whom the child may not face directly. All therapeutic work with children must be planned and conceptualized in the context of the child's current life and relationships and particularly in the light of the child's dependence on adult care. It cannot in itself offer a substitute for care and differs from friendship, although it includes an element of both.

Individual therapy

The use of the term 'therapy' when considering individual work with children is sometimes assumed to mean a very specifically defined, psychodynamically based method. In fact, only a minority of children can be offered help of this nature due to the considerable scarcity of appropriately trained child psychotherapists. Furthermore, not by any means all abused children require this degree of intensive help. Among those who do and would benefit from it, many children are not living in a sufficiently stable situation with parents or carers who would be able to support the child in necessarily prolonged and at times painful therapeutic process. Paradoxically, those children who find themselves in unstable situations of uncertain duration and future, may be the very ones who while in greatest need of more intensive therapy, are living in circumstances which preclude embarking on this process (Dyke 1987). In these cases, interim stability may need to be created by offering the child a placement in a therapeutic community, or occasionally special foster home, from which base the child can be supported in therapy. The therapeutic process here is dependent on the very special relationship created between child and therapist within which the child feels sufficiently safe to express and encounter his most persecuting, unconscious and avoided feelings through fantasy in play and art. The therapist's training enables her to contain and lend meaning to the child's participation during therapy (Boston and Szur 1983).

The indications for specialized individual psychotherapy are severalfold. The abuse would have so severely emotionally affected the child as to pervasively influence functioning, cognitive development, sense of self-preservation and especially her or his capacity to form and sustain positive attachments and relationships. The assumption is that the child has 'internalized' the damaging and negative aspects of the experiences. This may be due to the severity of the abuse itself, to the adverse and unsupportive nature of care or to the child's own constitutional vulnerability, and often to a combination of all these factors.

The advantage of reserving the term 'therapy' to this specific situation is the clarity of meaning conferred by it. There is, however, a great deal of important individual work which does not require this degree of specialized training and skill. The importance of less intensive aspects of therapeutic intervention is often underestimated by those who are in a position to offer it to the child. One of the central aspects of this work is offering the child the opportunity to talk about the abuse, feelings about the abuser and the family, to express her response to the intervention and its consequences and to seek and gain information about future events. Much of this work is concerned with the real events and the child's relatively consciously held but not articulated and expressed fears, anxieties, confusion, sadness and anger. Abused children gain enormous relief from the opportunity to talk and be heard unconditionally and uncritically, particularly when expressing feelings which might not be thought acceptable, such as positive feelings and a sense of loss and concern about the abuser. Some sexually abused children gain a degree of pleasure from the abuse but are unable to talk about this openly. While from a rational point of view these feelings might be considered inappropriate, their existence cannot be negated, and in having their legitimacy acknowledged, the child herself feels validated.

Sexually abused children often harbour particular fears and worries in relation to the abuse. For example, there is concern about possible physical damage to the genitalia, and to future sexual and reproductive functioning, caused by the abuse. Children may fear that they have been infected with AIDS. Sexually abused boys sometimes assume that the abuse has rendered them irreversibly homosexual in their orientation. Awareness of such anxieties enables the worker to explore their possible existence with the child. Jones (1986) illustrates some of these aspects in his account of individual work with an abused boy.

An important aspect of individual work with these children is keeping them informed and helping them prepare for future events in their lives. These may include changes in home and care, separations, a change in the circumstances of family members and court appearances. These latter will increase following recent changes in the status and hearing of children's evidence in abusers' trials. This aspect requires special attention and preparation. Maintaining continuity for the child across many changes which ensue after intervention in the abusive process is greatly valued by children as an indication of their own, sometimes doubted importance.

Group therapy

This modality has been increasingly offered to abused children, primarily where the abuse has included a sexual component. The most salient aspect of a group experience for these children is the fact that it counteracts the secrecy which almost invariably surrounds the abuse, and the isolation which so many abused children feel. Meeting other abused children, and witnessing the fact that sexually abused children bear no externally distinguishing features, is reassuring. Groups offer a very useful setting for observation and assessment of children's further therapeutic needs.

As with individual therapy, group work may be structured or unstructured, the latter tending to be offered to older children and adolescents who are developmentally more able to explore their feelings in such a setting. Younger children often benefit from shorter, structured and time-limited groups (Nelki and Watters 1989). This is particularly important in limiting the duration of the children's 'sexually abused' label. Participating children are usually within a similar age band, and apart from very young children, boys and girls are separated. Groups for children are far more likely to prove fruitful if parallel meetings are offered to the caregivers, who are thus supported in bringing the children regularly. These adults' groups also allow communication about certain aspects of the children's groups, particularly discussion about normal sexuality and the right not to keep secrets.

Although economically attractive, group therapy is in fact extremely time-consuming, requiring as it does two therapists, careful planning and preparation, post group de-briefing as well as supervision. The planning aspect include prior delineation of duration, membership, confidentiality, boundaries for acceptable behaviour as well as planning of aims and content of individual sessions. This work lends itself to evaluation, which does, however, require prior planning (Glaser and Frosh 1988).

Certain issues are particularly applicable to exploration in a group setting. These include acquiring appropriate language to describe anatomy, abuse and sexuality; establishing a 'comfortable' way of describing one's experiences and exploring the difficulties facing children in disclosure. Sex education as well as certain aspects of secondary prevention, especially the identification of trustworthy adults to whom a child could talk, are often easier to address in the group setting.

There is recent experience suggesting that groups for sexually abused boys may require particular skills and strict boundary setting due to the frequently encountered behaviour difficulties in these groups (Friedrich et al. 1988).

Family therapy

This aspect of work is being considered here specifically in relation to its contribution to the children's therapeutic needs. Sibling groups may be considered as representing one aspect of family work and is often very helpful in enabling abused siblings to share their experiences, this sometimes offering the first opportunity to do so. Sibling rivalry, hostility and blame may sometimes be safely aired in such a setting and an understanding gained about the respective children's predicament not previously recognized.

Family meetings offer an opportunity for children to express their feeling to their parents and other family members, often following a period of individual or group therapy. It is important to ascertain that the family is able to receive the child's expressions unconditionally. Otherwise the child could inadvertently be exposed to further emotional abuse. This setting enables children to hear their parents assume responsibility for past abusive acts. Family meetings also offer further opportunities for professionals to assess children's emotional needs.

Challenges, conflicts and issues facing therapists

Therapist issues

Questions are often raised about who should be working with abused children, including the therapist's gender, profession, training and experience. Concerns are often expressed about a therapist of the same gender as the abuser working single-handed. Some go as far as to suggest that men should not be involved in this work with sexually abused children. The child's wishes should be taken into account here, although a wish not to be working with a man merits exploration with the child about her or his reasons, since the child will continue to encounter and be likely to form future relationships with men. Both men and women are likely to arouse transference feelings in the child, and these may be explored. In group work, the ideal combination are a male and female therapist working together, since this enables the children to explore feelings in relation to both, as well as offering a role model of heterosexual co-operation in the interests of the child (Furniss et al. 1988). Particular dilemmas arise for men working in the field of child sexual abuse (Frosh 1987), and these are often fruitfully explored both individually and with colleagues. Men are also vulnerable to occasional false allegations by sexually abused children, although abuse by professionals is a reality.

In order to work with children, the professional should be familiar with children's language, cognitive and emotional development and the relevant therapeutic issues. Training in therapeutic work, particularly an awareness of the worker's own feelings and the appropriateness or otherwise of expressing these to the child, require careful exploration before work with abused children is embarked upon. It is likely that a significant proportion of workers will have undergone abusive experiences in their own childhood and in these circumstances, some form of therapy is often helpful in facing and coping with the feelings which abused children are likely to arouse.

Sensitivity, empathy and sympathy are all prerequisites, but the maintenance of a boundary which places the worker in a position different from a friend or carer is important, if the child is not to be further confused and later disappointed, particularly at the time of separation. Provided these attributes are broadly fulfilled, the professional designation of the worker matters less, and could be social work, psychology or child psychiatry. The special case of intensive child psychotherapy was mentioned earlier. In helping the child to establish trust in adults, continuity of work is desirable although often not possible. Work in this field is extremely stressful and calls for close team discussion and support, without which it is not possible to help children effectively.

Child abuse often arouses feelings of discomfort, anger and disapproval towards the abusers and non-protective caregivers. These, however, are at best only partially shared by most abused children and this difference requires resolution away from the child who should not be additionally burdened by them. Rather, the child's ambivalence requires acknowledgement and acceptance.

In the course of therapeutic work, the child may at times redirect anger belonging with the abuser towards the therapist. This requires containment and understanding but it is unhelpful for the child to be allowed to act this out.

Similarly but conversely, since many abused children have also experienced emotional deprivation and neglect, they may both seek and arouse strong feelings of attachment. It is the role of the designated caregiver, not therapist, to provide this love and care. The child may unconsciously attempt to create rivalries and splits between workers and carers. These can be minimized only by close co-operation between all those professionally involved with the child.

Therapy issues

The question of priorities and co-ordination of interventions is an important one, from the child's, professionals' and resources points of view. The child's paramount needs are for protection and permanency of care, neither of which can be directly met, only contributed to, by therapy. The fulfilment of these needs appropriately dictates the timing, content and type of help offered.

Confidentiality within therapy, whether group or individual, requires definition for the child. There is a certain risk that confidentiality and trust will be confused in the child's mind with the secrets so familiar from the abusive relationship. If it is considered appropriate for information given by the child to be shared with others, the child is entitled to know to whom and why this is being conveyed. The child's misgivings should be heard and considered, but cannot always be respected, in the child's own interests. Clear definition of this issue also minimizes confusion and mistrust between professionals.

Should the recollection of the abuse always be resurrected during therapeutic work? On the one hand, there is often an expectation that this will constitute a major part of the work. Others consider this a form of re-abuse. For future emotional adjustment and the formation of a 'good scar', it is important that at some point the opportunity has been provided and used by the child to describe her or his experiences as fully as possible. Thereafter, the child needs to know that any future therapist, and indeed carer, is willing and able to listen uncritically to any further accounts which the child may wish to give. Children vary greatly in the extent to which they continue to recount past events. They are the best judges of their needs.

Finally, therapy is likely to end at some point, either electively or due to circumstances beyond the therapist's control and hopefully in fulfilment of the child's future needs. If possible, the child should be prepared for the termination of this important relationship, and understand the reasons why. This rational approach, although necessary, is rarely wholly believed by the child who will nevertheless gain relief from this acknowledgement.

Conclusion

The essence of childhood is safe dependency which, it is assumed, abused children receiving therapeutic help can now enjoy. An aspect of this dependency and therefore interrelationship with at least one caring and protecting adult is that any work with the child must meet the approval and support of this adult. Furthermore, work with the child requires co-ordination with family and adult therapy. No two children, even when in similar circumstances, will have the same therapeutic needs. In planning for their fulfilment, the resultant is an individual one for each child.

References

Boston, M. and Szur, R. (eds) (1983) *Psychotherapy with Severely Deprived Children*, London: Routledge & Kegan Paul.

Briere, J. (1988) The long-term clinical correlates of childhood sexual victimization, *Annals of New York Academy of Sciences* 528: 327–34.

Briere, J. and Runtz, M. (1988) Post sexual abuse trauma, in G.E. Wyatt and G.J. Powell (eds) *Lasting Effects of Child Sexual Abuse*, London: Sage.

Conte, J.R. (1985) The effect of sexual abuse on children: a critique and suggestions for future research, *Victimology* 10: 110–30.

Conte, J.R. and Schuerman J.R. (1987) Factors associated with an increased impact of child sexual abuse, *Child Abuse and Neglect* 11: 201–11.

Crittenden, P.M. and DiLalla, D.L. (1988) Compulsive compliance: the development of an inhibitory coping strategy in infancy, *Journal of Abnormal Child Psychology* 16: 585–99.

Dyke, S. (1987) Saying 'no' to psychotherapy: consultation and assessment in a case of sexual abuse, *Journal of Child Psychotherapy* 13: 65–79

Eth, S. and Pynoos, R.S. (1985) *Post-Traumatic Stress Disorder in Children*, Los Angeles, Calif.: American Psychiatric Association.

Finkelhor, D. (1988) The trauma of child sexual abuse: two models, in G.E. Wyatt and G.J. Powell (eds) *Lasting Effects of Child Sexual Abuse*, London: Sage.

Friedrich, W.N., Berliner, L., Urouiza, A.J. et al. (1988) Brief diagnostic group treatment of sexually abused boys, *Journal of Interpersonal Violence* 3: 331–43.

Frosh, S. (1987) Issues for men working with sexually abused children, *British Journal of Psychotherapy* 3: 332–9.

Furniss, T., Bingley-Miller, L. and Van Elburg, A. (1988) Goal-oriented group treatment for sexually abused adolescent girls, *British Journal of Psychiatry* 152: 97–106.

Glaser, D. and Frosh, S. (1988) *Therapeutic intervention: in Child Sexual Abuse*, London: Macmillan Education.

Harter, S., Alexander, P. and Neimeyer, R. (1988) Long term effects of incestuous child abuse in college women: social adjustment, social cognition and family characteristics, *Journal of Consulting Clinical Psychology* 56: 5–8.

Haynes-Seman, C. (1987) Developmental origins of moral masochism: a failure-to-thrive toddler's interactions with mother, *Child Abuse and Neglect* 11: 319–30.

Jones, D.P.H. (1986) Individual psychotherapy for the sexually abused child, *Child Abuse and Neglect* 10: 377–85.

London Borough of Brent (1985) *A Child in Trust: Report of the Panel of Inquiry into the Circumstances Surrounding the Death of Jasmine Beckford*, London Borough of Brent.

Mrazek, P.J. and Mrazek, D.A. (1987) Resilience in child maltreatment victims: a conceptual exploration, *Child Abuse and Neglect* 11: 357–66.

Nelki, J.S. and Watters, J. (1989) A group for sexually abused young children: unravelling the web, *Child Abuse and Neglect* 13: 369–77.

Rosenberg, D.A. (1987) Web of deceit: a literature review of Munchausen Syndrome by Proxy, *Child Abuse and Neglect* 11: 547–63.

Selman, R.L. (1980) *The Growth of Interpersonal Understanding: Developmental and Clinical Analyses*, New York: Academic Press.

Summit, R.C. (1983) The child sexual abuse accommodation syndrome, *Child Abuse and Neglect* 7: 177–93.

6

School phobia

NIGEL BLAGG

. . . the whining schoolboy with his satchel
And shining morning face, creeping like snail
Unwillingly to school.

(Shakespeare, *As You Like It*, II. vii. 145-7)

Introduction

Judging by Shakespeare's brief description, school phobia has existed for centuries. However, it was Broadwin (1932) who first delineated the problem from other forms of non-attendance referring to it as 'a special kind of truancy':

> The child is absent for school for periods varying from several months to a year. The absence is consistent. At all times, the parents know where the child is. It is near the mother or near the home. The reason for the truancy is incomprehensible to the parents and the school. The child may say that it is afraid to go to school, afraid of the teacher or say that it does not know why it will not go to school.
>
> (Broadwin 1932)

The term 'school phobia' was coined in the states by Johnson and colleagues (1941), who felt that the basis of the problem was separation anxiety, with the mother exploiting the situation. The role played by the school in the condition was explained as follows:

> When the teacher as a more consistent disciplinarian frustrates the child, she rouses his rage. Being less dependent on the teacher, who is a diluted form of the mother, the child's rage, inhibited toward the mother, can now find expression through displacement and the teacher in her milieu becomes the phobic object. To avoid the teacher and school is now the defense against being placed in the situation in which the overwhelming anxiety is roused.
>
> (Johnson et al. 1941)

Since Johnson et al.'s (1941) paper, the majority of American workers have adopted the term 'school phobia', although many have regarded it as not one condition but rather a loose descriptor of any school attendance problem based on an emotional disturbance with phobic, hysterical and obsessional tendencies often overlapping.

In the UK, many researchers and therapists have regarded the term school phobia as too specific and/or too closely linked to psychodynamic interpretations. Thus, Hersov (1961), Khan and Nursten (1962) and Cooper (1966) have preferred the more inclusive term 'school refusal'. I prefer the term school phobia as it conveys to teachers and parents the emotion, fear, anxiety and helplessness which often accompanies the problem. School refusal, while being an inclusive term, sounds like a far less serious problem and, to the uninitiated, could even imply that the child has simply decided that school is not for him or her.

Graziano and colleagues (1979) comment that school phobia has generated twenty-five times as many research articles as any other childhood phobia. Perhaps this is not surprising, given the tremendous distress that the condition causes not only to those children affected by it but also to their families and school teachers. Nevertheless, although the problem has been recognized for centuries and seriously researched for almost sixty years, confusion reigns over the precise nature and cause of the condition and the best way to treat it. This chapter will briefly consider what is known about school phobia. The treatment literature will be reviewed in order to identify common conflicts and issues and the most efficient and effective strategies for managing them.

Clinical features

The clinical presentation of school phobia has been particularly well described by Hersov (1977).

> The problem often starts with vague complaints of school or reluctance to attend, progressing to total refusal to go to school or to remain in school in the face of persuasion, entreaty, recrimination and punishment by parents and pressures from teachers, family doctors and education welfare officers. The behaviour may be accompanied by overt signs of anxiety or even panic when the time comes to go to school and most children cannot even leave home to set out for school. Many who do, return home half way there and some children, once at school, rush home in a state of anxiety. Many children insist they want to go to school and are prepared to do so but cannot manage it when the time comes.
>
> (Hersov 1977)

Anxiety symptoms manifest themselves in various ways including headaches, stomach pains, nausea, dizziness, fevers and so on. Sometimes, the child protests with tears or temper tantrums which can become quite tyrannical leading to destructive and aggressive behaviour. Other children become withdrawn, lethargic, depressed and even suicidal. Typically, once the pressure to attend school has been removed, the symptoms accompanying the school avoidance appear to dissipate. However, the school phobia becomes even more pronounced as soon as the pressure to return to school is reapplied.

Whether the onset is sudden or incipient, parents frequently question whether something is wrong in school and/or whether the child is ill. Often, the child has a number of realistic worries (both home and school based) which are intertwined with irrational fears. Professionals such as GPs, social workers, teachers or educational welfare officers may not always be in a position to gain a holistic view of a problem and in these circumstances, it is not uncommon for parents to be offered conflicting advice. This can create uncertainty and further worry, fuelling a mutually reinforcing circle of anxiety involving parents, child and teachers. At this point, the child's unhappiness may be so marked that some parents and even some professionals allow the child to remain at home for a period. The child falls behind with school work, loses contact with friends and a return to normal education becomes even more difficult (for a fuller discussion of these issues, see Blagg 1987).

Distinguishing school phobia from truancy

School phobics who have been absent from school for some time often worry about being accused of malingering. Their concerns are echoed by some educationalists who have suggested that school phobia is a condition invented by psychologists to describe middle-class truancy. Hersov's (1961) classic studies clearly demonstrated that school phobia was part of an anxiety rather than conduct based disorder. However, his study has been criticized on grounds of sample bias by some researchers who suggested that differences between Hersov's groups were merely clinical artefacts of the social class differences existing between the phobic and truant samples. Nevertheless, a replication of Hersov's work with truants and phobics drawn from a similar social class distribution, reported in Blagg (1987), confirmed and extended Hersov's (1961) findings.

Briefly, whereas truants come from disrupted and disturbed family backgrounds, school phobics come from cohesive and protective families. Phobic children themselves are generally, reserved, introverted, socially conscientious and conformist types who are more inclined to worry than most pupils of their age. In contrast, truants are more extroverted, less inclined to worry and likely to be involved in a range of anti-social behaviours.

Treatment issues

Issues around the treatment and management of school phobia are intimately linked to theories about the etiology of the condition. Thus, if one favours the early psychodynamic perspective of the problem (simply a manifestation of separation anxiety), then the focus of treatment will be the mother–child relationship with relatively little attention being paid to school issues. Nowadays, there are relatively few therapists who would subscribe exclusively to this perspective. If on the other hand, one adopts the views espoused by Graham Chapman (a consultant psychiatrist) one might be inclined to almost ignore family dynamics and concentrate exclusively on schooling issues:

> There is something specific about the school situation. It is not entirely clear to me what it is but I have seen a number of children who have had several years out of school who have gone on and coped perfectly well with colleges of further education or even university.
>
> (Chapman 1990)

Indeed, in a recent interview on television (BBC2), Chapman (1990) appeared sympathetic to allowing school phobic children to remain out of school suggesting that he knew of no evidence that allowing a child to remain out of school would produce a neurotic adult or that forcing a child back to school would prevent the development of neurosis in adulthood. An entirely school-focused perspective on school phobia is rare among professionals today. Nevertheless, in recent years, an organization known as 'Education Otherwise' has actively campaigned for school phobia to be interpreted as 'acute school-induced anxiety'. The organization argues that the majority of children labelled school phobic are merely reacting rationally to unreasonable and unnatural pressures in school. On this basis, school is regarded as unendurable by some children and accordingly they suggest that local education authorities should help parents to educate their children at home (Knox 1989).

The etiological basis for school phobia probably lies somewhere between these extreme family/school positions. Certainly, schools cannot be absolved from all responsibility for the problem. School phobics are vulnerable pupils who do have many real and imaginary fears about school (Blagg 1987) which must be thoroughly investigated and sensitively managed. Nevertheless, many of these children also harbour fears and anxieties related to home life. For instance, there can be worries about the health of a parent and concerns that the mother or father will die while the child is at school. If such fears are not fully addressed but simply 'papered over' by allowing the child to remain at home, problems can be stored up for the future as Blagg and Yule's (1984) study demonstrated.

Moreover, one needs to look beyond legal issues and reflect on the wider benefits of schooling. While it is perfectly true that parents are entitled to ask for their child to be de-registered in order that they can be educated at home, one needs to consider the implications of this. It is very difficult for most parents to provide for children the range of curriculum experiences and educational opportunities that are available in schools. However, notwithstanding this, school is a major socializing experience. It is a relatively safe context beyond the family within which children can learn tolerance and respect for others (both children and adults), acquire the social skills to develop friendships and work as a member of a group or team.

It is for these and many other reasons that most therapists work towards the end of returning a school phobic to school rather than avoid a confrontation and opt for home education. Nevertheless, in both the psychodynamic and behavioural camps, there is still considerable debate about how a return to school should be accomplished. Answers to the following questions still divide many therapists.

1 What key factors should be attended to?
2 Who should be involved in treatment?
3 Should the child receive treatment before a return to school or should the return to school be part of the treatment process?
4 Should a return to school be immediate and enforced or a gentle, gradual process?

These and other issues will be considered in the subsequent sections, which briefly review some of the major psychodynamic and behavioural treatment studies. However, at this point it is worth emphasizing that there is now general agreement that school phobia is not one condition but a group of conditions of varying severity and pathology but in each case characterized by immense anxiety associated with school attendance. Most therapists now highlight the importance of recurring child, school and family themes that can guide therapy (Hersov 1977). Moreover, a detailed analysis of research to date (Blagg 1987) clearly indicates that certain treatment approaches are more successful than others and that some approaches still in use today may even make the problem worse. The treatment approach(es) favoured in different parts of the UK are often influenced more by availability of facilities, referral routes, therapist bias and personality, than by lessons learned from the research literature. Interestingly, the more successful treatment approaches transcend the psychodynamic/behavioural divide.

Psychoanalytically based treatment approaches

The earliest treatment studies (eg Klein 1945; Warren 1948; Thompson 1948) and the majority of large-scale treatment investigations (eg Rodriguez et al. 1959; Glaser 1959; Davidson 1961; Warnecke 1964) have used therapeutic approaches derived from psychoanalytic theory. Nevertheless, beneath the psychoanalytic umbrella, strategies and styles of intervention have varied enormously. In particular, there have been major differences of opinion with respect to whom to treat; where to treat; whether to insist upon an immediate return to school before treatment or organize a gradual return during or after treatment; and the extent to which factors outside the family have been deemed significant in terms of aetiology and treatment.

An initial and exclusive focus on the child (Jung 1911; Bornsteine 1949) was fairly quickly replaced by recognition of the need to consider the mother–child relationship. However, a review by Malmquist (1965) highlighted the fact that while many therapists attended to the mother and child, the role of fathers and other family members was rarely considered. More recent papers, including those by Skynner (1974), Framrose (1978), Hsia (1984) and Bryce and Baird (1986) argue that treatment should be based on a family system model with the father occupying a crucial role in therapy. On this model, the real problem is seen to lie in the relationships between the family members rather than in the mother, school phobic or any one individual or one relationship. Some family therapists also address school factors under the guise of 'additional practical measures'. Bryce and Baird (1986) take the systematic approach further arguing that therapists need to take care that dysfunctional relationships in families are not mirrored in parallel interprofessional conflicts.

Psychodynamic treatment has usually been supplied in the community at a clinic or on a hospital out-patient basis. However, in certain circumstances, hospital admission has been recommended for in-patient treatment in an adolescent unit (Hersov 1961; Weiss and Cain 1964; Barker 1968; Berg 1970). Weiss and Cain (1964) highlight the benefits of hospital admission. The sixteen adolescents involved in their study had all been highly resistent to community-based psychotherapy. These authors argued that hospitalization provided

1 managed separation experiences (with parents visiting according to an agreed plan)
2 removal of secondary build-up of worries related to falling behind with school work (by full-time attendance at the hospital school)
3 demonstration that the child's difficulties were more related to leaving home than going to school (by immediate success in hospital school attendance)
4 general benefits arising out of the 'therapeutic milieu' (such as the opportunity to develop new relationships and cope with new social situations).

As Table 6.1 shows, the treatment outcome for hospitalized school phobics is very poor. Similarly disappointing outcome figures were recorded for the hospitalized group in Blagg and Yule's (1984) comparative study. Only Barker's (1968) study, involving younger children (below 12 years) showed a highly successful treatment outcome.

The issue of whether to delay the child's return to school or insist on an immediate return has been viewed in different ways by various community-based therapists. A few have argued that it may be potentially harmful to confront the child's anxieties with an immediate insistence on returning to school. Indeed, some therapists advise, that the pressure to attend school should be removed while treatment is directed towards unravelling an over close unhealthy mother–child relationship (Thompson 1948; Woldfogel et al. 1957; Davidson 1961; Sperling 1961; Greenbaum 1964; Radin 1967).

> If psychotherapy is planned it is better to uncover the dynamics underlying the phobic behaviour and treatment and when this is achieved, the child will return to school voluntarily and assume responsibility for doing so himself. Any other method exempts the child from this responsibility and places it instead on parents, teachers, principal, truant officer or therapist.
>
> (Sperling 1961)

On the other hand, most psychodynamic therapists have favoured an early but gradual return to school via carefully agreed manageable steps as suggested by Berryman (1959). In more recent years, an increasing number of psychodynamic therapists favour an immediate, forced return to school using the threat of legal action as a therapeutic lever (Rodriguez et al. 1959; Warnecke 1964; Skynner 1974; Framrose 1978). Rodriguez et al. (1959) reported the first major trial with long-term follow-up of a rapid return approach. They support their methods with reference to an earlier paper by Eisenberg (1958), who observed that the school phobic's symptoms were a response to 'contradictory, verbal and behavioural

Table 6.1 Patient details and treatment outcome figures for a number of studies involving traditional psychotherapy and hospitalization

Study	N	Age range	Length of phobia	Length of treatment	Number returned to day school N	%	Follow-up period	Number in school at follow-up N	%
Warren (1948)	8	9–14 yrs	Not stated	Not stated	4	50	Not stated	–	–
Hersov (1961)	8	7–9 yrs	2 mths–2 yrs	6–12 mths	34	68	6–18 mths after discharge	29	58
	42	10–16 yrs							
Weiss and Cain (1964)	16	8–16 yrs	2 mths–2.5 yrs	Mean = 9 mths	6	37.5	No follow-up	–	–
Barker (1968)	6	All <12 yrs	Not stated*	3–14 mths	6	100	6–12 mths	6	100
Berg (1970)	29	10–15 yrs	3 days–2 yrs +	1–19 mths Mean = 9 mths			3–24 mths Mean = 13 mths	16	59

Note: * Details were given for only three cases
Source: Blagg (1987)

cues provided by his parents'. The involved parent 'initiated and recriprocated the child's anxiety'. It was argued that an immediate return to school broke the circle of anxiety but also provided other therapeutic advantages:

> it brings into sharp focus the primary issue of separation and dissociates the therapist from the family's displacement onto fantasised dangers in the school situation. Secondly, it emphasises our recognition of the core of good health in the child; the fact that we act upon this premise constitutes effective reassurance to a panic stricken family. . . . Finally, the return to school restores the child to a growth promoting environment and removes him from his emersion in the cycle of mutually reinforced anxieties in the home.
> (Rodriguez et al. 1959)

These authors argue that in contrast a de-emphasis on school attendance and a plan for prolonged therapy

> signal to the family that the physician, too, is uncertain and regards the child as being sick as they do despite verbal formulations to the contrary.
> (Rodriguez et al. 1959)

Moreover, the longer the child is out of school the more secondary fears arise.

Warnecke (1964) reports a long-term study of forty-seven cases in which treatment was modelled on Rodriguez et al.'s (1959) approach. Cases of school refusal were treated as emergencies with the primary concern being the return of the child to full-time schooling. Dealing with background psychopathology was put in second place. The diagnostic interview considered what steps would be needed to secure the child's return to school. Sometimes, discussions with family doctors were required to clarify medical issues. Eventually, it was agreed to apply pressure in all cases with the use of escorts and, if necessary, legal action. At the same time, changes within school such as a class transfer were arranged where necessary. The child and the parents were encouraged to live with their emotions in an active way. It was suggested that immediate confrontation played a critical role in treatment in that

> in dealing with these situations the ego of the child is supported and the feeling of inadequacy in the parents is diminished. Such an approach does not imply that unconscious determinants are ignored but that they should be dealt with at the proper time.
> (Warnecke 1964)

Out of the forty-six cases where a follow-up was possible, forty returned to 'satisfactory' attendance at school. Warnecke reports that twenty-four of the cases (64 per cent) were over the age of 11 years. The six failures all fell into this older age range, which means that for the children of 11 years plus, successful outcome in terms of satisfactory school attendance was 80 per cent.

In a retrospective study of twenty older school phobics, Skynner (1974) describes his conjoint family therapy approach in which an immediate and if necessary, enforced return to school is used as a focus for exposing and confronting inappropriate communications between family members. Skynner claims highly impressive outcome figures with 88.2 per cent successfully treated on long-term follow up. His results were surprising, given the amount of time devoted to treatment. In most cases only one interview was required. Skynner (1974) recognizes the overlap between his approach and other explicitly behavioural strategies like Kennedy's (1965) approach. However, he argues that Kennedy's success was probably more an outcome of the implicit focus on faulty family mechanisms rather than the explicit focus on behavioural techniques.

In the main, psychodynamic treatments have either ignored or paid relatively little attention to the role of school factors. However, a few therapists have written about the importance of co-ordinating family-based treatment with the school personnel (Eisenberg 1958; Davidson 1961; Framrose 1978; Hsia 1984; Bryce and Baird 1986).

Framrose (1978) vividly describes the successful treatment of four older, highly disturbed school phobics. The essential treatment elements are expressed in strategic family therapy terms but at the same time explicit use is made of behavioural techniques and a range of school factors are also addressed. Framrose places a strong emphasis on the establishment of a foolproof system of attendance checks once the child is back in school. One cannot help being impressed by the powerful sense of conviction and intentionality accompanying this paper. Framrose was clearly totally determined that the adolescent phobics would overcome their difficulties in a highly active, vigorous way.

School issues were very clearly addressed by Waldfogel and colleagues (1959) who dealt with incipient cases of school phobia and outlined a number of therapeutic advantages of operating directly in the school situation:

> the therapist can offer direct support to the child in a feared situation. In addition, he can help the principal and the teacher by relieving them of their sense of helpless bewilderment and guilt. By modifying their feelings toward the child, he is able to work with them towards altering whatever reality factors exist to aggravate the child's fears. Sometimes, adjustments need to be made, such as reducing the pressure of work and allowing the child to attend only part of the day. On rare occasions, the child must be transferred to another class.
>
> (Waldfogel et al. 1959)

Behaviourally based treatment approaches

The publication of Wolpe's (1954; 1958) work on systematic desensitization stimulated interest in behavioural treatment and from the early 1960s a large number of behaviour therapy studies were reported in the literature. In common with the early psychodynamic studies, the early behavioural studies were rather over-simplistic in that they focused attention almost exclusively on the child and often one aspect of his problem, such as separation anxiety (Lazarus 1960; Schermann and Grover 1962; Patterson 1965). As Berecz (1968) pointed out these early studies were 'one-shot attempts to prove the effectiveness of certain techniques'. Nevertheless, they were important in developing and refining the behavioural art.

In parallel with developments in the psychodynamic field, behavioural treatments have become increasingly sophisticated and complicated with treatment involving the application of a wide variety of behavioural techniques selected to address many child, family and school factors (Kennedy 1965; Phillips and Wolpe 1981; Blagg and Yule 1984). Moreover, it is now quite acceptable to attempt to modify feelings and perceptions as well as more observable and measurable phenomena (Croghan 1981).

Some authors (including Hersen 1971a; 1971b; Miller, et al. 1974; Blagg 1987) have drawn attention to the overlap between behavioural and psychotherapeutic approaches. Within the context of traditional psychotherapy, fear hierarchies may be worked through incidentally and informally in the course of discussions with desensitization happening in a variety of ways. The mere business of establishing a relationship between the child and the therapist may involve a non-specific desensitization effect. Moreover, as Miller et al. (1974) point out, the interpretation of unconscious material may involve 'a psychic shock process which combines emotional arousal with flooding of ideational material similar to that employed in implosive techniques'.

Just as traditional psychotherapists may informally use approaches that can be framed in behavioural terms, behaviour therapists may often incidentally rely upon techniques associated with traditional psychotherapy. For instance, Hersen (1970; 1971a) stresses that behavioural therapists often overcome resistance to treatment by utilizing support, interpretation and reality confrontation techniques. It seems likely that limitations on journal space and an eagerness to be purist leads many authors to report selectively only those aspects of treatment that illustrate their theoretical positions.

Miller and colleagues (1974) point out that treatments from different theoretical persuasions can all be reduced to four essential elements:

1 establishment of a relationship
2 clarification of the stimulus
3 desensitization to the stimulus
4 confrontation of the stimulus.

Each treatment approach satisfies these various elements in slightly different ways. Increasingly, behavioural work has adopted a problem-solving approach to therapy (Yule 1977) in which great care is taken to gather all relevant information, define and clarify the presenting difficulties, set up hypotheses to account for the observation and introduce clear, deliberate interventions which are carefully monitored and revised where necessary. With regard to desensitization and confrontation, a spectrum of approaches have been used that mirror the differences of opinion noted in the psychodynamic camp regarding gradual or immediate return to school. Thus, some behavioural therapists have favoured a gradual process of return using procedures from both the classical and operant conditioning paradigms.

On the classical conditioning paradigm, systematic desensitization procedures, imaginal or in vivo have been commonly used. Essentially, systematic desensitization (SD) involves taking the child through a carefully graded hierarchy of feared situations, starting with the least worrying and building up to the most frightening. At each stage the child is helped to overcome any anxieties by concentrating on a behaviour that is antagonistic to the anxiety (Wolpe 1958). The approach is often very time-consuming and highly dependent on a range of therapist skills including the ability to analyse the anxiety-provoking circumstances in the school phobia, construct a carefully graded fear hierarchy, and find and deploy a means of relaxing the child at each stage of the hierarchy. Imaginal approaches can be conveniently arranged in the therapist's office but rely on the ability of the child to visualize. Desensitization sessions in real life overcome the problems of poor visualization but may involve the therapist in more time and effort with frequent visits to the school. In spite of these various problems, a variety of single case studies have demonstrated the effectiveness of both imaginal and in vivo SD (Lazarus 1960; Lazarus and Abramovitz 1962; Schermann and Grover 1962; Garvey and Hegrenes 1966; Chapel 1967).

Systematic desensitization has also been used with techniques derived from the operant conditioning paradigm. For instance, Lazarus and colleagues (1964) deliberately set out to demonstrate the value of both classical and operant procedures at different stages in the treatment of a 9-year-old boy with a long history of unresolved separation anxiety in school situations. SD (imaginal) was abandoned in favour of SD (in vivo) because of the boy's 'inarticulateness and acquiescent response tendency'. On the fifteenth SD session, the boy appeared minimally anxious and the authors switched to an operant strategy as a means of securing school attendance, independent of the therapist. A comic book and tokens (to be exchanged later for a baseball glove) were given contingent on the boy returning to full-time schooling. In spite of this, the therapist was able to withdraw only after the mother had emphasized that school attendance was compulsory and would be enforced if the boy did not go to school. Tangible reinforcers were withdrawn three weeks later. All gains had been maintained at ten-months follow-up.

The theoretical implications of this study are interesting. Viewed in operant terms, in vivo SD may unwittingly reinforce dependent behaviour and avoidance reponses by allowing the child to return home after anxiety has been aroused during treatment. On the other hand, an operant-based approach might lead to premature exposure to the maximally feared situation, a rise in anxiety and a strengthening of the avoidance response should the child be able to escape. However, if the escape route is blocked and the child is held in the fear provoking situation, desensitization should occur through a process of extinction. If operant procedures were then implemented to enforce regular attendance, the classical and operant paradigms would not be in conflict. These authors suggest that high levels of anxiety indicate the need for desensitization whereas, low levels of anxiety call for the use of operant procedures.

Certainly, a number of authors have reported successful single case studies using operant techniques such as contingency management and contingency contracting with minimally anxious pupils (Hersen 1968; Cantrell et al. 1969; Welch and Carpenter 1970). In addition a number of therapists have successfully followed Lazarus et al.'s (1964) approach using a combination of SD and operant techniques (Tahmisian and McReynolds 1971; Phillips and Wolpe 1981).

In contrast to gradual return approaches, some therapists have preferred an immediate confrontation of the maximally feared situation (a return to school) without any careful preparation via graded exposure to less threatening circumstances. The approach is argued in terms of the classical extinction model (Stampfl 1967; 1968). When implemented in vivo it is referred to as 'flooding' (as used by Kennedy 1965; Rines 1973; Blagg and Yule 1984; Blagg 1987). The approach has the advantage of offering a very rapid approach to treatment but on the other hand, it typically results in heightened anxiety in the child (and often parents and teachers) before the process of extinction takes over. As a consequence, some therapists may find this approach rather stressful and difficult to manage.

Indeed, flooding may seem a rather drastic and extreme way of treating school phobia, especially from the point of view of the child and the parents. Not surprisingly, considerable effort needs to be expended upon a very detailed and thorough analysis of the child's problems as well as school and family circumstances, so that numerous practical measures can be taken to deal with any reality issues (Blagg and Yule 1984). The process of winning the parents' confidence and a detailed planning of practical arrangements probably has a desensitization effect upon the child, family and teachers (Blagg 1987). A less extreme way of confronting the child's worst fears could involve the therapist in helping the child to visualize highly threatening situations in school. This approach, known as 'implosion' was successfully implemented and illustrated by Smith and Sharpe (1970).

Kennedy's (1965) paper reports the first large-scale treatment study recorded in the behavioural literature. Kennedy's treatment package draws on both classical and operant paradigms and involves

1   an immediate and enforced school attendance
2   positive reinforcements for school attendance
3   contingency management to deal with somatic complaints.

The author acknowledges the importance of establishing good interprofessional relations to ensure consistency of management and the ability to inspire confidence in the parents so that they give the treatment approach a chance. The study involved fifty school phobics who fitted Kennedy's criteria of less severe, type 1 school phobics. All fifty cases returned to school with only three days' treatment. Furthermore, gains were maintained over eight years. However, only thirty of these cases were older than 11 years and the subjects were not a treatment series. Kennedy doubted that this approach could be used with more severe cases but this was subsequently refuted by Rines (1973) and Blagg and Yule (1984). However, it is important to remember that only thirteen of his cases were above 11 years.

Comparative treatment studies

Blagg and Yule's (1984) paper reports the only recorded comparative treatment study dealing exclusively with adolescent school phobia. A treatment series of thirty cases (10 to 16 years) was helped by a systematic, problem-solving approach which addressed many child, family and school factors. The approach deployed a comprehensive range of behavioural measures including

1 *desensitization* of the child, parents and teachers, using a variety of techniques including humour, role rehearsal and emotive imagery
2 *flooding* an immediate return to school using an escort if necessary
3 *contingency management* at home and at school, to deal with somatic complaints and the reinforcement of appropriate behaviours.

These thirty cases were compared with sixteen children admitted to an adolescent psychiatric unit and a further twenty cases who received psychotherapy and home tuition. Treatment outcome details are summarize in Tables 2 and 3.

Table 6.2   Comparing treatment outcome for the hospital unit (HU), home tuition (HT) and behavioural treatment approach (BTA) groups

Child attending school at follow-up	HU		HT		BTA		χ^2 Values and significance levels		
	N	%	N	%	N	%	HU × HT	HU × BTA	BTA × HT
Failure	10	62.5	18	90	1	3.3	No	$\chi^2 = 20.21$	$\chi^2 = 38.27$
Partial success	0	0	0		1	3.3	significant	P < 0.001	P < 0.001
Success	6	37.5	2	10	28	93.3	difference		
Total N	16		29		30				

Source: Blagg and Yule (1984)

Table 6.3   Comparing treatment outcome for each group in terms of percentage attendance at follow-up

Attendance at follow-up %	HU		HT		BTA		χ^2 Values and significance levels		
	N	%	N	%	N	%	HU × HT	HU × BTA	BTA × HT
0–80	11*	68.8	20	100	5	16.7	$\chi^2 = 4.88$	$\chi^2 = 10.29$	$\chi^2 = 30.08$
81–100	5	31.3	0		25	83.3	P < 0.05	P < 0.001	P < 0.001
Total N	16		20		30				

Note: * Three cases in this group were attending boarding school at follow-up. They had been placed in residential schools because their return to normal day school was not possible. In the circumstances, they were placed in the 0–80 per cent attendance group.
Source: Blagg and Yule (1984)

It can be seen that 93.3 per cent of the behavioural group returned to school and were attending regularly without further problems at two-year follow-up. This compared to similar improvements in only 37.5 per cent of the hospitalized group and 10 per cent of the home tutored group. Moreover, children in the behavioural group took an average of 2½ weeks to treat compared to 45 weeks and 72 weeks respectively for the hospitalized and home-tutored groups.

Blagg and Yule's (1984) comparative study revealed that the hospitalized cases were closely matched to the two community-treated groups on all significant indices even though they were not randomly allocated. Indeed, variations in outcome could not be explained by differences in the make-up of the treatment groups. Children in the three groups were closely matched on the length and severity of their phobia; the nature of their symptoms; their age; family background and other significant characteristics.

Summary

Of course, it is always difficult to compare treatment studies because the majority are bedevilled by methodological flaws. For example, very few authors clearly define what they mean by school phobia; outcome figures are not always broken down by age; some studies have not included long-term follow-ups; and subject details at follow-up are often sketchy with relatively few studies providing details of attendance rates, social adjustment and enquiries about symptom substitution. The majority of behavioural accounts have involved single case studies and only one treatment study has involved a comparison of treatment approaches. Nevertheless, methodological inadequacies are not uniform across studies and a careful analysis of both the psychodynamic and behavioural treatment literature does point to some tentative conclusions (Blagg 1987).

1 The treatment outcome for younger children (of 10 years and below) is extremely good irrespective of the treatment approach. This applies to psychodynamic and behavioural studies both hospital and community based. Studies that have dealt exclusively with younger children (Glaser 1959; Barker 1986) and investigations that have broken down outcome in terms of age (Rodriguez et al. 1959; Warnecke 1964; Miller et al. 1974) consistently report that for the 5–10 year olds there is a treatment success rate of 95 per cent or more.
2 The treatment outcome for older children (in the 11–16 years age range) seems far less predictable and has varied widely from study to study. In general the outcome for this age range is far less favourable and more dependent upon the type of treatment employed.
3 The treatment outcome figures for hospitalized school phobics are generally very poor, as illustrated by the studies summarized in Table 6.1 as well as Blagg and Yule's (1984) comparative study. Undoubtedly, hospitalization represents the most intensive and costly treatment intervention. At the same time there is no conclusive evidence to suggest that this kind of help is reserved for the most profoundly disturbed cases. It seems more likely that hospitalization is an outcome of patterns of referral and the restrictions and bias of professionals involved rather than a carefully considered intervention weighed against alternative community-based approaches (Blagg 1987). As the outcome figures for studies involving hospitalization are no better for younger or older children than many community-based approaches, it seems wholly unreasonable to use hospitalization as the first treatment option. Barker's (1968) study is especially open to criticism in this respect.
4 Apart from Blagg and Yule's (1984) paper, there appears to be no other recorded trial of home tuition with psychotherapy. This is rather worrying as the treatment outcome for the home-tutored group was so appallingly poor that this kind of intervention may inhibit spontaneous remission or, even worse,

reinforce the school phobia pattern. Clearly, experimental evidence for these statements is limited but nevertheless the clinical experience of the author suggests that school phobics who have been put on home-tuition and given psychotherapy prior to a more direct attack on the problem are much more difficult to treat than those who have been out of school for the same amount of time but have had no previous treatment. It is not uncommon for home tutors to become over-involved with the child and the family and to become unwittingly a powerful maintaining factor.

Although the prognosis for older school phobic children looks poor a few psycho-dynamic and behavioural studies report high success rates with this more difficult age range. These studies have not only produced highly impressive treatment results (maintained at follow-up) but also have been very economic on therapist time (Warnecke 1964; Rines 1973; Skynner 1974; Framrose 1978; and the behavioural approach reported in Blagg and Yule 1984). Each of these studies emphasize

1 An implicit or explicit problem-solving approach recognizing the uniqueness of each case and the importance of addressing a complex interplay of child, family, schooling and community factors.
2 The importance of eliminating medical problems and dealing with many practical issues and realistic concerns *before* dealing with irrational fears.
3 The importance of attending to numerous practical issues at home and at school to enable an immediate return to school to be effective. In practice this means winning the confidence of parents and teachers; painstaking attention to detail in planning flexible arrangements that anticipate potential blocks to treatment and minimize the chances of secondary problems arising.
4 A vigorous, energetic approach to treatment in which there is never any question of if the child will return to school but only when and how it will be accomplished. This may mean that a special escort system is arranged for the child during the early confrontational stages. Legal intervention is regarded as a legitimate, therapeutic lever.
5 A watertight system of attendance checks and follow-ups with particular care being taken after weekends, holidays and illnesses.

References

Barker, P. (1968) The inpatient treatment of school refusal, *British Journal of Medical Psychology* 41: 381–7

Berecz, J.M. (1968) Phobias of childhood aetiology and treatment, *Psychological Bulletin* 70: 694–720.

Berg, I. (1970) A follow-up study of school phobic adolescents admitted to an inpatient unit, *Journal of Child Psychology and Psychiatry* 11: 37–47.

Berg, I., Marx, I., McGuire, R. and Lipsedge, M. (1974) School phobia and agoraphobia, *Psychological Medicine* 4: 428–34.

Berryman, E. (1959) School phobia: management problems in private practice, *Psychological Reports* 5: 19–24.

Blagg, N.R. (1979) The behavioural treatment of school refusal, unpublished PhD thesis, Institute of Psychiatry, University of London.

Blagg, N.R. (1987) *School Phobia and its Treatment*, London: Croom Helm.

Blagg, N.R. and Yule, W. (1984) The behavioural treatment of school refusal: a comparative study, *Behaviour Research and Therapy* 22: 119-27.

Bornstein, B. (1949) The analysis of a phobic child, *Psychoanalytic Study of the Child* 3 and 4: 181-226.

Broadwin, I.T. (1932) A contribution to the study of truancy, *Orthopsychiatry* 2: 253-9.

Bryce, G. and Baird, D. (1986) Precipitating a crisis: family therapy and adolescent school refusers, *Journal of Adolescence* 9: 119-213.

Cantrell, R.P., Cantrell, M.L., Huddleston, C.M. and Woolridge, R.L. (1969) Application of contingency contracts to four school attendance problems, *Journal of Applied Behavioural Analysis* 2: 215-20.

Chapel, J.L. (1967) Treatment of a case of school phobia by reciprocal inhibition, *Canadian Psychiatric Association Journal* 12: 25-8.

Chapman, G. (1990) Speaking on Patricia Knox's BBC2 *Open Space* television programme *An Education in Fear*.

Coolidge, J.C., Hahn, P.B. and Peck, A.L. (1957) School phobia: neurotic crisis or way of life, *American Journal of Orthopsychiatry* 27: 296-306.

Cooper, M.G. (1966) School refusal, *Educational Research* 8(2): 115-27.

Croghan, L.M. (1981) Conceptualising the critical elements in a rapid desensitisation to school anxiety: a case study, *Journal of Paediatric Psychology* 6: 165-9.

Davidson, S. (1961) School phobia as a manifestation of family disturbance: its structure and treatment, *Journal of Child Psychology and Psychiatry* 1(4): 270-87.

Eisenberg, L. (1958) School phobia: study in the communication of anxiety, *American Journal of Psychotherapy* 10: 682-95.

Framrose, R. (1978) Outpatient treatment of severe school phobia, *Journal of Adolescence* 1: 353-61.

Garvey, W.P. and Hegrenes, J.R. (1966) Desensitisation techniques in the treatment of school phobia, *Behavioural Psychotherapy* 6: 7-10.

Glaser, K. (1959) Problems in school attendance school phobia and related conditions, *Paediatrics* 23: 227-48.

Graziano, A.M., DeGiovanni, I.S. and Garcia, K.A. (1979) Behavioural treatment of children's fears: a review, *Psychology Bulletin* 86(4): 804-30.

Greenbaum, R.S. (1964) Treatment of school phobias: theory and practice, *American Journal of Psychotherapy* 18: 616-33.

Hersen, M. (1968) Treatment of a compulsive and phobic disorder through a total behaviour therapy program: a case study, *Psychotherapy* 5: 220-5.

Hersen, M. (1970) The complementary use of behaviour therapy and psychotherapy, some comments, *Psychological Record* 20: 395-402.

Hersen, M. (1971a) Resistance to direction in behaviour therapy: some comments, *Journal of Genetic Psychology* 118: 121-7.

Hersen, M. (1971b) The behavioural treatment of school phobia, *Journal of Nervous and Mental Disease* 153: 99-107.

Hersov, L.A. (1961) Persistent non-attendance at school, *Journal of Psychology and Psychiatry* 1(2): 130-6.

Hersov, L.A. (1977) School refusal, in M. Rutter and L.A. Hersov (eds) *Child Psychiatry: Modern Approaches*, Oxford: Basil Blackwell.

Hsia, H. (1984) Structural and strategic approach to school phobia/school refusal, *Psychology in the Schools* 21: 360-7.

Johnson, A.M., Falstein, E.K., Szurek, S. and Svendsen, M. (1941) School phobia, *American Journal of Orthopsychiatry* 11: 702-11.

Jung, C.G. (1911) A case of neurosis in a child, in *The Collected Works of C.J. Jung*, New York: Bollington Foundation.

Kennedy, W.A. (1965) School phobia: rapid treatment of 50 cases, *Journal of Abnormal Psychology* 70(4): 285-9.

Khan, J.H. and Nursten, J.P. (1962) School refusal, *American Journal of Orthopsychiatry* 32: 707-18.

Khan, J.H., Nursten, J.P. and Carroll, H.C. (1981) *Unwillingly to School*, 3rd edn, Oxford: Pergamon Press.

Klein, E. (1945) The reluctance to go to school, *The Psychoanalytic Study of the Child* 1: 263-79.

Knox, P. (1989) Home-based education: an alternative approach to 'school phobia', *Educational Review* 41(2): 143-50.

Lazarus, A.A. (1960) The elimination of children's phobias by deconditioning, in H.J. Eysenck (ed.) *Behaviour, Therapy and the Neuroses*, Oxford: Pergamon Press.

Lazarus, A.A. and Abramovitz, A. (1962) The use of emotive imagery in the treatment of children's phobias, *Journal of Abnormal Psychology* 70: 225-9.

Lazarus, A.A., Davidson, G.C. and Polefka, D.A. (1964) Classical and operant factors in the treatment of a school phobia, *Journal of Abnormal Psychology* 70: 225-9.

Malmquist, C.P. (1965) School phobia: a problem of family neurosis, *Journal of the American Academy of Child Psychiatry* 4: 293-319.

Miller, L.C., Barrett, C.L. and Hampe, E. (1974) Phobias of childhood in a prescientific era, in A. Davies (ed.) *Child Personality and Psychopathology: Current Topics*, vol. 1, New York: Wiley.

Patterson, G.R. (1965) A learning theory approach to the treatment of the school phobic child, in L.P. Ullman and L. Krasner (eds) *Case Studies in Behaviour Modification*, New York: Holt, Rinehart, Winston.

Phillips, D. and Wolpe, S. (1981) Multiple behavioural techniques in severe separation anxiety of a twelve year old, *Journal of Behaviour Therapy and Experimental Psychiatry* 12(4): 329-32.

Radin, S. (1967) Psychodynamic aspects of school phobia, *Comprehensive Psychiatry* 8(2): 119-28.

Rines, W.B. (1973) Behaviour therapy before institutionalisation, *Psychotherapy: Theory, Research and Practice* 10: 281-3.

Rodriguez, A., Rodriguez, N. and Eisenberg, L. (1959) The outcome of school phobia: a follow-up study based on 41 cases, *American Journal of Psychiatry* 116: 540-4.

Schermann, A. and Grover, V.M. (1962) Treatment of children's behaviour disorders: a method of re-education, *Medical Procedures* 8: 151-4.

Shapiro, T. and Jegede, R.O. (1973) School phobia: a babel of tongues, *Journal of Autism and Child Schizophrenia* 3: 168-86.

Skynner, A.C.R. (1974) School phobia: a reappraisal, *British Journal of Medical Psychology* 47: 1-16.

Smith, R.E. and Sharpe, T.M. (1970) Treatment of a school phobic with implosive therapy, *Journal of Consulting Clinical Psychology* 35: 239-43.

Sperling, M. (1961) Analytic first aid in school phobics, *Psychoanalytic Quarterly* 30: 504-18.

Stampfl, T.G. (1967) Implosive therapy: I. The theory, in S.G. Armitage (ed.) *Behaviour Modification Techniques in the Treatment of Emotional Disorders*, Battle Creek, Mich: Veterans Admin.

Stampfl, T.G. (1968) Implosive therapy: a behavioural therapy?, *Behaviour Research and Therapy* 6: 31-6.

Tahmisian, J.A. and McReynolds, W.T. (1971) Use of parents as behavioural engineers in the treatment of a school phobic girl, *Journal of Counselling Psychology* 18: 225-8.

Thompson, J. (1948), Children's fears in relation to school attendance, *Bulletin of the National Association of Social Workers* 24: 1.

Vaal, J.J. (1973) Applying contingency contracting to a school phobic: a case study, *Journal of Behaviour Therapy and Experimental Psychiatry* 4: 371-3.

Waldfogel, L., Coolidge, J.C. and Hahn, P.B. (1957). The development, meaning and management of school phobia, *American Journal of Orthopsychiatry* 27: 754–80.

Waldfogel, L., Tessman, E. and Hahn, P.B. (1959) A program for early intervention in school phobia, *American Journal of Orthopsychiatry* 29: 324–32.

Warnecke, R. (1964) School phobia and its treatment, *British Journal of Medical Psychology* 37: 71–9.

Warren, W. (1948) Acute neurotic breakdown in children with refusal to go to school, *Archives of the Disturbed Child* 266–72.

Weiss M. and Cain, B. (1964) The residential treatment of children and adults with school phobia, *American Journal of Psychiatry* 23: 103–14.

Welch, M.W. and Carpenter, C. (1970) Solution of school phobia by contingency contracting, *School Applications of Learning Theory* 2: 11–17.

Wolpe, J. (1954) Reciprocal inhibition as the main basis of psychotherapeutic effects, *Archives of Neurological Psychiatry* 72: 205–26.

Wolpe. J. (1958) *Psychotherapy by Reciprocal Inhibition*, Stanford, Calif.: Stanford University Press.

Yule, W. (1977) Behavioural approaches to treatment, in M. Rutter and L. Hersov (eds) *Child Psychiatry: Modern Approaches*, London: Blackwell Scientific Publications.

Yule. W., Hersov, L. and Treseder, J. (1980) Behavioural treatments of school refusal, in L. Hersov and I. Berg (eds) *Out of School*, Chichester: Wiley.

7

Bullying

DAVID A. LANE

Where do you start? With those involved

> Just walking through the school you can feel the undercurrent of violence;
> to continue to send my son to the school is unthinkable.
>
> (Parent visiting son's school)

> This is a boys' school. You have to accept bullying. If a child can't take it
> they should be in another school.
>
> (Teacher at the same school)

> There is this boy in my school, he gets bullied a lot, I admit I do it myself
> sometimes, but that is because if I didn't I would get bullied as well.
>
> (Professional Development Foundation letters file)

> Bullying is the one issue which makes me most angry and one which I, as
> a teacher, feel least able to deal with.
>
> (Professional Development Foundation letters file)

> At school I do not succeed, I am daily taunted by one teacher and my mates.
> I feel a deep sense of failure.
>
> (After writing this, Roberto, aged 15, from Caserta in Italy, took his father's
> gun and killed himself: Basalisco 1989)

These quotes make clear not only that bullying is not a minor issue which can be
left unattended but also that bullying is a complex process involving victims,
perpetrators, relationships, and the attitudes of adults and schools. Understanding the phenomenon is likely to involve a variety of factors and not simplistic ideas
about bullies as louts and victims as wimps (or whipping boys). Dealing with the
problem is not attainable through tighter discipline, suspensions, or therapy for
victims. A structure for dealing with bullying must do justice to the complexity
of the process and any such structure is likely to be more effective if informed by
an empirically based model of bullying.

This chapter begins the task of establishing a framework for individuals to build such models and from them a structure for intervention. No more than a beginning is possible given the current level of research in this area. We know a great deal about the characteristics of those labelled bullies and victims; unfortunately more recent research casts doubt on this simple dichotomy and therefore renders less useful earlier findings. Similarly many authors have concentrated on what can be done with or for victims and bullies with only scant attention paid to the role of the school as causative and the impact this has on the bullying relationship. An agreed model is not provided by any of the current texts, although Roland (1989) has made a valuable start.

Any consideration of bullying must begin with the work of the pioneers from Scandinavia, although the literature is much older (Dukes 1905).

Introduction

Research into bullying owes a substantial debt to the work of several Scandinavian pioneers (most notably Heinemann 1973; Olweus 1984; Pikas 1975; 1976; 1989; Roland 1983; 1988; 1989). They have given us perspectives and models of working which have been only slowly influencing UK practitioners.

Tattum (1988) has made the point that, in contrast, bullying in the UK has received scant attention from national and local authorities or from the teachers' unions. Schools have given it a low priority compared with disruptive behaviour and truancy. In the UK research into the problem has lagged far behind the lead offered by Pikas and others. There have been some attempts to place it on the national agenda (Orton 1982) but UK efforts have been patchy. Some case study material has appeared (Lane 1973; 1975) and some research data have been forthcoming (Lowenstein 1978). The publication of the first UK book devoted to bullying (Tattum and Lane 1988) and Roland and Munthe (1989) on international perspectives changed the agenda. Both books were widely covered in all media, both in the UK and abroad. No longer could anyone claim that it was not a problem and calls for a wider debate and the need to take the issue seriously appeared even in official reports (Elton 1989).

In response a variety of ideas for intervention have appeared and government funding has finally been made available to a research team from Sheffield University to follow up their work first published in Roland and Munthe's book. The emphasis in much of the activity that has followed the initial publication has centred on the question of what to do about the problem. Little attention has been paid to developing an understanding of why bullying takes place. The two-step model of problem-solving has been used:

1 The problem is defined . . . bullying
2 The solution is . . . x, y or z (depending upon whom you talk to).

As I have argued elsewhere (Lane 1974b; 1978; 1990a) behavioural problems which are complex require an approach which builds a model of the behaviours in question out of which solutions are defined, implemented and evaluated. A five-phase model of analysis was proposed.

In spite of the debt the Scandinavian research has left us with certain difficulties. These include both the models used and the contrast in emphasis on work with victims and bullies rather than on the school as a whole. This chapter will consider both of these issues but will concentrate on the broader perspective to intervention which has characterized the UK position and which is increasingly influencing work in Scandinavia.

The process starts with the *definition* of the problem, leads on to an *exploration* of factors of influence, attempts the *formulation* of a model of the behaviour, develops ideas for *intervention* which arise from the formulation, and provides an *evaluation* of outcome in so far as it is possible with the limited data available.

What is bullying, or how do we choose to define it?

Bullying is one of those hidden subjects. We all know it goes on and certainly when confronted with it we would take action, but there have been few attempts to find out how much misery is being experienced by children in school every day. If the incidence in Norway, for example, was reflected in the UK statistics, then there could well be (according to Tattum 1988) 870,000 children involved. This would make them the largest group with special needs in England and Wales.

There have been many tragic cases reported in the press over the years. There are examples of handicapped pupils being terrorized, children being driven to suicide and even cases of murder. Many children have been driven out of the system altogether and into truancy according to several studies (Reid 1988; Knox 1989). However, only limited data on the phenomenon are available in the UK literature, and the international data are even more limited (Roland and Munthe 1989).

The first problem concerns the definition of the act. Heinemann (1973) originally reported on an activity he called 'mobbing', referring to a group attack on an individual who had disturbed the group's ordinary activity. Later work has referred to both individual and group action (Olweus 1978). This (according to Pikas 1989) serves to confuse the issue and he advises that 'mobbing' should be reserved for group activity, whereas bullying could refer to both forms. The inclusion of psychological or physical threat in definitions of bullying also raises problems since there are established sex differences for these types of bullying (Roland 1988).

The intention of the aggressor and belief of the victim are considered key aspects by some researchers (Stephenson and Smith 1988; Lane 1988) and therefore school reports cannot be relied upon to reflect the situation accurately. Sparks (1983) provides a clear account of this difficulty in comments reported from teachers and pupils at private schools. The distinction between individual bullying and group activity was certainly recognized in the nineteenth century (Dukes 1905).

The definition used is of more than academic interest, for it has led to different perspectives on intervention. Pikas (1989) for example has concentrated on a concept of mobbing closer to Heinemann's original definition. He has developed very effective techniques for working with mobbers and victims. Olweus and

Roland (1983) and Roland (1988) have taken a different route and developed anti-bullying campaigns for use in schools. Unfortunately, these have sometimes been seen as alternatives in opposition rather than the ends of a dimension of potential approaches. This confusion over definition has led to difficulties in determining the level of such activities and the interventions which might be appropriate.

If we choose to define bullying in terms of the threatening acts of one individual against another, we limit the potential explanations to characteristics of bullies and victims. The choice of definition is not neutral for it is normally imposed by those with the power to label. A definition which excludes the role that those who apply the label may play, serves their own interests. It may excuse them from changing their own behaviour or from the necessity to confront the idea that not all is well with the way they run their school. Some of the research and recommendations which have appeared certainly reinforce that avoidance. They may provide a cosy picture in which a tightening of procedures and a whole school policy is advocated without the necessity to actually deal with bullying behaviour wherever and from whomever it originates. As Pikas (1989) has pointed out, while an immense need to deal with the problem may be expressed by society the need 'is not proportional to the willingness of that Society to deal with those cases which actually occur'. He is talking about Sweden who as a nation are much further along the path of awareness of bullying than people in the UK or anywhere else.

The impact of particular definitions is, therefore, very real. It also extends to difficulties in determining how much bullying takes place.

How much bullying takes place?

The answer will depend on how the theoretical perspectives are viewed. Are we to separate group violence and call that 'mobbing' and individual violence and call that 'bullying', or are we to view them as part of one set of social aggression in which a dominant individual or group intends and causes distress to another. It is this later perspective which has influenced UK work and which is used in various forms in the UK incidence studies.

Establishing the level, type and duration of bullying has not proved easy even in the well-financed research studies in Scandinavia. Figures reported there vary between 5 per cent and 25 per cent.

Some welcome clarity was offered in the UK by an important study from Stephenson and Smith (1987). Based on research with over 1,000 primary children (aged 7–11), they estimate that 23 per cent of children experience bullying. The incidence figures for pupils referred for behaviour problems are very much higher in this study. Bullying is not a passing phase, they point out; for many children their pain continues over years.

Lane (1988), based on four secondary school samples (N = 480) collected several years earlier and then followed-up, produces figures very similar to those found in the primary study with a level of 19 per cent; the study also confirms the extended duration of pain and humiliation suffered by many children. Elliott (1989) has reported from her sample of 4,000 primary aged children that 38 per cent had experienced a particularly frightening experience or been bullied twice or more. A substantial difference is found between studies using pupil report and those relying on teacher report. Lowenstein (1978) for example put the figure no higher than 5 per cent in a sample of nearly 5,000 pupils, whereas Newson and Newson (1984) based on a sample from their Nottingham studies suggest that 26 per cent of mothers are aware of their child having been bullied. Arora and Thompson (1987) reported incidents of various types involving up to 50 per cent of pupils.

The international data show similar variability. The figures from Scandinavian researchers summarized by Munthe (1989) vary from 2 to 15 per cent for girl victims and from 6 to 27 per cent for boys, with similar divergence in the figures for bullies. An analysis of pupils' essays produced a figure of 4 per cent in an Italian sample, which as Basalisco (1989) points out is a low estimate, but an alarming one given the way that the data were collected. Garcia and Perez (Fonseca et al. 1989) in a Spanish investigation produce figures varying up to 17–21 per cent. O'Moore (1989) reviewing the Irish data found that about 10 per cent were involved in serious bullying (once a week or more) and 55 per cent had been bullied occasionally. In a cross-cultural study of youth violence, Pulkkinen and Saastamominen (1986) refer to figures from the USA indicating an increase in assaults on pupils of 85 per cent during the 1970s. They report that 40 per cent of pupils indicated that violence had hindered their school work but only 3 per cent regarded it as severe. In respect of bullying 8 per cent of pupils were involved.

These figures illustrate the mess that bullying research is in, with no consistent definitions being used in research studies, hence widely varying estimates occur with no method to determine the meaning of the differences.

An attempt was made to deal with this problem by a Sheffield University team (Yates and Smith 1989). They used Roland's definition from the Norwegian studies and the same questionnaire so that comparisons became possible. They estimated that 22 per cent of pupils were bullied 'now and then', with 10 per cent bullied 'once a week or more'. These figures are of course higher than comparable Norwegian or Irish figures and lead to discussions about the place of Britain in comparison with other European countries. Subsequent studies by the team from Sheffield University with larger samples confirmed these levels.

None of the UK studies represents nation-wide data, equivalent to those obtained in Norway, but it appears that the estimate by Tattum (1988) of levels of bullying in UK schools may be on the low side. The great advantage of the Sheffield study is that it makes the process of international comparison manageable and it is to be hoped that, at least for incidence studies, other researchers will follow their lead. Following Roland (1988) an agreed definition of bullying might be

> Bullying is longstanding violence, physical or psychological, conducted by an individual or group and directed against an individual who is not able to defend him/herself in the actual situation.

This definition would have to be expanded in questionnaires used with children to assess incidence and Yates and Smith (1989) have provided a definition based on the original one used by Olweus with only slight adaption to differing cultures. Future researchers could usefully follow the same method to provide a more valuable basis for comparison. However, this still leaves the question of how bullying might be defined in intervention studies. We might want to use a single definition for before and after measures but the meaning of the behaviour to those involved varies. It is necessary to consider those involved in the bullying process who might have a stake and whose definition of the situation influenced outcome.

Roland (1989) has described a 'bullying structure', which is a social system consisting of bullies, victims and bystanders. Each of those will be defining the situation from a different perspective. The perspective of the bystanders has received particular attention from Kelly (1990), who has demonstrated that bullying has significant effects on those who see, but are not direct victims. Their own self-esteem can be lowered as a result of the impotence they feel. There are similarities in her descriptions of the impact with those reported for victims of trauma and the so called peripheral victims (there but for the grace of God go I), and also in the helplessness bystanders report that they feel (Taylor 1991).

The impact of racial bullying has also been investigated by Kelly (1990) and she makes the important distinction between racial attacks, of a random type, and racial bullying which involves a relationship between victims and perpetrators. The impact of each will have differing consequences. Her work does emphasize the importance of looking at the relationship that exists within bullying groups. The discussion by King and colleagues (1992) clearly illustrates the importance of the structure involved. What is the 'story' behind the act, its meaning in terms of the place of bullying within the school in a racial, gender, socio-economic and differentially abled context must be made explicit. The roles taken by each party legitimize both the act and meaning ascribed. Thus it becomes 'O.K.' to devalue an individual or social group because those in positions of power choose not to actively seek information about bullying but instead rely on the occasional report which emerges.

Lister (1990) has concentrated attention on the perspective of the victim and drawn the parallels with other forms of abuse, the secrecy, shame and self-doubt that victims often feel. Davies (1990) has explored the way that pupils and teachers define the experience, and has indicated that bullying is one subject about which teachers feel both angry and impotent. Similarly pupils feel that teachers are incapable of acting to protect them, consequently a 'conspiracy of silence' builds up (O'Moore 1989). This sense of impotence has been explored by Lane (1990b) in terms of an analysis of the conversations (discourse) of participants. That is, the way those involved in the bullying structure define and redefine the behaviour. Understanding and dealing with bullying requires a sense of that discourse within the particular institution. Is bullying seen by some adults as a preparation for life? Are bullies viewed as evil characters who need to be punished? How is bullying viewed? An approach to intervention, using such a model, investigates the social exchange of meaning which emerges from the discourse. For example, if we think in terms of 'provocative victims' our definition as professionals will relate to their psychological characteristics, the bully will define those things that the victim does which mean that they deserve to be punished, and the victim may define him or herself as worthless. The bystander will see the injustice of the bullying, but be exhausted by efforts to help the victim which are rendered useless by repeated failure. If we choose not to use the term 'provocative victim' we might try to define the problem in terms of system events which generate such feeling of worthlessness. Repeated analysis of the discourses which actually take place in any given context, leads to the idea that you define the problem in terms of three elements, each examined from the perspective of those involved in the bullying structure. The three elements include the way each party defines the problem, the objectives they set, and the roles they expect to play in resolving the problem. The differences between them form the basis of a negotiation around the alternative behaviours which are to replace those seen as problematic. A shared concern emerges from this negotiation which forms the basis for the definition of bullying to be used.

It can be seen that such an approach renders useless a standard definition. However, the approach has been used with both individuals and groups and as a basis for negotiating a whole school policy with pupils, teachers and parents contributing. Once a shared concern is obtained a very powerful commitment to change is engendered. Everyone becomes a stakeholder in the change process.

Who, then, might be at risk?

It could be anyone. The following examples quoted in Tattum and Lane (1988) illustrate this point. Chazan (1988), based on infant schools in south Wales, has described both individual bullies and bullying gangs of 6 and 7 year olds. Herbert (1988), a head of year at a high school in Huddersfield, has referred to the incidents of intimidation, extortion, physical threats, the destruction of homework, and psychological bullying. He argues that it is not only physical violence that children fear but also the constant condemnation, isolation and loneliness. Askew (1988), from her research in London schools, has referred to clever children who have just given up, and children constantly feeling that they have to be careful in case they became the next victim. She makes the key point that it is not only the victim who suffers but also every child who has to keep his or her head down, just in case. Walford (1988), although describing the long history of gross violence in the public schools as days of Flashman that may have passed, still calls for vigilance. For, as he points out, unlike day school pupils, for the victim in the boarding school there is no escape from the tormentors.

These patterns describe pupil-to-pupil activity, but Lane (1988) has pointed to the social psychology of a process which labels children as bullies but not teachers. The pupils in his research identified about 10 per cent of teachers as bullies. The reverse of this is those teachers who felt bullied by children (Sparks 1983). Bullying is a more complex process than is implied by popular stereotype of bullies and victims.

What are the causes of bullying? An exploration

If we are to develop effective methods to deal with bullying we must understand the causes of the problem in a way that does justice to the complexity of the behaviour. Tattum (1988) in his review of the subject pointed to the importance of this complexity. He too makes the point that bullying affects not only those directly involved but also those who witness it, and indeed the whole atmosphere of the school. The tragic murder of a child in a Manchester school, he argues, provides an example of this. The language we use to describe bullying may contribute to a simplistic view. We must, according to Tattum, when we are considering potential action look at bullying in terms of its nature, intensity, duration, intentionality, numbers involved, and motivation.

Additionally, and drawing upon a 'sketch theory' from Olweus (1984) we should, Tattum maintains, consider school setting, external characteristics of potential victims and bullies, psychological behaviour of victims and bullies and socio-economic background.

Chazan (1988), drawing on a varied literature also points to the combination of a difficult temperament and adverse parental attitudes and practices. Stephenson and Smith (1988) have taken these arguments a stage further and point to similar characteristics in their survey but also raise additional factors. They point to a relationship between social deprivation and bullying (for bullies and victims). They also identify different groups of bullies and victims who vary on a number of physical, personality and social dimensions. There is not a standard profile of bully and victim. These findings raise serious difficulties for research and intervention models which have worked from a simple dichotomy and introduces the prospect of different possible interventions for these groups. However, they also argue for the importance of differences between schools. There are high and low bullying schools. The distinctions between these schools are not only those of catchment area and intake, but also those of policy decisions by the schools. The school's own role in promoting or reducing bullying therefore becomes an important consideration.

Lane (1974a; 1978; 1988) in his research into disruption, truancy and bullying also points to features of the individual, the family and the school. In relation to bullying the model would involve a combination of factors.

1 *Behaviour is predictive of future behaviour* Early patterns of bullying are likely to predict later activity.
2 *Preferred action style* Personality differences are predictive of patterns of behaviour. In particular individuals who describe themselves as tough-minded, stable extraverts are more likely to be involved in violent activity. The tough-minded dimension is especially predictive of bullying and later violent crime. Individuals may have a preference for violence.
3 *Multiple stress* Those involved are more likely to suffer from multiple stresses. They are more likely to be found in groups with more health problems, lower social class membership, poor peer relationships, larger families, higher levels of social disadvantage, and fewer compensating positive features in their families.
4 *Schools matter* However, most importantly the action taken by schools was a key component of both the level of difficulty and its continuation.

A similar range of issues were reviewed by Besag (1989) and O'Moore (1989) but the latter raises the important issue of the attitude of teachers to the problem. She contrasts the strong views expressed on protecting teachers from assault with the comparative silence on protecting children. The ambivalence in attitudes of adults to aggressive behaviour has also been identified by Titman (1988). It is this issue of 'attitude' which is missing from the more traditional reviews of the problem which effectively see it as a matter between victims and bullies rather than one in which the school plays a part in the solution and is also part of the problem. (Authors who have begun to explore these more complex aspects include Askew 1988; Roland 1989; Kelly 1990; Davies 1990; Lane 1989; 1990b; Lister 1987; 1990; King et al. 1992.) From a separate perspective the work of Pikas (1989) has touched upon the issue. Within this broader perspective, views taken of the act and its labelling are crucial. If in fact bullying is a complex social labelling process, then understanding its causation requires more than looking at bullies and victims. The possibility of a broadly based model of bullying behaviour is beginning to be possible.

The work of Olweus and Roland (1983) offers a starting-point since they have provided data from large-scale surveys. Roland (1988) has summarized the key findings and more recently provided a more detailed account of the motivation for bullying (Roland and Munthe 1989). Roland has argued that bullying is more likely to be a group than an individual activity and it must be seen as part of the social process of group activity. Bullying for boys is more likely to be part of power based social relationships and for girls affiliation activities are more frequently the source of bullying activities. Within that structure there are differences between those involved and those less likely to be involved. Both bullies and victims are likely to have fewer close friends. Physical characteristics are a factor, particularly differences in physical appearance and strength but these are generally over-estimated in importance. Any feature could be picked on as a pretext for bullying. Low self-esteem seems to be a common feature of victims with some coming to see themselves as deserving of their fate. For Roland the socialization process is a key feature, whereas Olweus refers to 'personality' factors and the role of early learning in particular a tolerance of aggressive behaviour.

It is this later factor which requires modification in view of the increasing data on differences between schools. Levels of bullying do vary between schools but also importantly between classes within schools and even year by year. These intra-school differences cannot be explained by individual and family difference models. Features within the school need to be isolated. Lane (1988) argues for a number of factors including school policies on bullying and the extent to which the school feels like a safe place to pupils, teachers and parents alike. Arora and Thompson (1987) have similarly demonstrated that differences between school years may relate to the approach taken by the year head teacher.

Underlying these differences, Lane (1988) identifies an ambivalence in some schools in their attitudes to power and masculinity. A violent macho ethos may be promoted by staff as well as pupils which leads to bullying becoming a status activity. A failure to deal with these issues clouds attempts by a school to state a clear policy on equal opportunities by race, sex, class, disability or life-style preferences. If, for example, women teachers in a school feel intimidated by the tactics of some male staff towards them and feel that they will not get a fair hearing, how safe will children feel in reporting incidents of bullying? Askew (1988) has presented a clear argument for the role played by these issues in research into boys' schools. She has also provided evidence that action even by one form teacher can have positive effects. The arguments by King and colleagues (1992) strengthen this view.

If the perspective presented by research such as that by Stephenson and Smith (1987), Askew (1988) and Lane (1988) is confirmed in other studies then our approach to intervention for bullying needs to be very broadly based. Is such an approach possible?

A model of bullying: the formulation

Our model of bullying has to start with the discourse. How is bullying defined by those involved in the particular bullying structure we are investigating. Davies (1990), working with groups of schools, has illustrated how they can begin to reach shared definitions leading to a shared concern and action. He has used an action research model, with a team within the school taking responsibility for a study prior to involving the whole school in data collection about the problem as they perceive it. Once the problem is defined, the contexts within which bullying occurs can be explored. The settings for the occurrence of difficulties, places, people, times, and so on, can be compared with those in which problems do not occur. With an understanding of those contexts in place, the question of developing models which influence the occurrence of the behaviour can be addressed.

The issues from the literature in terms of constitutional features of individuals and schools, prior experience in the family, peer groups, the class, etc., which are hypothesized to give rise to less or more likelihood of bullying can be examined. The particular events happening at the time bullying occurs can be explored in terms of antecedents and consequences and the beliefs which support the bullying structure can be contextualized. However, because the model developed by the school can identify contexts which make bullying more or less likely the value of any of the hypothesized factors of influence can be sorted, weighed and judged. Those which do not stand up to scrutiny can be discarded. In this way a formulation of the bullying structure appropriate to the context can be established. It is likely to lead to ideas for intervention which will be effective in that context, whereas general purpose approaches imported from elsewhere might not. In this way an empirically based model of bullying is established which can inform action.

What can be done? A framework for intervention

A model of bullying constructed as discussed above would carry a number of implications for intervention. The most effective starting-point for any school would be to build their own model along the lines suggested by Davies (1990). Thus an action research/systems approach would be possible. Those contemplating such an approach would need to complete some preliminary steps to ensure the necessary commitment. Preliminary steps for an action research/systems approach include the following.

Step 1   If you think bullying is worth looking at go back to colleagues in your school, talk it through and raise it as part of the school agenda.

Step 2   Assign priority: there is a lot going on in schools at the moment; do you want to deal with this?

Step 3   Think about how your school deals with similar issues, crisis management or as part of co-ordinated structure.

Step 4   Think about the implications for the school's existing problem-solving style of using an action-oriented approach, which is exploration focused not solution focused.

Step 5   If action research seems viable get an agreement to form an action team, supported by an adviser, psychologist and so on: get organized and get going.

If this level of analysis and action is not viable within the school then a decision is still required on where to place the priority for action. Five areas for action could be justified in terms of the literature:

1 deal with victims and bullies direct
2 work through the curriculum
3 work through support agencies
4 work through school systems
5 work through training events.

These areas are now discussed further.

Deal with victims and bullies direct

A number of ideas have been developed for dealing with bullying. A bullying action plan (Priest 1989) identifying factors of influence and strategies for action is viable and can be applied in direct work with the individuals concerned. Similarly Besag (1989) has provided a number of suggestions. Unfortunately few of the interventions which have appeared have been evaluated. As Besag points out the situation is very different in Scandinavia. Pikas (1989) for example has provided programmes for those involved in group bullying (mobbing) trained others to use the methods and obtained positive results based on case study data. Chazan (1988) has also provided examples from infant schools. The work of Lister was featured in a BBC TV *40 Minutes* programme ('Bullies', 30 November 1989). This approach based on an educational therapy model has much to recommend it. Lister, unusually, has evaluated her work and provided a detailed account for the purpose of replication (Lister 1987). The model of analysis and intervention used at the Islington Educational Guidance Centre (Lane 1975b) was used extensively with children involved with bullying and it has been the subject of evaluation (Lane 1983; 1990a). At the therapeutic end of the dimension the case study reported on pp. 151–3 provides an example.

Work through the curriculum

The development of a pastoral curriculum in schools can provide a starting-point for dealing with a wide range of issues including bullying. Group work techniques are now widely available and lists of resources have been provided by Titman (1988), Besag (1989) and Herbert (1988). The value of pastoral approaches is also featured in the international literature (see Roland and Munthe 1989).

Five ideas from within this general approach are worth particular attention. Walker (1989) has placed the issue of bullying in the context of non-violent conflict resolution. She has argued that conflict management is a major task of the teacher and the methods used to deal with it will have a more general impact. The development of non-violent conflict resolution models in the classroom places the issue in the broader peace education movement and that concept has had some influence on work in the USA and Europe. Peace education has had a more difficult reception in the UK. Herbert (1988; Tattum and Herbert 1990) has demonstrated that effective action can take place through the curriculum. Careful selection of books, discussion periods and role-plays are effective and begin to change the climate of opinion. A more elaborate development along the same lines is found in the work of the Neti-Neti Multi-lingual Theatre Company (Casdagli et al. 1990) They use plays, playscripts and workshops to raise awareness and generate ideas for solutions from children themselves. That one person can make an impact, if children are empowered, is evident in the work of Askew (1988). She has outlined the work undertaken with one school class and the effect it had on their behaviour and attitudes to each other. A major programme of work within the tradition of empowering children is found in the Kidscape programmes designed to teach children the skills to keep themselves safe. Elliott (1988; 1989) has provided a detailed scheme which involves children, teachers and parents. Her programmes have been used extensively in UK schools.

Work through support agencies

For some children the level of difficulty they face, and the degree of anguish they experience will leave them de-skilled and even self-hating. For such children a detailed programme of work will be necessary. This may involve support within the school, or referral to an external agency. It may involve contact with social services, the courts, or telephone helplines such as Childline. Some children may write to magazines or television programme presenters, and some of those have prepared detailed advice leaflets (for example, 'How to deal with bullying', from the children's *MotorMouth* programme).

The problem with external services is the sometimes limited impact they can have on the situation back in school. However, some external agencies have taken that on board and ensure that therapeutic interventions are tightly woven into school response. Bayley (1989) has described therapeutic groups for victims in schools based on the work of the Southwark Educational Guidance Service. Social skills based groups have also been used effectively by support agencies in this area (Lane 1975). The case study discussed on pp. 151–3 presents a therapeutically led approach. Other approaches such as play therapy (Newson 1992) could easily be adapted to deal with this problem (see also Chapter 4).

Work through school systems

If impact is to take place through school systems the issues raised by Davies (1990) need to be considered, but as he demonstrates it is possible to influence systems in this way. An interesting alternative from a systems perspective is found in work on bullying in school playgrounds. The playground represents an important social system in its own right. Several ethnographic approaches to playground work were used by the Islington Educational Guidance Centre and were presented at workshops. Titman (1988) has provided a valuable discussion of play-based work and drawn attention to the contrast between the barren tarmac of most school playgrounds and the exciting atmosphere of adventure playgrounds. Ross and Ryan (1990) have recently developed a detailed guide to playground work from pilot projects with primary schools.

Work through training events

A number of practitioners have looked at the impact of training workshops with teachers to raise awareness and generate action. Examples include the work of Askew (1988) and Burden et al. (1990). The one-day training event can provide a powerful impetus for change if those present are provided with a mechanism to convert the desire to act into an action plan. The impact is particularly noticeable when a commitment to act is publicly made at the end of a workshop event with an agreed follow-up date stated.

A wide range of possibilities for action exists. However, as Tattum (1988) has pointed out, these are not likely to be effective except as part of an overall school policy. He has listed eleven pointers for action, but that is the single most important measure.

Can the problem of bullying be overcome? The evaluation

There is a considerable amount of descriptive material in the literature to suggest that effective action is possible. Most of the authors whose work has been discussed above have provided such descriptive evaluations. However, there is a substantial shortage of experimental evidence. In part this is inevitable since the literature itself is very young and perhaps the lack of interest in evaluation is no more than a reflection of the general failure of the child therapy literature. It is also perhaps a response to the enormous cost of such an enterprise. Few governments or funding bodies have been prepared to meet the costs involved.

The notable exception is the Norwegian government which has actively supported a research process from the inception of the campaigns they launched. The UK government recently responded to the increasing demands for action by the UK media and funded a study at Sheffield University (1991). An alternative approach is being supported by the Professional Development Foundation (1990) to encourage and integrate small-scale studies by various practitioners so that comparisons can be made. Until the evaluations are available (in the mid-1990s) the only large-scale studies are those based on whole school campaigns. These provide mixed results. Olweus (1989: reported in Yates and Smith 1989) has pointed to the effectiveness of the approach. Roland (1988) and Munthe (1989) indicate a more varied set of findings. Roland makes the point (perhaps obvious but important) that the programmes work better in schools that make active use of them. It also appears that schools that already have less of a problem become even more effective at dealing with bullying following a campaign. This illustrates more potently than anything else could the importance of looking at a particular system and the context for understanding the bullying structure which it presents.

A case study in context

While 25 per cent of teachers feel that it is sometimes helpful to ignore the problem the majority of children look to teachers to act (Stephenson and Smith 1988). Given the misery that many thousands of children endure for several years of their lives and the fact that the school is itself part of the problem, schools cannot afford to take an ostrich-like position of bullying. The concept of the 'safe school' which has begun to take hold in the USA is perhaps one that should be explored here (Lane 1989).

Is there anything that a programme of therapy can contribute? The ideas presented in this chapter suggest that something can indeed be done at a number of levels. One of these levels is direct intervention with individuals or groups. For many the issue has become very complex and the impact on their lives has been devastating. For them a therapeutically based intervention will be necessary. Nevertheless, the issues that I have raised are likely to feature in any such endeavour. A case study is therefore presented which illustrates a number of the points raised.

John is the youngest of five children. His father was in regular work but had always been aggressive towards the children according to the mother's and child's accounts. She used to intervene to prevent the children being hit, but gave up after receiving beatings herself. She reported that the father had a poor relationship with all the children. Attempts over the years to involve the family in family therapy failed. The older brother had been suspended from school for bullying and was increasingly involved with the police. John spent several months in hospital in his early years, for a series of operations to correct birth defects. He remembered that period clearly, and his feelings of fear. Difficulties with language development added to his problems. Speech therapy over several years, two years in a specialist unit for language difficulties and, later, a period in a unit for the 'emotionally disturbed', preceded his transfer to mainstream secondary education. At this time, he was still a non-reader and had poorly developed social skills, although his speech had improved. He developed a severe stutter at the age of 12. He was becoming increasingly involved in violence and vandalism and, subsequently, football hooliganism.

The school he attended made extensive use of the cane as a punishment, in spite of the fact that, as the deputy head said, 'You might as well cane the wall as some of these children for all the good it does'. However, there were also several positive compensatory features. John had established a very good relationship with the special needs teacher in the school, who made a determined and successful attempt to teach him to read. A number of other teachers felt there were positive aspects in his behaviour, although they neither accepted nor tolerated his bullying. Several teachers wanted him further beaten, suspended, prosecuted or 'xxxxed'. His mother, although powerless against the father, did provide a compassionate model and he felt loved by her. The school decided to make a referral for Child Guidance but that broke down. They then made a referral to the Islington Centre. A complex analysis and intervention followed. In brief, it identified certain key elements:

1   Both his father and some male teachers provided models of aggressive behaviour. John disliked them but saw them as powerful models.
2   He valued the compassion he was shown but saw it as weakness.
3   He greatly valued being in school, at least that part of it which gave him some sense of success. He feared the prospect of further suspension.
4   His speech difficulty and lack of social skills prevented his expressing/asserting himself effectively. When confronted, he found that hitting out worked: children did not tease you if you terrorized them, and being unpredictable made teachers uncertain about confronting you. Violence worked; reason did not.
5   The school did not have a consistent policy, and conflicts were apparent between staff dealing with these issues and this pupil.

One particular aspect of the case will be considered. Point (4) above looked at the problem of hitting out as a result of stress. Three situations of violence were identified for consideration:

1   bullying other children
2   attacks on certain teachers
3   fights in other contexts.

The initial hypotheses explored linked the idea of stress to violence as follows.

When faced with a confrontational situation, John's level of stress is increased. As a result, his speech difficulty becomes worse, he has difficulty expressing himself, and he hits out – which reduces his anxiety. The various components in this sequence can be tested. The situations in which confrontations occur can be listed, the levels of stress he feels can be established on a scale on which he rates the level (say 1–10). Speech fluency could be checked, and the occasions on which he hits out could be recorded. Specific 'Attribution' or 'ABC' techniques could be used to provide a fine-grain analysis of the contexts in which violent or non-violent outcomes were observed (see Lane 1990a for discussion of the techniques).

This process of observation led to the realization that there were in fact at least four different patterns.

1   *Cognitive justification*   In some settings when faced with stress, John became angry, told himself that it was wrong that he was treated that way and chose to hit out.
2   *Stress management/skills deficit*   In some settings he would become anxious, be unable to talk his way out because of his stutter, and hit others in frustration.

3 *Just world* In some settings where he saw someone acting unjustly he would 'punish' the offender by hitting them. This was cold, calculated violence.

4 *Sheer pleasure* Certain settings, mostly involving football, were ones in which he sought out fights, for the pleasure involved. This was entertainment, not stress.

Given these very different patterns, the hypothesis that stress leads to violence cannot be sustained. It might do, but the circumstances in which it did were very specific. A programme was introduced to teach John mechanisms to deal with stress situations and to develop his social skills. A review of the models in his environment took place, to help him to identify power as legitimate assertion rather than aggression. A contracted set of relationships was established with teachers, so that events were rendered predictable, with defined consequences. It was made clear that any incident of bullying would be followed by a suspension, but that the issue of provocation by others would also be tackled, that is, he saw it as fair (just world). Over a nine-month period, the programme took effect with only two incidents being reported. No violence was reported in his final year at school. He left without qualifications but did eventually obtain work.

The one area not covered in the original programme was 'sheer pleasure', and it is not surprising, to discover on follow-up, that no change had occurred in that area. Two years later, he was involved in an incident with others (his old football gang) but, following a period of probation and good social work support, he stayed out of further trouble. Five years on he was working, developing an ongoing relationship and feeling positive about himself.

Conclusion

Bullying presents major problems for child and adolescent therapy. It is a problem which affects a vast number of children yet which has been curiously ignored. Its effects can be long term (Lane 1988) and therapeutic intervention may be necessary. Yet it illustrates the dilemma facing therapy. It cannot take place or be effective without impacting on the context in which the problem occurs. While the child guidance movement has taken a step away from individual analysis of the child towards family therapy, there has still been a reluctance as Howarth (1992) points out to get involved directly in the community or schools. The challenge for child therapy is to become involved in messier issues which represent the areas where problems exist for the overwhelming majority of children. A 'good enough therapist' can no longer treat an elite few.

A comparison of the suggestions by Pikas (1975) and those more recently by Tattum (1988) indicates the emerging trend. Both share concern with awareness of the problem and careful work with bullies (or mobbers) and victims, but Tattum points to the greater emphasis on the victim in the USA, and the involvement of parents, and the community in taking responsibility and the role of the academic and pastoral curriculum in the UK. In fact the emergence of a broad spectrum approach is beginning. In many ways the origins of such a policy lay with both ends of the original Scandinavian dimension. Within such a broadening perspective therapy can take its place, but it requires a more robust therapy (and therapist?) based on models of bullying behaviour which accurately reflect the context within which bullying appears.

References

Arora, C.M.J. and Thompson, D.A. (1987) Defining bullying for a secondary school, *Education and Child Psychology* 4(4): 110–20.

Askew, S. (1988) Aggressive behaviour in boys: to what extent is it institutionalised, in D.P. Tattum and D.A. Lane (eds) *Bullying in Schools*, Stoke-on-Trent: Trentham Books.

Basalisco, S. (1989) Bullying in Italy, in E. Roland and E. Munthe (eds) *Bullying: An International Perspective*, London: Fulton Books.

Bayley, J. (1989) *School Support*, Southwark London Borough: Southwark Educational Guidance Centre.

Besag, V.E. (1989) *Bullies and Victims in Schools*, Milton Keynes: Open University Press.

Burden, R., Davies, R., Kelly, E., Lane, D.A. and Lister, P. (1990) *Bullying: A Programme for Action*, London: Professional Development Foundation.

Casdagli, P., Gobey, F. and Griffen, C. (1990) *Only Playing Miss*, Stoke-on-Trent: Trentham Books.

Chazan, M. (1988) Bullying in the infant school, in D.P. Tattum and D.A. Lane (eds) *Bullying in Schools*, Stoke-on-Trent: Trentham Books.

Davies, R. (1990) Bullying: an action research approach, Conference Paper, Exeter University.

Dukes, C. (1905) *Health at School*, London: Rivingtons.

Elliott, M. (1988) *Keeping Safe: A Practical Guide to Talking with Children*, London: Hodder & Stoughton.

Elliott, M. (1989) Bullying: harmless fun or murder?, in E. Roland and E. Munthe (eds) *Bullying: An International Perspective*, London: Fulton Books.

Elton Report (1989) *Discipline in Schools: Report of the Committee of Inquiry*. London: HMSO.

Fonseca, Viera da, M.M., Garcia, I.F. and Perez, G.Q. (1989) Violence, bullying and counselling in the Iberian Peninsula, in E. Roland and E. Munthe (eds) *Bullying: An International Perspective*, London: Fulton Books.

Heinemann, P.P. (1973) *Mobbing*, Oslo: Gyldendal.

Herbert, G. (1988) A whole curriculum approach to bullying, in D.P. Tattum and D.A Lane (eds) *Bullying in Schools*, Stoke-on-Trent: Trentham Books.

Howarth, R. (1992) The Child Guidance Clinics: problems and progress for the 1990s, in D.A. Lane and A. Miller (eds) *Child and Adolescent Therapy: A Handbook*, Milton Keynes: Open University Press.

Kelly, E. (1990) Multi-cultural issues in bullying, Conference paper, Exeter University.

King, O., Keise, C., Kelly, E. and Lane, D.A. (1992) *Culture and Child Services*, in A. Miller and D.A. Lane (eds) *Silent Conspiracies*, Stoke-on-Trent: Trentham Books.

Knox, P. (1989) *School Phobia*, London: Readers and Writers Collective.

Lane, D.A. (1973) The problem of order, *Remedial Education* 8(3): 9–11.

Lane, D.A. (1974a) Truancy in the disruptive pupil, Conference paper, ILEA, London.

Lane, D.A. (1974b) *The Behavioural Analysis of Complex Cases*, London: IEGC.

Lane, D.A. (1975a) *Dependency: Techniques of Prevention*, London: Kings Fund Centre/ IEGC.

Lane, D.A. (1975b) *Dealing with Behaviour Problems: A New Approach*, London: Kings Fund Centre.

Lane, D.A. (1978) *The Impossible Child*, Vols 1 and 2, London: ILEA.

Lane, D.A. (1983) *Whatever Happened to the Impossible Child*, London: ILEA.
Lane, D.A. (1988) Violent histories: bullying and criminality in D.P. Tattum and D.A. Lane (eds) *Bullying in Schools*, Stoke-on-Trent: Trentham Books.
Lane, D.A. (1989) I'll see it when I believe it: a behavioural search for meaning, in D.A. Lane (ed.) *Attributions, Beliefs and Constructs in Counselling Psychology*, Leicester: British Psychological Society.
Lane, D.A. (1990a) *The Impossible Child*, Stoke-on-Trent: Trentham Books.
Lane, D.A. (1990b) Bullying: an integrated approach, Conference Paper, Exeter University.
Lister, P. (1987) *The Management of Behaviour Problems: An On Site Unit*, London: Lister Consultancy Services.
Lister, P. (1990) Bullying: the victim's perspective, Conference Paper, Exeter University.
Lowenstein, L.F. (1978) Who is the bully? *Bulletin of the British Psychological Society* 31: 316–18.
Munthe, E. (1989) Bullying in Scandinavia, in E. Roland and E. Munthe (eds) *Bullying: An International Perspective*, London: Fulton Books.
Newson, E. (1992) The barefoot play therapist: adapting skills for a time of need, in D.A. Lane and A. Miller (eds) *Child and Adolescent Therapy: A Handbook*, Milton Keynes: Open University Press.
Newson, J. and Newson, E. (1984) Parents' perspectives on children's behaviour at school, in N. Frude and H. Gault (eds) *Disruptive Behaviour in Schools*, Chichester: Wiley.
Olweus, D. (1974) *Hakkekyllinger og skoleboller. Forskning om skolemobbing*, Oslo: Cappelen.
Olweus, D. (1978) *Aggression in the Schools: Bullies and Whipping Boys*, Washington, DC: Hemisphere Press.
Olweus, D. (1984) Aggressors and their victims: bullying in schools, in N. Frude and H. Gault (eds) *Disruptive Behaviour in Schools*, Chichester: Wiley.
Olweus, D. (1989) Bully/victim problems among schoolchildren: basic facts and effects of a school based intervention programme, in K. Rubin and D. Pepler (eds) *The Development and Treatment of Childhood Aggression*, Hillsdale, NJ: Erlebaum.
Olweus, D. and Roland, E. (1983) *Mobbing-Bakgrunn og tiltak*, Oslo: Kirke-og under visningsdepartementet.
O'Moore, A.M. (1989) Bullying in Britain and Ireland: an overview, in E. Roland and E. Munthe (eds) *Bullying: An International Perspective*, London: Fulton Books.
Orton, W.T. (1982) Mobbing, *Public Health* 96: 172–4.
Pikas, A. (1975) *Sa stoppar vi mobbing*, Stockholm: Prisma.
Pikas, A. (1976) *Slik stoppar vi mobbing*, Oslo: Gyldendal.
Pikas, A. (1989) The common concern method in the treatment of mobbing, in E. Roland and E. Munthe (eds) *Bullying: An International Perspective*, London: Fulton Books.
Priest, S. (1989) Some practical approaches to bullying, in E. Roland and E. Munthe (eds) *Bullying: An International Perspective*, London: Fulton Books.
Professional Development Foundation (1990) Bullying Research Programme (in progress), London, PDF.
Pulkkinen, L. and Saastamominen, M. (1986) Cross-cultural perspectives on Youth Violence, in S.J. Apter and A.P. Goldstein (eds) *Youth Violence: Program and Prospects*, Oxford: Pergamon Press.
Reid, K. (1985) *Truancy and School Absenteeism*, London: Hodder & Stoughton.
Reid, K. (1988) Bullying and persistent school absenteeism, in D.P. Tattum and D.A. Lane (eds) *Bullying in Schools*, Stoke-on-Trent: Trentham Books.
Roland, E. (1983) *Strategi mot mobbing*, Stavanger: Universitetsforlaget.
Roland, E. (1988) Bullying: the Scandanavian research tradition, in D.P. Tattum and D.A. Lane (eds) *Bullying in Schools*, Stoke-on-Trent: Trentham Books.
Roland, E. (1989) A system oriented strategy against bullying, in E. Roland and E. Munthe (eds) *Bullying: An International Perspective*, London: Fulton Books.

Roland, E. and Munthe, E. (eds) (1989) *Bullying: An International Perspective*, London: Fulton Books.

Ross, C. and Ryan, A. (1990) *'Can I Stay in Today, Miss?'*, Stoke-on-Trent: Trentham Books.

Sheffield University (1991) Department of Psychology Research Programme into Bullying (in progress).

Sparks, J.P. (1983) Mobbing in an independent secondary boarding school, *Public Health* 97: 316-19.

Stephenson, P. and Smith, D. (1987) Anatomy of the playground bully, *Education* 18 August: 236-7.

Stephenson, P. and Smith, D. (1988) Bullying in the junior school, in D.P. Tattum and D.A. Lane (eds) *Bullying in Schools*, Stoke-on-Trent: Trentham Books.

Tattum, D.P. (1988) Violence and aggression in schools, in D.P. Tattum and D.A. Lane (eds) *Bullying in Schools*, Stoke-on-Trent: Trentham Books.

Tattum, D.P. and Herbert, G. (1990) *Bullying: A Positive Response*, Cardiff: South Glamorgan Institute of Higher Education.

Tattum, D.P. and Lane, D.A. (1988) *Bullying in Schools*, Stoke-on-Trent: Trentham Books.

Taylor, A.J.W. (1991) The field of disasters and disaster stress, *British Journal of Guidance and Counselling* 19(1): 1-7.

Titman, W. (1988) Adult responses to children's fears, in D.P. Tattum and D.A. Lane (eds) *Bullying in Schools*, Stoke-on-Trent: Trentham Books.

Walford, G. (1988) Bullying in public schools: myth and reality, in D.P. Tattum and D.A. Lane (eds) *Bullying in Schools*, Stoke-on-Trent: Trentham Books.

Walker, J. (1989) Resolving classroom conflicts non-violently, in E. Roland and E. Munthe (eds) *Bullying: An International Perspective*, London: Fulton Books.

Yates, C. and Smith, P.K. (1989) Bullying in two English comprehensive schools, in E. Roland and E. Munthe (eds) *Bullying: An International Perspective*, London: Fulton Books.

8

The management of trauma following disasters

WILLIAM YULE AND RUTH M. WILLIAMS

Introduction

Children have been victims and survivors of large- and small-scale disasters from time immemorial. Therapists of all disciplines are used to helping children adjust after an individual trauma, but few have experience of managing trauma caused by a major disaster. The second half of the 1980s in Britain witnessed a number of large-scale disasters that have made people much more aware of the effects of such disasters on victims, survivors and their relatives. Children were at the football stadium at Bradford when it caught fire; children and adolescents were aboard the *Herald of Free Enterprise* when it capsized outside Zeebrugge, and on the *City of Poros* ferry when it was attacked by terrorists outside Athens, and on the cruise ship, *Jupiter*, when it sank, again outside Athens. Such disasters will continue to happen. How should schools and mental health professionals prepare to help survivors?

Much less is known of the manifestations of post-traumatic stress reactions in children than in adults. In part, this is because of the difficulty in mounting adequate studies in the immediate aftermath of a disaster; in part, it is because adults are understandably very protective towards children who have survived a disaster; and in part, it is because adults, unwilling to acknowledge what children may have suffered, deny that children have major psychological sequelae that warrant investigation. Thus, there are very few systematic studies of the effects of major trauma on children, and most of the published ones suffer major methodological weaknesses (Garmezy 1986).

Garmezy and Rutter (1985) summed up the distilled wisdom from published studies. Regarding the effects of a variety of stressors on children, they concluded:

> behavioural disturbances appear to be less intense than might have been anticipated; a majority of children show a moderate amount of fear and anxiety but this subsides; regressive behaviour marked by clinging to parents and heightened dependency on adults appears and then moderately

mild sleep disturbance persists for several months; a later less severe stressor such as a storm may lead to a temporary increase in emotional distress, although this is variable; enuresis occurs in some cases, while hypersensitivity to loud noises may be evident in others.

(Garmezy and Rutter 1985: 162)

In their view, severe acute stressors such as occur in major disasters result in socially handicapping emotional disorders in some children, but in the majority of those cases, the disturbances are short lived. Because children tend not to show amnesia for the event, nor to show 'psychic numbing' or intrusive flashbacks, they argue that there is no need for a specific diagnostic category for stress reactions in children parallel to post-traumatic stress disorder (PTSD) in adults.

While these conclusions fit reasonably with the bulk of the evidence surveyed, the difficulty is that the studies themselves have rarely dealt with the aftermath of major disasters in which the children have been exposed to life-threatening factors. For example, Handford et al. (1986) carried out a detailed study of thirty-five children aged 5 to 19 years eighteen months after the Three Mile Island nuclear accident. This study is important in establishing that parents under-report the extent and severity of their children's reactions and in demonstrating that the widely used Quay and Peterson (1979) Behavior Problem Checklist completed by parents is insensitive to the children's reactions. However, it must be seriously questioned whether this is really a study of the effects of a major disaster in that, as the authors put it, Three Mile Island was a silent disaster with no apparent physical damage to people or property, and the children were not separated from their parents during the time of the evacuation that some of them experienced.

Galante and Foa (1986) undertook a very impressive study of children badly traumatized by the massive earthquakes in a remote mountainous region of central Italy in November 1980. Many thousands of people were killed and many more made homeless. As part of a co-ordinated response to dealing with the tragedy, Galante and Foa set up treatment groups for the children. Before the groups started, 300 children aged 6 to 11 years were rated on an Italian translation of the Rutter (1967) behaviour rating scale for completion by teachers. Detailed notes were taken of the content of discussion during the group meetings that were spaced over a one-year period, and the Rutter scales were completed again at the end of the period, some eighteen months after the earthquake.

The authors were disappointed that many of their predictions relating the teachers' ratings to indices of trauma and bereavement were not substantiated in their data. However, in our view, they analyse their data inappropriately and do not give the distributions of rating scores. Rather, they report on correlations which are probably inappropriate as the B-scale scores are usually not distributed normally. Much more importantly, the Rutter scales were developed as screening instruments for use in general population studies and were not intended to screen out rare conditions. The authors seem aware of this when they raise somewhat belatedly the question of the validity of the scales for their purposes.

Rutter's screening scales were also favoured by McFarlane in his large-scale studies of the effects of the February 1983 bush fires in south-east Australia

(McFarlane 1987; McFarlane et al. 1987). The children studied were aged 5 to 12 years and lived in one rural community in which large tracts of agricultural and forest lands were burnt, a quarter of a million livestock perished, fourteen people died and many homes were burnt out or partially devastated. As has been found in other studies that attempt to research survivors, many teachers were unwilling to participate fully and while McFarlane tried to get repeated measures two, eight and twenty-six months after the fire, the attrition rate in his sample was very high.

In the immediate aftermath of the fire at two months, the children were rated as less disturbed than a comparison group studied elsewhere. However, by eight months, both parents and teachers report significant increases in the numbers of children at high risk of psychiatric disorder; these high rates maintained at twenty-six months. In fact, close inspection of the data shows that teachers lagged behind parents in reporting problems; overall the study demonstrates a consistent increase in reported morbidity from eight months after the disaster.

McFarlane et al. (1987) concluded that the delayed recognition of problems suggests that many problems do not spontaneously resolve. Indeed, they 'challenge Quarantelli's (1985) hypothesis that the mental health effects of disasters are short-lived and of little practical importance'. They subjected their data to many complex analyses, but these could not overcome one of the major weaknesses of the study – namely that it relies mostly on the completion of scales that were never intended to measure the effects of trauma on children. Unfortunately, there does not appear to have been any attempt to interview the worst affected children to ascertain how they themselves reported the effects of the traumas. Indeed, one has to ask, as with the Three Mile Island study, whether all the children were really traumatized by their experiences of the fires. That is not to say that the effects of bush fires are not awful, but it is vital to ascertain the exposure of, and threat to each individual child.

In a related paper, McFarlane (1987) reports his investigations of family reactions and functioning and their relationship to children's adjustment. Again keeping the caveats about sample attrition, inappropriate measures and doubts about the strength of the trauma in mind, the questions that he poses are very apposite in trying to understand why some children are affected more than others and why some remain affected for longer. He concludes that at the eight month follow-up, the families showed increased levels of conflict, irritability and withdrawal, with maternal overprotection being quite common. The adjustment of the parents themselves was an important determinant of the adjustment of the children. In particular, he comments that 'families who did not share their immediate reactions to disaster may have had more trouble with their long-term adjustment . . . and experienced a greater degree of estrangement'. Equally important, the child's reactions to the fire affected the adjustment of the family, emphasizing the reciprocal interactions among members of a family system.

Pynoos and his colleagues have undertaken among the most systematic studies of children suffering post-traumatic stress disorders following a variety of trauma from witnessing a parent being murdered or raped to themselves surviving an attack from a sniper in their school playground (Pynoos and Eth 1986; Pynoos et al. 1987; Pynoos and Nader 1988). To avoid the weaknesses of previous studies, they sampled 159 children (14.5 per cent of those attending the school) who were exposed to a sniper attack on the school in which one child and a passer-by were killed and thirteen other children were injured. Many children were trapped in the playground under gunfire and others were trapped in classrooms. Many were separated from siblings and, of course, parents. The siege lasted a number of hours.

Pynoos and his colleagues used a structured interview to obtain information on the children's reactions and codified this into a PTSD Reaction Index. On average the children were 9.2 years old at the time of the trauma. Nearly 40 per cent of the children were found to have moderate to severe PTSD approximately one month after the event. A particularly striking finding in this study was the very strong relationship between exposure and later effects in that those children who were trapped in the playground scored much higher than those who had left the vicinity of the school before the attack or were not in school that day, as can be seen in Figure 8.1.

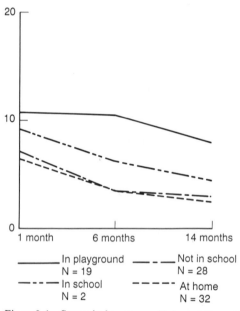

Figure 8.1 Stress index scores (Adapted from Nader et al. 1990)

At fourteen-month follow-up, Nader and colleagues (1990) report that 74 per cent of the most severely exposed children in the playground still report moderate to severe levels of PTSD, contrasted with 81 per cent of the unexposed children reporting no PTSD. Earlier PTSD Reaction Index scores were strongly related to those obtained at follow-up. In a more detailed analysis of the data, Nader et al. (1990) investigated the effect of the survivors' knowledge of the victim on their PTSD Reaction Index scores. They found that only among the less exposed children did greater knowledge of the victim increase the strength of the emotional reaction to the trauma. In other words, the level of exposure to the life-threatening trauma was more important than other factors such as knowledge of the victim.

In this study, the moderating effects of families' reactions was not reported but the strength of the relationships noted challenges McFarlane's (1987) claim that most effects are mediated by parental reaction.

Yule and Williams (1990) report their experiences in assessing and treating children who survived the capsize of the *Herald of Free Enterprise* in Zeebrugge harbour in March 1987. They assessed thirteen of the then known twenty-two surviving children under the age of 16 years. At six to nine months post accident, over half the children were reported by parents to be showing significant disturbance, while only two of eight children rated by teachers were said to be disturbed. The authors used the Rutter parent and teacher rating scales and, despite the small numbers, concluded that these screening scales were not sensitive to the subjective distress that is the hallmark of PTSD. In interviews, children revealed much more pathology than was known to parents or teachers.

After getting to know the children better, those authors were able to ask the children to complete Horowitz's Revised Impact of Events Scale (Horowitz et al. 1979). Children as young as 8 years found the scale meaningful and on that basis it was concluded that the children scored higher than adult patients attending Horowitz's clinic for treatment. At twelve to fifteen months post accident, the children repeated their ratings and it was found that the overall level had scarcely dropped, as can be seen in Figure 8.2.

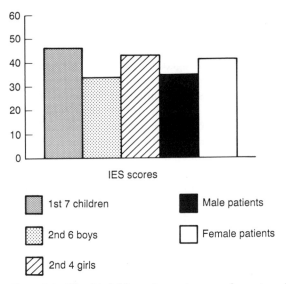

Figure 8.2 Herald child survivors, impact of events scale

On the basis of their continuing work with the children as well as the assessments based on interviews with children and parents, Yule and Williams (1990) concluded that children in the 8 to 16 year range do show symptoms that are very similar to those shown by adults presenting with post traumatic stress disorder. They also cautioned against the use of instruments developed as screening instruments for general childhood psychopathology and suggested using the Impact of Events Scale and measures of depression.

When the cruise ship, *Jupiter*, sank outside Piraeus harbour, Athens, in October 1988 after being hit by an oil tanker, there were nearly 400 children and 90 adults, mainly teachers, aboard. One pupil, one teacher, and two seamen helping with the rescue were killed. However, the children experienced a major trauma in that many had to take to the water, many were not reunited with their classmates and teachers for many hours, they were in a foreign country where they did not speak the language, and they were far away from their homes and parents.

Yule and Udwin (forthcoming) offered to help the survivors at one school. An account of the preliminary 'debriefing' work is given below. They screened all twenty-four survivors on three scales: the Impact of Events Scale, Birleson's Depression Scale (Birleson 1981; Birleson et al. 1987) and the Revised Children's Manifest Anxiety Scale (Reynolds and Richmond 1978). On the basis of their scores ten days after the sinking, ten girls aged 14 years were thought to be at high risk of developing problems. When help was offered on an individual or group basis, and without saying which girls were considered to be at high risk, eight of the ten high risk group came forward for help on the first day. The other two attended the second meeting. Only five others ever attended any group meeting. This was a highly significant relationship between scores on the screening scales and later help seeking, and the authors conclude that the battery shows considerable promise in identifying children who most need help after a disaster.

Most of these studies of the effects of disasters on children have been descriptive and few have attempted to use the opportunity to test theories relevant to emotional processing in children or to evaluate different approaches to treatment. Dollinger and colleagues (1984) studied the effects of a lightning strike on twenty-seven soccer players and two spectators all aged 10–13 years. All had been knocked flat by a lightning strike in which one boy was killed and six required immediate medical treatment. The survivors later completed the Louisville Fear Survey for Children: 104 items rated on a five-point scale (Miller et al. 1972; Staley and O'Donnell 1984). A respondent conditioning theory of children's fears predicts that '(a) a high-intensity stimulus can result in a conditioned fear, and (b) this conditioned fear can generalize to other similar stimuli' (Dollinger et al. 1984: 1,028). The investigators found that the children on the soccer field showed more fears of storms than did matched controls, and these fears were more intense. Detailed analyses of their responses showed a clear generalization gradient effect, in keeping with the theoretical prediction, with fears of storms being strongest, followed by fears related to sleep, noise and disasters, death and dying, while there was no effect on fears of people or embarrassment. Thus, Dollinger et al. (1984) have shown how a carefully conducted study of children who survive a disaster can contribute to our understanding of the conditioning theory of children's fears.

Following on this model, Yule and colleagues (1990) asked all fourth-year girls in one school which had had a party of twenty-four aboard the *Jupiter* when it sank, to complete the Revised Fear Survey Schedule for Children (Ollendick et al. 1991). Effectively, there were three subgroups of girls: those who went on the cruise and were traumatized, those who had wanted to go but could not get a place, and those who showed no interest in going in the first place. However, this latter group could not be considered as an unaffected control group as the whole

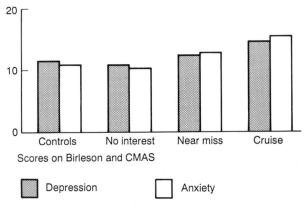

Figure 8.3 Depression and anxiety at 5 months

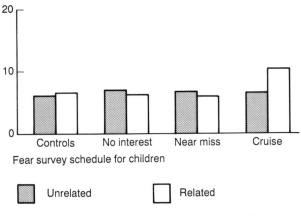

Figure 8.4 Unrelated and related fears at 5 months

school was badly affected by the aftermath of the disaster. Accordingly, fourth-year girls in a nearby school also completed the fear schedule, along with the depression and anxiety scales.

Two sets of results should be noted. As can be seen in Figure 8.3, the girls on the cruise were significantly more depressed and anxious than the other groups five months after the disaster. Indeed, there is a strong suggestion of an exposure/ effect gradient on these two measures, reminiscent of that reported by Pynoos et al. (1987). The fear survey items were rated as being related to the events on the cruise or not. There was agreement among the authors that eleven items were related and thirty-three were unrelated. Scores on these set of items were standardized by dividing the score on unrelated items by 3. The results can be seen in Figure 8.4, where it is evident that there are no differences across the four exposure groups on unrelated fears. By contrast, on related fears, only the girls who experienced the traumatic events show a significant increase in reported fears. Thus, the authors took the opportunity of the disaster to examine the effects on children's fears and conclude that the effects are specific to stimuli present and thereby provide more confirmatory evidence of the conditioning theory of fear acquisition.

The adult PTSD literature is increasingly full of examples of the successful application of behaviour therapy to reduce intrusive thoughts, startle reaction and phobic and avoidance behaviour. The child literature is so sparse that there appears to be only one published report by Saigh (1986) of the in vitro flooding treatment of PTSD exhibited by a $6\frac{1}{2}$ year old Lebanese boy who had been traumatized by a bomb blast. Two years after the event, he suffered nightmares, intrusive thoughts and avoided areas associated with the bombing. Four scenes were successively worked on in therapy and rapid improvement was obtained in ten sessions; improvement was maintained over six months. Saigh (1986) notes that earlier attempts to treat other children with systematic desensitization failed, and in this case, each session began with fifteen minutes' relaxation followed by twenty-four minutes of in vitro flooding. This extended exposure to the fear-inducing stimuli fits in well with Rachman's (1980) views on factors that accelerate successful emotional processing.

From this review of the scattered but relevant literature, we conclude that after major disasters, a high proportion of children are likely to suffer from a variety of post traumatic stress disorders. As many as 30–50 per cent of children will show significant symptomatology, at least when carefully assessed. Sadly, their problems are not always recognized by their parents and teachers. The three studies that have followed children over a year post trauma agree in finding that there is only a slow resolution of the problems in that time. Two of the studies find that the initial level of reported distress is highly predictive of later adjustment, and they also report a strong linear relationship between the level of exposure to life threatening situations and subsequent psychopathology. Before going on to consider how services should respond to these identified needs, let us look at the phenomenology presented by children in greater detail, paying particular attention to the question of the developmental changes that may occur in the expression of the distress.

Common stress reaction in children

Sleep disturbance

Almost all children had major sleep problems in the first few weeks. They reported fears of the dark, fear of being alone, intrusive thoughts when things are quiet, bad dreams, nightmares, and waking through the night. Problems persisted over many months. Use of music to divert thoughts helped.

Separation difficulties

Initially, most wanted to be physically close to their surviving parents, often sleeping in the parental bed over the first few weeks. Some distressed parents found their clinginess difficult to cope with.

Concentration difficulties

During the day, children had major problems concentrating on school work. When it was silent in the classroom they had intrusive memories of what had happened to them.

Memory problems

They also had problems remembering new material, or even some old skills such as reading music.

Intrusive thoughts

All were troubled by repetitive thoughts about the accident. These occurred at any time, although often triggered off by environmental stimuli, for example movement on a bus, noise of glass smashing, sound of rushing water, or sight of tables laid out like the ship's cafeteria. Thoughts intruded when they were otherwise quiet.

Talking with parents

Many did not want to talk about their feelings with their parents so as not to upset the adults. Thus, parents were often unaware of the details of the children's suffering, although they could see they were in difficulty. There was often a great sense of frustration between parents and children.

Talking with peers

At some points, survivors felt a great need to talk over their experiences with peers. Unfortunately, the timing was often wrong. Peers held back from asking in case they upset the survivor further; the survivor often felt rejected.

Heightened alertness to dangers

Most were wary of all forms of transport – not willing to put their safety into anyone else's hands. They were more aware of other dangers. They were affected by reports of other disasters.

Foreshortened future

Many felt that they should live each day to the full and not plan far ahead. They lost trust in long-term planning.

Fears

Most had fears of travelling by sea and air. Many had fears of swimming and of the sound of rushing water.

Irritability

Many of the children found themselves much more irritable than previously, both with parents and peers. Some found that they got much more angry than before the disasters.

Guilt

'Survivor guilt' has long been discussed as a paradoxical reaction following a disaster. Inexplicably, this symptom, so characteristic of post traumatic disorders, is not considered in DSM-III-R although it was regarded as a central feature of the earlier definition. Child and adolescent survivors often feel guilty that they are alive when others have died. They feel guilty that they might have done more to help others during the disaster. Less frequently discussed, but present nevertheless, they sometimes also feel guilty about things they did during the crisis in order to survive. Guilt has been a particularly strong theme among adolescents surviving the *Jupiter* sinking.

Depression

As noted in Figure 8.3 adolescents from the *Jupiter* report significantly higher rates of depression than do controls of the same age. While those figures refer to self-report on questionnaires, similar findings are confirmed on detailed clinical interviews. A small but significant number of children became clinically depressed; some had suicidal thoughts and even took overdoses in the year after the accident.

Bereavement

Particularly in the *Herald of Free Enterprise* disaster, a number of children were bereaved and no treatment plan could ignore the children's grief. Bereavement reactions complicate the presenting picture of symptoms, but must be attended to.

Anxiety and panic

A significant number of children became very anxious after the accidents, although it is our impression that the appearance of panic attacks was sometimes considerably delayed. Usually, it is possible to identify stimuli in the child's immediate environment that trigger off panic attacks, hence the need to get very detailed accounts of the impact of the trauma on all the child's senses.

These commonly occurring symptoms are almost identical with those recognized by the American Psychiatric Association (1987) in its Diagnostic and Statistical Manual, Third Edition Revised (APA, DSM-III-R, 1987) as comprising post traumatic stress disorder. The defining characteristics are summarized in Figure 8.5. It should be noted that there is not complete agreement on how best to define PTSD, especially as it manifests in children. Indeed, the World Health Organization (1988) in its *International Classification of Diseases: 10th Edition* (WHO, ICD-10, 1988) regards numbing of affect as a frequent but not necessary component of PTSD.

(A) The person has experienced an event that is outside the range of usual human experience and that would be markedly distressing to almost anyone, e.g., serious threat to one's life or physical integrity; serious threat or harm to one's children, spouse, or other close relatives and friends; sudden destruction of one's home or community; or seeing another person who has recently been, or is being, seriously injured or killed as the result of an accident or physical violence.

(B) The traumatic event is persistently re-experienced in at least one of the following ways:

    (1) recurrent and intrusive distressing recollections of the event (in young children, repetitive play in which themes or aspects of the trauma are expressed)

    (2) recurrent distressing dreams of the event

    (3) sudden acting or feeling as if the traumatic event were recurring (includes a sense of reliving the experience, illusions, hallucinations, and dissociative [flashback] episodes, even those that occur upon awakening or when intoxicated)

    (4) intense psychological distress at exposure to events that symbolize or resemble an aspect of the traumatic event, including anniversaries of the trauma

(C) Persistent avoidance of stimuli associated with the trauma of numbing of general responsiveness (not present before the trauma), as indicated by at least three of the following:

    (1) efforts to avoid thoughts or feeling associated with the trauma

    (2) efforts to avoid activities or situations that arouse recollections of the trauma

    (3) inability to recall an important aspect of the trauma (psychogenic amnesia)

    (4) markedly diminished interest in significant activities (in young children, loss of recently acquired development skills such as toilet training or language skills)

    (5) feeling of detachment or estrangement from others

    (6) restricted range of affect, e.g., unable to have loving feelings

    (7) sense of a foreshortened future, e.g., does not expect to have a career, marriage, or children, or a long life

(D) Persistent symptoms of increased arousal (not present before the trauma), as indicated by at least two of the following:

    (1) difficulty falling or staying asleep

    (2) irritability or outbursts of anger

    (3) difficulty concentrating

    (4) hypervigilance

    (5) exaggerated startle response

    (6) physiologic reactivity upon exposure to events that symbolize or resemble an aspect of the traumatic event (e.g., a woman who was raped in an elevator breaks out in a sweat when entering any elevator)

(E) Duration of the disturbance (symptoms in B, C, and D) of at least one month.

Specify delayed onset if the onset of symptoms was at least six months after the trauma.

Figure 8.5 DSM-III-R criteria for post traumatic stress disorder

Developmental perspectives

Having said that the diagnostic category of PTSD has heuristic value, it is also important to consider some developmental aspects that will affect children differently from adults. There are very few, even anecdotal, accounts of the effects of disasters on preschool children. The younger the child, the more one relies on information from parents and if they, too, have been traumatized, it is difficult to sort out direct effects of the trauma on the children from those mediated by effects on the parents. Various 'authorities' write that very young children may show all sorts of regressive behaviour or antisocial behaviour, and they may well do, but there is little hard evidence. Parents may avoid talking to the child about what happened. However, it is possible to get children as young as 4 to 6 years old to describe vividly what they had experienced, much to their parents' surprise.

A number of the pre-school children who survived the sinking of the *Herald* were reported by their parents and teachers to get involved in repetitive play or drawings involving themes about the ship. One 4-year-old girl involved her playmates in endless games of nurses patching up the injured, and this went on for many months. A 6-year-old boy drew many pictures of 'the bad ferry' and spoke about it often in class with an understanding teacher. The day that the headteacher took the class, she forbade him talking about it again. That night he began having nightmares and a few months later he tried to kill himself by poking a metal rod into the electric socket. He said he wanted to die to stop the pictures of the bad ferry in his head.

Three other pre-school boys became aggressive and antisocial both at home and at school. In all three cases, their parents knew they were still upset thinking about the ferry, but they could never talk about it to anyone. When things got bad, they would gouge out pieces of plaster or destroy toys or pick fights with other children.

Very young children have only limited understanding of the life-threatening nature of disasters. Even so, we know from other studies of the concepts of death and dying that some pre-school children have very adult concepts of these. It is important that we remember the range of individual differences in cognitive awareness when discussing (or not discussing) the effects of disasters with children.

Children over 10 years of age have usually a very good understanding that their lives were threatened. Young teenagers often report a sense of foreshortened future: what is the point of planning anything when the fates can be so capricious? This realization is very difficult for parents to cope with.

Indeed, parents are often at a loss to know how best to react. If they were directly affected by the same disaster, they are having to cope with their own reactions at the same time as trying to support their children. Following the Australian bush fires, McFarlane (1987) found that eight months on, the families showed increased levels of conflict, irritability and withdrawal, with maternal overprotection quite common. The adjustment of the parents themselves was an important determinant of the adjustment of the children. In particular, he comments that 'families who did not share their immediate reactions to disaster may have had more trouble with their long-term adjustment . . . and experienced a greater degree of estrangement'. Equally important, the child's reaction to the fire affected the adjustment of the family, emphasizing the reciprocal interactions among members of a family system.

Teenagers who survived the *Herald of Free Enterprise* capsize often found it very hard to share their feelings with their parents. They would go out of the house a lot to avoid talking about it. Parents were often frustrated that they wanted to reach out to their children but did not know how to. Behaviourally, the children looked as if they had developed lots of interests outside the home; in reality, they were avoiding dealing with the effects of the trauma.

When child survivors of a mass transport disaster are scattered over many schools, there is, perhaps, more excuse for teachers being ill-prepared to deal with problems that manifest in the classroom. When children have returned from a traumatic school outing, there can be no such excuse. Children may well have enormous problems concentrating in class and in doing their homework. If they are not sleeping properly, all this gets exacerbated. Children are sensitized to a wide variety of stimuli, mention of which may trigger an emotional reaction, as in the child who had to read about the evacuation from Dunkirk. Teachers need to make arrangements for child survivors to leave the classroom when such events occur.

For example, children returning to a very caring school after the sinking of the *Jupiter* entered a geography classroom where the walls were covered with projects on 'great disasters of the world'. Their upset was immediate and the connection obvious. Less obvious was the pressure put on a boy whose GCSE project had not survived the sinking of the *Herald*. Unable to concentrate on new learning, he was still pressurized to rewrite his missing project, until the problem was drawn to the school's attention. The teacher had, understandably, focused more on the impending exams than the current problems and these were then very quickly resolved.

Teachers need to be aware, too, of the reactions of other pupils towards the survivors. One 8 year old suffered silently for weeks after a classmate said, 'I wish you'd died in the ferry'. A 12-year-old girl had to cope with taunts about being orphaned. These episodes only came to light during a group run for the child survivors (Yule and Williams 1990).

Treatment needs

Beverley Raphael's (1986) book, *When Disaster Strikes*, is an excellent introduction to the whole area of disasters and their emotional aftermath. Unfortunately, little is written about treating child survivors. In many cases of natural disasters – flooding, fires, tornadoes, earthquakes – people emphasize the need to facilitate the rebuilding of the community, to treat people in groups in which children can participate. In the case of mass transport disasters, there is no natural group and with survivors scattered over thousands of square miles, it is difficult to get useful groups established. In the case of school journey disasters, there are clear groups to work with. So what work needs to be done?

In the immediate aftermath, children usually need to be reunited with their parents and family. Even teenagers may go back to sleeping in their parents' bed. Tolerance and understanding are called for. Survivors need to talk over what happened so as to get the sequence of events clear in their minds as well as to master the feelings that recall engenders. Repetitive retelling is not enough alone. Professionals can help by creating a relatively safe environment in which such recounting can take place. Experiencing that the world does not come to an end when feelings are shared between parent and child can be very facilitating.

Learning that other survivors share similar, irrational guilt about surviving can help to get things in perspective. Learning how to deal with anxiety attacks, how to identify trigger stimuli, how to take each day as it comes – all are important therapeutic tasks.

However, these things should not be left to chance. Mental health professionals are rapidly learning that formal psychological debriefing can help adult victims of disaster (Dyregrov 1988). Yule and Udwin (forthcoming) describing their experience with girls who survived the sinking of the *Jupiter*, suggest that this can also be helpful with teenagers.

Ten days after the accident, they met with the teachers, the pupils, and many of the parents initially in separate groups throughout an afternoon. During this preliminary session, the pupils were encouraged to describe and share their reactions. By anticipating some of these, they were able to emphasize that their reactions were understood and were normal reactions to an abnormal experience. At the end of the afternoon, they brought the pupils and parents together and got them to share publicly some of their feelings. Hopefully, that gave permission for such discussions to take place more readily at home. Subsequently, they saw the more seriously affected girls in small groups to treat more specific fears, panic disorders and depression.

Rachman's (1980) paper on emotional processing is very helpful in formulating what to do with child survivors. Saigh (1986) gives one of the few accounts of therapy with a 6 year old who suffered PTSD after a bombing in Beirut. A flooding treatment proved very successful, but longer exposure sessions than normal were needed. There is a great need for similar treatment studies involving children from other types of disaster. Ayalon (1988) provides sensible suggestions culled from a variety of theoretical perspectives. She, too, emphasizes the need to help children make sense of what happened to them and to gain mastery over their feelings. To this end, many practitioners agree that children should be treated in small groups. They should be asked to write detailed accounts of their experience and to be helped to cope with the emotions that brings up. In addition, it is advised that they be given specific treatment for fears, phobias and any other avoidant behaviours. They should get practical help with sleep disorders. Given that intrusive thoughts seemed worse at night just before dropping off to sleep, many children have been advised to use portable tape-recorders to play music to distract them and blot out the thoughts. With better sleep, they were better able to face the thoughts in the safety of daylight.

Intervention in groups

Elsewhere (Yule and Williams, 1990), we describe in more detail what we actually did in treating children and parents who survived the *Herald of Free Enterprise* sinking. We began by assessing children and their parents as they were referred to us by their solicitors. Most were keen to receive help when offered, but then, as often happens with disaster victims, they took some time to engage. The problems of engaging all the members of a family who had been traumatized were immense.

One of the first things to strike us was the different levels of distress reported when children were seen separately from the parents. Parents who had also been on the ferry were having to cope with their own distress as well as try to comfort their children. Children proved acutely aware of their parents' distress and often were unwilling to describe their innermost thoughts in front of their parents for fear of distressing them further. Parents were uncomfortably aware that their children, particularly their teenagers, were distressed, but they did not know the content of that distress nor how to broach any discussion. Thus, as part of the assessment procedure, we would see the family together initially to get a brief overview of what they had experienced, having usually already received a witness statement prepared by the family's solicitors. Then each member would be separately interviewed and finally we would see them all together for a few minutes. During this final meeting, we would put to them that it had been very hard to share each others' experiences for fear of upsetting each other further. By showing that we understood some of the difficulties (which we soon began to do) we were able to get them talking a little among themselves about what happened to them on the boat and how they had been subsequently. Most families seemed to find this systematic history taking and discussion of their reactions within a relatively safe setting to be quite helpful.

The groups were open to any survivor to attend and met initially at monthly intervals over about one year, tailing off to every six to eight weeks thereafter. They seem to be drawing to a natural close some three years after the disaster. It is our impression that the children appreciated an opportunity to share their feelings with others who had been there, without having to explain everything to outsiders. They took advantage of the cognitive-behavioural, problem-solving approach whereby efforts were made to help them identify things they were finding difficult, to place these within a framework that suggested that most of the problems were understandable reactions to abnormal circumstances, and to use the resources of the group to develop solutions to the identified problems. The therapist working directly with the children also acted as go-between with the parents' group.

The parallel group with parents had the dual task of addressing the parents' and other relatives' own distress as well as discussing how best they could support the children. As with the children, the adults were very supportive of each other and the group quickly became very cohesive. Two years after the disaster, it was deemed appropriate to organize a group crossing of the channel by ferry. The first attempt at organizing the crossing was abortive as a group member volunteered to make the arrangements and then could not face up to them. It was not until September 1989 that we managed to organize a trip. Two weeks before the due date, the pleasure boat, *Marchioness*, sank in the Thames with considerable loss of life. Not surprisingly, most of the families called off and we crossed with only one family. The ferry company was very sensitive to the family's needs and the trip was very successful. The 10 year old who had previously been unable to face up to a crossing showed some signs of anxiety but was quickly calmed by his parents and the welfare officer. He felt a great sense of achievement at the end of the day.

Involvement of schools

At various points above, we have noted the reluctance of schools to get involved in studies of child victims and the sometimes inexplicable insensitivity to children's distress. For example, after one well-publicized disaster, a party of children returned to their school to be banned from discussing their experiences. Whereas another party who had been abroad at the same time were allowed to display photographs of their trip in the school hall as usual, the traumatized children were forbidden to put up any photographs at all. Needless to say this resulted in the children feeling very unsupported and very angry.

And yet at other schools, teachers have been very sensitive and supportive, although at times unsure how best to react to the problems the children present. It is as much a dilemma for teachers as for parents to know how much of subsequent problems to attribute to the disaster and how much to adolescence. There is also a feeling that after a few months, people should stop making allowances and survivors should settle down and get on with things. Our evidence would suggest that in as many as half the children who have experienced a life-threatening trauma, there will still be significant psychopathology manifesting at school for at least fifteen months after the event. Clearly, school teachers will need support from mental health professionals to ensure that they can cope with these problems.

Having said that, one has recently heard the comment that it is fashionable to lay on disaster counselling for survivors. Some people are clearly concerned lest automatic intervention does more harm than good. Given that part of any intervention necessarily forces children to confront unhappy, distressing memories, it is understandable that parents and teachers become protective towards the children when they see them being upset by the therapists. Without hard evidence on the efficacy of various interventions, it can be difficult to convince all parties that such upset may be healthy. However, once again one must take note of individual differences in reactions and individual needs in treatment. Following the recent earthquakes in San Francisco, it was said by a very experienced child psychiatrist that there could not have been a single child in the school system who was not asked to draw an earthquake in school over the next few days! Such well-intentioned interventions overlook the differing needs of children and may indeed do harm to some if conducted insensitively.

Earlier, we have argued that it is possible to identify high risk groups at an early post trauma stage. Our own data and those of Nader and Pynoos (1990) show that the scores of high risk groups on measures of distress remain remarkably stable over a one-year period. We conclude from this that even in these early stages, it is possible to do some screening and ensure that services are delivered to the most needy.

Implications for service delivery and training

By their nature, disasters are unpredictable and yet one can predict that they will happen somewhere and sometime when least expected. This implies that it would be very cost-ineffective to have all services at a high state of readiness to cope with a disaster which may never happen in a particular health or education authority. Equally, now that we know the high levels of morbidity that follow a disaster, it would be irresponsible of any authority not to have plans as to how they will respond to the emotional needs following a disaster. Thus, each responsible authority should examine its civil disaster plan and decide on who will take the lead responsibility for responding after a disaster. Key statutory and voluntary groups should be identified and key people within those agencies should be trained in the rapidly emerging literature on how to cope with disasters.

It is a well-documented fact that after a disaster, many individuals and agencies offer help. Such altruism is to be applauded, but such offers need to be co-ordinated if chaos is to be avoided. All too often one sees rivalry and dissent with the victims and survivors being the losers. Each area disaster plan therefore needs to identify lead agencies who can co-ordinate the necessary help.

In our view, it is vital that the multiplicity of needs and their complexity are adequately recognized. This means that all helpers, from whatever discipline or background, need to be able to screen for serious problems and know when to refer on.

Discussion

It seems to us that it is now well established that children do show intense behavioural disturbances when the stressor is as massive as experienced at Zeebrugge. Some children can show amnesia for parts of the event and most experience intrusive thoughts and some experience full-blown flashbacks. We agree with Frederick (1985) that it is much more difficult to detect 'psychic numbing' in children. If anything, their pressing need to avoid situations that remind them of the accident drives them out of the house, where it will be discussed, and into a frenzy of social activities. They need to be constantly occupied and never silent in order to avoid intrusive, unwelcome thoughts. However, it should be noted that the draft form of ICD-10 also has difficulties with the concept of 'psychic numbing' and has relegated it from a necessary sign to one that may or may not be present. Thus, we would argue not only that most of the children whom we assessed suffered from Acute Adjustment Reactions that lasted upwards of a year, but also that their presenting symptoms justified the diagnosis of PTSD.

We were surprised at the failure of teachers to note the problems that children were experiencing at school. In part, this must be because they did not wish to acknowledge the horrors the children experienced and did not know how to respond to the needs. Similar reactions happened after the Bradford fire disaster when many schools refused to acknowledge that children who had been at the stadium but were not burned might have any psychological after effects. McFarlane (1987) in Australia was thwarted in his attempts to study the children who saw the bush fires because schools would not co-operate, saying it was best to let past things remain in the past. Thus, there is a consensus in recent literature that teachers report less psychopathology among child survivors than do parents, and that both report far less than the children themselves (McFarlane et al. 1987; Earls et al. 1988; Wolfe et al. 1987).

We have also raised the question of the validity of screening scales in studying the detailed effects of major disasters on children and concluded that on their own, without detailed interviews with the children, they are of limited value. Moreover, we have found that it is possible, and indeed valuable, to use the IES with children aged 8 upwards. The use of a children's depression inventory reveals the amount of sadness and depression felt by the child survivors as much as a year after the disaster. Pynoos et al. (1987), in their study of the effects of a fatal shooting attack on children in a school playground in Los Angeles, also found that traumatized children can report their experiences through completing questionnaires.

Finally, we have described the interventions we were able to mount. Undoubtedly the groups were of considerable value to the children and their parents. There are other problems that resources, time and distance have not allowed us to tackle. Thus many children still have phobias of travelling by ferry, of swimming and of other travel. Clearly, these could be treated by well-known behavioural means.

The capsize of the *Herald of Free Enterprise* and the sinking of the *Jupiter* were both major mass transport disasters and as such illustrate many important differences from disasters that hit already cohesive communities. The passengers on the *Herald* had nothing in common with fellow travellers, other than being on the ferry at the fateful time. They were scattered throughout England shortly afterwards, and it was only at considerable personal cost and inconvenience that those attending our groups were able to come so regularly. In our view they would not have been able to obtain the sort of support otherwise, and this has clear implications for those local authority and government officials who have responsibility for planning for the aftermath of major disasters. In the case of the *Jupiter*, it was potentially easier for schools to organize help in groups, but it was surprising how many did not do this.

Acknowledgements

We would like to thank our colleagues in the Psychology Department of the Institute of Psychiatry who shared with us the task of assessing the victims, and particularly Dr V. Rippere who suggested some of the measures used. Our thanks are also due to the solicitors who referred the clients and took the initial load of obtaining witness statements. But above all, we would like to thank the survivors themselves for agreeing to allow us to use this material in order to advance all our understanding.

References

American Psychiatric Association (1987) *Diagnostic and Statistical Manual of Mental Disorders* (Third Edition – Revised), Washington, DC: APA.
Ayalon, O. (1988) *Rescue! Community Oriented Preventive Education for Coping with Stress*, Haifa: Nord Publications.

Birleson, P. (1981) The validity of depressive disorder in childhood and the development of a self-rating scale: a research report, *Journal of Child Psychology and Psychiatry* 22: 73–88.

Birleson, P., Hudson, I., Buchanan, D.G. and Wolff, S. (1987) Clinical evaluation of a self-rating scale for depressive disorder in childhood (Depression Self-Rating Scale), *Journal of Child Psychology and Psychiatry* 28: 43–60.

Dollinger, S.J., O'Donnell, J.P. and Staley, A.A. (1984) Lightning-strike disaster: effects on children's fears and worries, *Journal of Consulting and Clinical Psychology* 52: 1,028–38.

Dyregrov, A. (1988) Critical incident stress debriefings, unpublished manuscript, Research Center for Occupational Health and Safety, University of Bergen, Norway.

Earls, F., Smith, E., Reich, W. and Jung, K.G. (1988) Investigating psychopathological consequences of a disaster in children: a pilot study incorporating a structured diagnostic approach, *Journal of the American Academy of Child and Adolescent Psychiatry* 27: 90–5.

Frederick, C.J. (1985) Children traumatized by catastrophic situations, in S. Eth and R. Pynoos (eds) *Post-Traumatic Stress Disorder in Children*, Washington DC: American Psychiatric Press.

Galante, R. and Foa, D. (1986) An epidemiological study of psychic trauma and treatment effectiveness after a natural disaster, *Journal of the American Academy of Child Psychiatry* 25: 357–63.

Garmezy, N. (1986) Children under severe stress: critique and comments, *Journal of the American Academy of Child Psychiatry* 25: 384–92.

Garmezy, N. and Rutter, M. (1985) Acute reactions to stress, in M. Rutter and L. Hersov (eds) *Child and Adolescent Psychiatry: Modern Approaches*, 2nd end, Oxford: Basil Blackwell.

Handford, H.A., Mayes, S.O., Mattison, R.E., Humphrey, F.J., Bagnato, S., Bixler, E.O. and Kales, J.D. (1986) Child and parent reaction to the TMI nuclear accident, *Journal of the American Academy of Child Adolescent Psychiatry* 25: 346–55.

Horowitz, M.J., Wilner, N. and Alvarez, W. (1979) Impact of event scale: a measure of subjective stress, *Psychosomatic Medicine* 41: 209–18.

McFarlane, A.C. (1987) Family functioning and overprotection following a natural disaster: the longitudinal effects of post-traumatic morbidity, *Australian and New Zealand Journal of Psychiatry* 21: 210–18.

McFarlane, A.C., Policansky, S. and Irwin, C.P. (1987) A longitudinal study of the psychological morbidity in children due to a natural disaster, *Psychological Medicine* 17: 727–38.

Miller, L.C., Barrett, C.L., Hampe, E. and Noble, H. (1972) Factor structure of children's fears, *Journal of Consulting and Clinical Psychology* 39: 264–8.

Nader, K., Pynoos, R.S., Fairbanks, L. and Frederick, C. (1990) Children's PTSD Reactions one year after a sniper attack at their school, *American Journal of Psychiatry* 147: 1526–30.

Ollendick, T.H., Yule, W. and Ollier, K. (1991) Fears in British children and their relationship to manifest anxiety and depression, *Journal of Child Psychology and Psychiatry* 32: 321–31.

Pynoos, R.S. and Eth, S. (1986) Witness to violence: the child interview, *Journal of the American Academy of Child Psychiatry* 25: 306–19.

Pynoos, R.S., Frederick, C., Nader, K., Arroyo, W., Steinberg, A., Eth, S., Nunez, F. and Fairbanks, L. (1987) Life threat and posttraumatic stress in school-age children, *Archives of General Psychiatry* 44: 1,057–63.

Pynoos, R.S. and Nader, K. (1988) Psychological first aid and treatment approach for children exposed to community violence: research implications, *Journal of Traumatic Stress* 1: 243–67.

Quarantelli, E.L. (1985) An assessment of conflicting views on mental health: the consequences of traumatic events, in C.R. Figley (ed.) *Trauma and its Wake*, New York: Brunner/Mazel.

Quay, H.C. and Peterson, D.R. (1979) *Manual of the Behavior Problem Checklist* (unpublished).

Rachman, S. (1980) Emotional processing, *Behaviour Research and Therapy* 18: 51–60.
Raphael, B. (1986) *When Disaster Strikes: A Handbook for the Caring Professions*, London: Hutchinson.
Reynolds, C.R. and Richmond, B.O. (1978) What I think and feel: a revised measure of children's manifest anxiety, *Journal of Abnormal Child Psychology* 6: 271–80.
Rutter, M. (1967) A children's behaviour questionnaire for completion by teachers: preliminary findings, *Journal of Child Psychology and Psychiatry* 8: 1–11.
Saigh, P.A. (1986) In vitro flooding in the treatment of a 6-yr-old boy's posttraumatic stress disorder, *Behaviour Research and Theory* 24: 685–8.
Staley, A.A. and O'Donnell, J.P. (1984) A developmental analysis of mothers' reports of normal children's fears, *Journal of Genetic Psychology* 144: 165–78.
Wolfe, V.V., Wolfe, D.A. Gentile, C. and LaRose, L. (1987) Children's Impact of Traumatic Events Scale, unpublished manuscript, University of Western Ontario, London, Ontario, Canada.
World Health Organization (1988) *International Classification of Diseases*, 10th Edition (ICD-10), WHO: Geneva.
Yule, W. and Udwin, O. (forthcoming) Screening child survivors for post-traumatic stress disorders: experiences from the *Jupiter* sinking (submitted for publication).
Yule, W. and Williams, R. (1990) Post traumatic stress reactions in children, *Journal of Traumatic Stress* 3(2): 279–95.
Yule, W., Udwin, O. and Murdoch, K. (1990) The *Jupiter* sinking: effects on children's fears, depression and anxiety, *Journal of Child Psychology and Psychiatry* 31: 1051–61.

PART III

Settings

9

The residential community as a therapeutic environment

MARTIN SCHERER

Introduction

Between the 1944 and 1981 Education Acts residential special education and child care grew substantially. Contemporary research showed that segregated residential provision may present as many dangers as benefits. This research provided the moral justification for drastically reducing government expenditure on residential provision. Many local authorities no longer maintain residential special education or child care. The freedom of choice is curtailed for children in need.

The residential therapeutic community approach started in the 1930s and pioneered a radically different approach for a minority of children and adolescents whose behaviour caused them to be rejected by society. This chapter seeks to describe and critically examine this approach. Its practice is examined in the light of predominant theories and the current demands of good provision. It finds that the practice of therapeutic communities predates the expectations of the Education Act 1981 and the Children Act 1989. Therapeutic communities similarly grew during the period to 1981, but remained a relatively minority provision. They existed outside the mainstream of educational provision, training and research.

By rejecting residential provision as a whole we may be guilty of throwing out the baby with the bath water. The growing rates of school truancy and suspension suggest that the needs of children with emotional and behavioural difficulties are not being met by integration. We may then be forced to reinvent the wheel that is today the therapeutic community.

What is a therapeutic community?

Origins

Bridgeland (1971) provides a comprehensive account of therapeutic communities, their origins in the 1930s, and points to some of the notable examples: New Barns (Franklin and Wills), Mulberry Bush (Docker Drysdales), Cotswold

Community (Balbernie), Peper Harrow (Rose) and some of the originators of innovative residential education such as Aichorn, Homer Lane, A.S. Neil and Bettleheim. We may include Shotton Hall (Lenhoff), Warleigh Manor, and in Canada, Warrendale (Brown). The name of the community is often synonymous with the name of its originator (in parentheses). Therapeutic communities were often established as a radical alternative to existing and traditionally punitive approaches.

Definition

The term 'community' suggests common rights of its members and common ownership of property and social structures. The term 'therapy' suggests some attempt to meet and resolve the problems of its members. Readers involved in therapeutic communities today or in the past will find this definition too extensive, wanting or inaccurate. This is merely testimony to the nebulous nature of the term and that different approaches within the field have failed to reach a broad agreement by sharing experiences and methods.

From Wills (1973; 1979), we can take the specific term Planned Environment Therapy (PET) and apply it generically to all therapeutic communities that display one common feature, a use of everyday shared living experiences between the worker and clients to jointly achieve solutions to the problems faced by the clients. Given such a broad definition a whole range of establishments and approaches may claim to be therapeutic communities, including those using a behavioural approach, such as Chelfham Mill (Burland). In his definition of PET, Wills (1979) specifically excluded behavioural approaches. The problem with definitions is that they do not expose the reader to the behavioural expectations and consequences embodied in those phrases. A more detailed description is required to bring the reader into close contact with the living experience of a therapeutic community.

Description

A written description is only a valid example in the experience of the author. However, it will serve to illustrate the practice of Franklin and Wills's definition. Contrast with some aspects of traditional organizations will serve the illustration.

Leadership and authority

All stable organizations maintain an authority and social structure that orders the lives of its participants towards the goals and aims of the organization. A system of establishing rules, or codes of conduct, the consequences for breaking the rules and how the consequences are applied. The status of the individual within the organization will vary by employed position, duration of service, age, sex and wealth. The higher the status, the greater the power of an individual to establish and maintain rules, and be excused for transgressing the rules. The participants see the system as legitimate to the extent that the authority brings order and predictability out of chaos and meets their needs and aspirations.

We may identify four ideal types of authority: traditional, bureaucratic, charismatic and democratic (Pugh and Higson 1989). Few organizations fit neatly into any one of these categories. Most organizations maintain more than one authority system. One will order the actions of individuals in their occupations, another may order individuals' social interaction. The systems may coexist independently, complement or compete with each other. Organizations that manage clients may feel that they order the social interaction, but the clients are equally likely to establish their own authority system. Organizations that maintain a strict hierarchy among staff with a clear demarcation between staff and clients, often result in client peer structures that mimic and exaggerate that structure. The peer group will establish its own 'pecking order', its own leaders and secret code of conduct, that are strongly anti-establishment. It will evolve a highly intuitive complex of non-verbal signals in which group discipline and loyalty can be maintained by the merest flicker of a muscle (Owen 1974).

Schools and children's homes often meet the problem of bullying. **Bullying** is an example of abuse where a socially or physically stronger individual or group extract entertainment (pain or ridicule), obedience, possessions or sexual favours from a weaker individual. Boarding schools developed extensive systems, including initiation rituals such as debagging, pinning and hedging. **Debagging** is an emotionally brutal sexual degradation, where the child's shorts are removed and the genitals abused. **Pinning** is where pins are stuck into the buttocks during a public ceremony. **'Hedging'** is where the new child is pushed through a hedge so that clothing is soiled or damaged. These rituals aim to silence the victim's complaint to the organization's authority by shame (debagging), fear of adult condemnation (crying out from pinning) or actually gain adults' complicit support (hedging, punishment for dirty clothes). Children who do report incidents are ostracized or 'Sent to Coventry'. Initiation rituals occur in the first term while bullies were usually in the second year. The bullies are often obliged to participate by the social system. The system is often generalized across the school, where all first years became 'fags'; that is obliged to run the errands of older pupils.

Traditional authority　The bullying system held an advantage for the school's authority: it taught obedience without question. However, it could also become a direct challenge as pupils were bullied into actions against the school. The solution was to incorporate the bullying system into the school's authority system, by the creation of prefects. Prefects had their 'fags', and punishments they could administer. The bullying thereby gained legitimacy: the school's authority, pupils and even victims became silent conspirators. If revealed, the initiation ceremonies were often justified – 'It did no harm to me, makes a man a man'. Unquestioning obedience to authority is functional to many organizations. Without any rational analysis of why the system exists it is difficult to question or justify reasons for change. Traditional authority systems are very resistant to change.

Bureaucratic authority　Therapeutic communities also maintain dual systems. First, to meet the overt goal of the establishment, staff are employed in specific roles as teachers, child-care staff, secretaries, cooks and cleaners. Their role is determined by the employer, whether it is an independent establishment or one managed by the local authority. The employed role reflects national conditions of service and pay. Teachers, child-care staff and nurses therefore receive very different pay and conditions for similar work. This often creates divisions and sometimes conflict in residential work. In some rare examples staff are paid according to personal need. In a bureaucratic authority system the rules are more clearly stated and often written in contracts or standard procedures. They are usually designed to meet the goals of the organization, more than the needs of its individuals. It is easy to confuse the goals of education and social service establishments. It may seem that children are the consumers of education, but the real consumers are those who pay; local and national government, parents and employers. Children are the products of the education system and like any raw material that is shaped into a product, children have little say in the process. This is also true of child care establishments that serve the state's duty to house a child where the parent is absent or considered incapable.

Charismatic authority Charismatic organizations are usually those originated by an individual or small group, such as religious sects, political or ideological movements, and small businesses. Christ, Marx, Fox (Quakers) and Henry Ford are prominent examples of each. The leader is seen as endowed with exceptional qualities, knowledge or power. When that knowledge is put into practice by the participants their needs or aspirations may be met as never before. To survive and grow a charismatic organization needs to be remarkably successful, resilient to, or protected from the predominant and perhaps antagonistic ideas and practices of the wider society.

The leaders of therapeutic communities may be seen as charismatic. This is true whether they were the early pioneers (eg A.S. Neil, Wills) or those who followed in their footsteps (eg Balbernie). Their exceptional knowledge and quality were the new ideas, theories and practices they brought. Those of the Quakers and Freud show in the origins of therapeutic communities. Therapeutic communities usually cater for individuals who have been rejected by society. They are often established in the countryside and socially self-sufficient. The more self-sufficient the organization, the more likely that those new practices will gain stability and assurance. The more the practice appears to meet the needs of its members, the less likely society is to intrude. The geographic isolation and resulting social insulation may provide the protection necessary to enable disturbed clients to develop within a non-punitive environment and enable the establishment to develop new practices.

The strength of charismatic authority is also a source of weakness. While the insulation may protect it from hostile external influences it also denies it positive external influence. The organization then stagnates. Few, if any, therapeutic communities are so insular. Most provide education or social provision and so are subject to the expectations and inspection of relevant statutory authorities. Most have staff who either work or live, were trained or gain training, outside the community. All depend on referral of clients from external agencies and therefore exist within a market-place of available provision. To compete they must be seen to provide a high standard of provision. Charismatic leaders usually seek an influence that is wider than the boundaries of their establishment. Compared to traditional leaders they often attend more conferences, publish more about their practice and entertain more visitors and students.

A second problem with charismatic authority is that it makes inordinate demands of the leader. Any new situation requires the ruling of the leader who must regularly be available. Failure to meet the problem undermines the authority of the leader. Such organizations are essentially immature. This is often understood within therapeutic communities where the leader declines to provide a solution but requires the community to find an acceptable and successful solution for itself.

Finally, if authority is embodied in a single leader, it dissolves when that leader dies, retires or leaves through promotion. Within the organization there is competition between those who consider themselves to be the 'true heirs'. A new leader from outside will not be accepted, especially if they seek change. While therapeutic communities often have some very experienced staff who may share the burden of leadership, many therapeutic communities have not survived the departure of their founder.

Democratic authority Democratic authority rests on the equal voting right of its members. A true democracy will not only elect its leaders but also determine the rules of conduct and the consequences of breaking those rules. The leaders are then its servants who implement the rules and undertake specified tasks of the organization.

The authority of a therapeutic community Like most real organizations therapeutic communities do not fit the simple ideal types of authority. Generally they tend to be originated by a charismatic leader, an influence that may be maintained in all small organizations. Having established, therapeutic communities tend to rest on two other forms of authority: first, the bureaucratic authority of employed staff roles, and second and more importantly for a discussion of therapy, the democratic authority of the community.

Membership

Most therapeutic communities exist to meet the need of adults, young people and less frequently young children, who may be described as maladjusted, delinquent, criminal, enduring emotional and behavioural difficulties or psychiatric illness. The approach of therapeutic communities tends to be applied in a residential context where most and perhaps all members, including staff, are resident. There is no reason the approach should not be extended to geriatric, mentally handicapped or even the so-called normal child or adult, in any context. The approach has been applied in day school units with considerable success.

Therapeutic communities often consist of sixty or more members, of whom approximately two thirds will be clients. The membership is fluid as clients resolve their problems and return to their families or move to independent living.

All residents are usually members; clients and staff including teachers, childcare staff and ancillary staff. Non-resident staff, such as cooks, cleaners, part-time staff and voluntary workers may assume membership if they wish. Individual involvement varies by the nature of their employed position, extent of the residence and personality.

Community property and shared responsibility

Each community member pays a small but equal membership subscription. The community uses this fund to pay for those items or services it chooses to purchase: stationery, records, tape recorders, cycles, trips out. Communal ownership entails communal responsibility, so there is a Treasurer and a person responsible for each item. The community needs a regular members' meeting to manage its affairs and will elect its own officers. As the areas of responsibility grow the community may need subcommittees. A common one is an entertainments committee that may organize a variety of events from discos and barn dances to concert revues and sports events to which parents, relatives, neighbours, friends and colleagues are invited. Those responsible are elected for a limited term by a majority, often secret, ballot. Given that most members are clients, they have the power to ensure that elected officers are clients. It is rare for a member of staff to become an elected officer. The roles are also used for therapeutic purposes. Within a supportive and protective environment clients are able to learn responsibility and service to the community. Unlike role-acting or teaching methods, the responsibilities of officers are very real in a therapeutic community. Officers will discuss their responsibility and any changes in procedures with the community. There is competition over the use of resources. The principles for resolving this competition and occasional conflict will be discussed in the community. Where the discussion results in new rules these are recorded as resolutions for all to read. A new member is encouraged to read the book of resolutions. By this means all members learn that there is a higher authority than the responsible individual alone, one to which they can make any complaints about abuse of the position of responsibility. That authority is not invested in an individual but the community itself.

Like bureaucratic authority the community is a rational and legal system. It establishes rules or conduct that aim to meet its goals. Unlike a bureaucratic system the authority is not invested in one person but the community. Voting within a therapeutic community is not the imposition of the will of the majority over the minority but an expression of consensus. Matters that do not reach a consensus generally are not seen as resolved.

The property of the community is separate from the property of the establishment. As the community grows in its responsibility, the establishment pass responsibility for items or areas of the building to the community. The community's ability to fulfil its responsibilities will fluctuate with the client group. If privileges are abused they may be withdrawn after discussion. The community itself may ask to be relieved of responsibility. The community and its members are allowed to make mistakes and learn from the consequences unless the personal damage or loss is greater than the benefit from learning. If the latter, staff may intervene and assume responsibility to protect clients or their property.

While community members may not determine the working role of staff they often have an influence over it. The community may form consumer subcommittees whose representatives may criticize, question, request changes or compliment the performance of the role in the way it affects the community and its members. The staff may equally comment on the actions of the community in the way they help or burden the staff's work. Where inmates of an institution have little influence or freedom of choice, they often receive a poor standard of provision. This is especially true of food. By enabling consumer influence, therapeutic communities often enjoy an enviable standard and variety of meals.

Community social structure

Any community sharing communal residence and possessions will experience conflicts, especially so when the community is one seeking to meet the needs of clients who lack social skills. The method of resolving those conflicts illustrates the social structure. A hierarchical authoritarian approach will refer conflict to a higher authority, who will punish the offender or assess the offender's special needs and make provision. This is not unlike the criminal courts where the victim is often forgotten as the state assumes the role of victim. The victim may be compensated by the state or may seek compensation through the civil courts. The offender may feel equally alienated by the circumstances of a court, where they have little personal opportunity to express their position and punishment is handed from 'betters'. Alienated, they may feel resentful against the system as a whole.

The community meeting   In a therapeutic community every member has the right to bring a complaint, apology or question to the community: for example, a complaint by a victim of offence, an apology by an offender wishing to resolve the matter before it escalates any further, or a question by a person who feels disturbed or even curious about the actions of other members. The complaint, apology or question is listened to and all participants are asked to give their account of the event and what lead up to it. An illustration will help. A member walks through a common room, sees one boy hit another and subsequently brings a question to the community. Therapeutic communities do not tolerate assault. In silence the offender refuses to explain his behaviour. He looks deeply ashamed, unable to face his accuser or the community. One may interpret the behaviour as showing remorse, an appropriate response that promises an early apology enabling the matter to be quickly resolved. However, another member states that the day before he heard the victim saying that the offender's mother was a prostitute. The offender starts to cry and seeks to leave the meeting but is encouraged to stay, supported by the community as the attention is turned on to the apparent victim. In his defence the victim states that he was told it was true by another who was also an observer to the event. The attention turns to the observer, asked why he was spreading malicious gossip. Again there is silence. Gradually the community pieces together the circumstances. The observer was until recently a close friend of the offender and to him the offender had admitted his feelings about his mother's 'boyfriend'. Since then the offender had found a new friend. Feeling rejected, the observer sought revenge. However, the offender was bigger than him and he feared him. So he got someone else to fulfil the revenge by feeding him with the most damaging information. The roles now reverse. The observer may now be seen as the offender, the victim as the dupe and the offender the victim of damaging verbal abuse. The community will be deeply concerned about the person who originally heard the offensive remark the day before but didn't question it in the community meeting. The meeting does not seek to punish, but to help those involved understand the causes of their behaviour and how they may behave differently. The community will tolerate and support them while they do and may seek to monitor the situation. There is a high status to be gained by explaining, understanding and learning, which compensates for disapproval. Bullying and peer rebellion against adults are problems that the therapeutic community system was designed to resolve. In the place of a hierarchical structure the community offers equality. The community may disapprove of offensive behaviours but in the place of punishment by adults, the community offers understanding by peers. In the place of a conspiracy of silence it expects all members to question disturbing or threatening behaviour.

Community officers and staff may sometimes have to make decisions or act in a way that requires explanation and may deserve apology even though they were required to undertake it because of their employed or elected position. The most obvious but rare example is where a child out of control and endangering themselves or others may need to be controlled, and removed from the situation. Such an incident is threatening and disturbing to all about, not least the adult who has to undertake it. The community meeting will want to know what happened and why, how the person was cared for and are they now happy about the outcome. Explaining the situation relieves much of the pressure. The resulting discussion may conclude how others about may help, if only in removing themselves from it, thereby removing the need to control the child. Carers and adults who explain themselves may find that some part or all their actions are criticized, but they will find understanding and maybe support in future situations. The position of adults is then not so lonely or vulnerable.

Generally, such matters wait until a regular community meeting, which may occur after each meal. However, every member has the right to call an emergency meeting at any time. All members attend such meetings unless they have some reason preventing their attendance. A poorly attended meeting will avoid reaching any decisions as it feels under-represented. If the discussion reveals that a key participant is missing, then the matter will not be discussed in their absence. Before deferring any unfinished business the community will satisfy itself that the participants to an event can reasonably survive until the next meeting. If not, the meeting may ask a member to support the individual until that time. Conflicts that threaten the stability of many members will not be deferred until the matter is resolved or all involved are adequately supported.

The community will not seek to impose its conclusion on any individual, instead seeking compromise, preferring the suggested resolution to come from those who bear its consequence. In this sense the therapeutic community's resolution of conflicts and transgressions of rules is very unlike a court.

The community may reach the conclusion that it itself is responsible for the conflict in failing to recognize that such an incident may arise and establishing guidance for conduct in such circumstances. New resolutions are then decided and recorded; resolutions that fall out of date may be questioned and altered or abandoned.

The organization of the therapeutic community illustrates the sharing of responsibility for social conduct. This removes the conditions that create the traditional 'them and us' between clients and staff, where the staff hand down decisions to the clients. Instead the clients share the responsibility for property and decisions of the community. There are no peer groups to conspire with, to rebel against adults, for the property is largely owned by peers and the decision largely taken by peers. If an individual feels aggrieved by a decision they have the opportunity to have the grievance aired and possibly influence the decision, seek a compromise, or gain an understanding of why.

Equality or parity of esteem?   People are not equal within a therapeutic community: the notion of equality is idealistic and never achieved in any context. People have different skills and attributes that are differentially valued. A member of staff with an employed role that may be externally perceived as lowly, may nevertheless gain a high status among the community for their contribution to community living and therapy. This may cause conflict. A new senior member of staff may feel inadequate and undermined as the group pays more attention to the therapeutic contribution of an experienced but junior member of staff or even child. Similar conflicts exist for children where an older new member finds themselves subject to the authority of the community chairman who is younger than themselves. The equality that therapeutic communities seek to establish is parity of esteem where every individual has the right to express their views, be listened to, considered and have their contribution valued. Parity of esteem provides the basis for development of self-esteem and personal adequacy from which the individual may feel confident in learning and personal development.

Social or self-control   The community meeting is a very successful and subtle method of social control. However, social control is usually administered by a power group over a less powerful group. The community meeting transcends this limited control. It is self-control of the community over itself and its individual members. By learning to participate in mutual self-control, children may develop the skills of self-control. In the same way that staff may hand items of property or running of events to a mature and responsible community, staff may hand responsibility for social conduct to the community.

Skills required of new members

Clients   The basic skills required of new members are the abilities to converse, recall and reflect. The method therefore seems to exclude certain client groups, but it can be adapted to suit their needs. Children who repeatedly fail to respond to the community meeting may be placed by the community in the care of an adult they appoint. Being 'in care' is a limited use of the term used in social work. It means that the person holding the care, 'the carer', holds responsibility for their behaviour. For the duration of the care the child is denied full community membership, voting rights and unsupervised access to community property. Any complaint would be brought against the person holding the care, and not the person 'in care'. If the complaint was upheld, the carer, not the child, apologized or made amends. The relationship is not unlike that of parent and young child, where the child is forgiven but the parent held accountable. We may note the increasing trend in society to hold parents legally accountable for their children's behaviour. Bearing the consequences of misbehaviour the carer will not permit the child to participate in social events until they are confident that the child can do so without causing offence.

In appointing a 'carer' the community gives special privileges of control and authority to the carer. The community will therefore frequently wish to question the actions of the carer to ensure the position is not abused, that the person in care is given every encouragement to learn socially appropriate behaviour and the care is ended as soon as possible. Being denied full community membership, including the right to vote and hold office, is a loss of personal liberty, one taken very seriously.

Some staff will have their families with young children living in the community. If their children are afforded the freedom of the establishment they themselves may inadvertently cause offence. Hence the children are often implicitly considered 'in care' of their parent, who is answerable for their behaviour. Staff children grow and may wish for full and equal membership of the community. In their application, the community will want to know if they have fully discussed it with their parents. The community will be reluctant to intervene in family matters, and may seek deferment giving more time for both parent and adult to discuss. The application may be rejected, taken on trial for a probationary period or accepted, even in the face of parental objection.

Staff The skills required of staff are not dissimilar to those required of clients; the abilities to listen, accept criticism, understand social behaviour and the events in which it occurs, accept the view of the majority and apologize or make reparations. Most adults, parents, teachers, care staff and nurses are familiar with a clear demarcation between roles of clients or children and staff. Working in a therapeutic community requires a radical change in the perception of these relative positions. It is an abrupt and sometimes threatening challenge. Adults often find it extremely difficult to learn from or apologize to children or adolescents. Admitting error may be felt to threaten the authority of their position and the security of those for whom they have a duty of care. Failings are shamefully hidden or covered by a show of authority. Many staff will unconsciously or even consciously defend 'being adult' with its traditional rights and unquestioned power. They may even see the community meeting as an abdication of staff responsibilities and duty of care.

Without acceptance by staff of their equal position, the approach may degenerate into lip-service to idealistic notions of equality. An abrupt lesson of early adolescence is that adults and parents are human and fallible. Adults who are able to learn and apologize provide children with a model from whom to learn how to apologize, how to put things right and how to openly overcome their shame of their misbehaviour.

Within children's establishments, adults are usually staff. Within a therapeutic community they are equal members who happen to be adults. The greatest danger of adults is that they will dominate the community meeting. While it may be efficient to give the 'right' answers to a problem, it denies the community the opportunity to stumble towards and discover its own 'right' answers. The contribution of adults is better guided through elucidating or suggesting questions rather than directly framed. However, adults do have equal rights in the community and may sometimes bring personal complaints. Adults need to learn when to step out of the role of a member of the community and into the role of a member of staff. This is usually when they are fulfilling the specific role they are employed for, as a house parent or teacher.

Many therapeutic communities assume that adults may have their problems and recognize that living and working together in a residential context with disturbed clients leads to conflict and personality clashes. Hence staff meet regularly, initially to discuss the business of the week but also to permit the resolving of conflicts (Browne 1991). The same care and support is given as by the community meeting.

Therapy

Terms used to describe a client also direct the user to certain remedies. Hence if described as psychiatrically ill or delinquent, the therapist is directed to medical treatment or methods of control. The current term of emotional and behavioural difficulties does little to prescribe treatment. Therapeutic communities tend to prefer the term 'maladjusted', which suggests that the client is wrongly adjusted. The client has either not learnt appropriate social responses or has learnt the wrong ones.

Community meetings

The community structure is most frequently observed by visitors through observation of meetings and notice boards containing committee officers, sub-committee functions and members. Seen this way the community meeting may seem an ideal way of encouraging the participation of children. However, the principal function is therapeutic. The community meeting provides a child with the opportunity to learn the skills required of adolescence and adulthood in a living and non-punitive environment. The community meeting is the most obvious therapeutic aspect of a therapeutic community and often its core.

Key-worker role

A therapeutic relationship Many establishments present a child with a significant adult who may be called a key-worker or as in this case a 'special friend'. The term 'special friend' applies to both adult and child, so the adult is the child's special friend and vice versa.

The purpose and nature of the key-worker role is different for each establishment. The key-worker may support the child through early days, make assessments, design treatment programmes and write reports. The material included in reports, such as self-offending rates, child's view and personal aspirations, may be obtained only by developing a trusting relationship. The key-worker role may therefore give the impression of a supportive friendship. The relationship may develop into a personal one where the adult becomes a 'significant other' in the child's life, similar to that of close friend, older brother, sister, uncle or aunt or even as close as a substitute parent. However, a key-worker relationship rarely asks the adult to advocate the child's case, especially where that advocacy argues against the authority employing the adult. At this point the loyalty to one's employer becomes stronger than the loyalty to a friend.

While special friends maintain case histories, write case reports and attend case conferences, their role vastly exceeds the key-worker role. The relationship is not given to the adult and child concerned. Within a therapeutic community developing a special friendship is a common and natural process. As with all natural friendships it is a personal choice between child and adult, one that slowly emerges. Normally it is the child who initiates the friendship.

Few people go to bed at night without saying goodnight to someone or giving a loved one a kiss. Even the most assertively independent adolescent says goodnight. Children go through the ritual of a story, a kiss and a tuck of the sheets. Going to bed at night in a new, strange institutional context is a most lonely experience. Like most pain, psychological pain is felt most when alone in the dark of the night. It is here in children's homes and hospitals that people, quietly and sometimes shamefully, cry themselves to sleep. It is common in residential contexts to hear a child whimpering at night as they feel lonely, separated from family and home, rejected by peers and isolated. When a child says, 'Will you say goodnight to me tonight', both know that the emerging friendship has begun. Before making the request, both may have discussed their intentions with others, the house-parent, teacher and existing special friends, but it is a private request and a private act. Others may show their pleasure that the child has found a friend but not without a little caring concern: was this the right friendship for both?

As most parents know, the attention that children demand at night depends on the day they have experienced. Goodnights in a therapeutic community may merely be a quick goodnight, a short story or a discussion reflecting on the day and a look at the next day's demands. It is a time to relax at the end of the day, put the world to rights and sleep peacefully. The age of the child is largely irrelevant. So adults tend to structure their special friendships to the needs of the child rather than their age. Consequently an adult may reject a request to say goodnight, but not without accepting responsibility for the failure and offering support until the child had found a 'better person' to be their special friend.

Child advocacy   It is difficult to explain a special friendship without reference to what special friends will typically do. In community meetings they will support the child through elected responsibilities. When special friends are the subject of complaints and find difficulty in answering, the special friend may help, acting the role of advocate. The special friend may be accused of bias and even admit it, after all, this is their friend under criticism. The special friend will support the child through acceptance of the conclusion of the meeting and in making amends. While adults predominantly guide and support children it should not be assumed that predominant practice illustrates the principle. Particularly in understanding the dynamics of peer groups, children may guide adults. When an adult is the subject of a complaint, their special friend may act to support and defend that adult.

Community meetings tended to sit in friendship groups. Those without special friends would sit with their house-mother's or teacher's group. With existing special friends a new friendship may lead to feelings not unlike sibling rivalry. The child's ability to cope with such reactions may reflect previous problems in the child's natural family. A child objecting to a new special friend, may be encouraged to discuss their feelings in the community or therapy groups.

A family existence
Children tend to develop a definite cycle of special friendships:

1 adult
2 adult's spouse
3 husband and wife jointly
4 family of husband and wife including the couple's own children and other special friends
5 the wider community including peers, school friendships and natural home.

The social structure is one of nuclear families existing within a larger extended family that comes to include natural family and external friends. As the child develops greater ability and personal autonomy, the special friend, like any good parent, would know the moment to stand aside as the child takes his or her own tentative steps, to wait and watch and yet always be ready to provide support when necessary. In time those steps would be towards home or out into the wider community as a young adult. The therapeutic friendship would then change its form with the adult becoming a good friend of the young person or the family to which the child returned.

Like many residential establishments, most therapeutic communities have 'houses' with eight or nine children in each and separate but adjacent houseparent's accommodation. This is an institutionally convenient arrangement but one that does little to reflect normal life experience. Special friendships mitigate against this institutional arrangement. Friends seek permission to spend the evening, or day, out shopping, visiting the local cinema, or in the flat of the special friend. Professional responsibilities are retained, inasmuch that a houseparent or teacher would be asked for permission for the special friend to be absent. The member of staff would wish to assure themselves that due care was being taken.

Being a family experience there are very few closed doors in a therapeutic community. As in any large family children freely roam through and play in each other's bedrooms. Where there are single bedrooms, these are usually given for some specific purpose, such as children needing to study for mainstream day school or college. Privacy is not a matter of a private place but respecting the privacy and possessions of another. That respect extends to overhearing private conversations. At least one external door is left open all night so that children never feel 'locked in'. Within a therapeutic community it is the relationships and loyalties that children develop that keep them from running away.

The special friend

The role of the adult special friend may then be seen as an advocate and an 'enabler': one who will speak on their friend's behalf and may adopt a variety of roles as determined by the needs of the child at different stages of personal development; one who enables the child to learn the skills required of life. The approach shows a marked contrast to the current vogue for detailed assessment of personality or social skill deficits, where these become the goals of therapeutic programmes and children are the subject of those goals. The staff of therapeutic communities do plan therapy and set goals recorded by case conferences. However, the therapeutic community deliberately uses everyday living experiences of the community and social relationships to reveal social skill deficits and then meet them within the protection and support of the special friendship and community. The special friendship is then a process of continuous dialogue that involves preparation for predictable problems in the day-to-day environment, interpretation of those events, support and protection whenever necessary and follow-up examination of each significant experience. Special friendships endure beyond the child's stay. Contact is maintained by letters, phone calls, visits and holidays. Professional after-care is a poor substitute for sincere and lasting personal friendship (Owen 1973).

While the obvious core of the approach is the community meeting and social structure, the special friendship is the principal vehicle of therapy and pervades all aspects of the community. Describing any context in a few words is to do it a disservice. No mention has been made here of educational provision and its use of local day schools and colleges in the preparation of a child for integration to home and day school, college or work or the joint responsibility held by both care staff and teachers for the success of that provision. Space does not permit description of the role of field social workers, consultant psychiatrists, educational psychologists, the various voluntary workers, holiday and crisis provision, therapy groups, the place of ex-pupils and shared houses in the community, and the position of parents. Therapeutic communities are living communities with a variety of provision. They are continually evolving according to the contribution of its members and their needs. The principal concern here is to describe what is potentially unique about residential therapeutic communities in the current provision for people in need.

What theories guide the practice of therapeutic communities?

There are almost as many theories that guide the practice of therapeutic communities as there are pioneers that established them (Bridgeland 1971). Further, the extent to which the staff of an establishment are guided by the predominant theory will vary considerably. Staff tend to learn by the experience of living within the community (Owen 1973).

We may briefly examine the two basic approaches that have held greatest influence in applied work with children and adolescents. Freudian psychotherapy has held greatest influence so far. Behaviour therapy is increasingly gaining influence. It is worth noting that in academic psychology Freud has held little influence for some decades, while the influence of behaviour therapy is now waning. Two of the major proponents of these approaches in the residential context are David Wills (New Barnes School) and Roger Burland (Chelfham Mill School).

Freudian psychotherapy

Basically Freud argued that a person was born with certain instinctual drives: these he termed 'sexual' and are known collectively as the Id. As the person grew he or she internalized the norms, expectations and morals of those adults around. This Freud termed the Super Ego. During adolescence the individual developed his or her identity that Freud termed the Ego. Berne (1975) popularized this explanatory structure by terming the three elements the child, adult (or self) and parent. Berne argued that when faced with a decision people could hear three voices in their head; the child or id demanding gratification of instinctual urges; the parent or super ego suppressing those demands with ideals and rules; and the adult or ego finding a reasonable socially acceptable compromise between the two. Freud pointed to the use of severe punishment as the cause of personality problems resulting in the individual becoming fixated at a given stage of development. The treatment that Freud consequently prescribed was 'talk therapy' whereby the client would regress to those early stages, talk it out and transfer their feelings to the therapist.

There are two aspects of psychoanalysis that make it strange for it to be adopted by those operating therapeutic communities along the lines of Planning Environment Therapy (Wills 1973; 1979). First, PET uses the environment to change the behaviour of the client. Freud saw no role for the environment in psychoanalysis. The problems lie within the psyche of the client and the therapy may occur within any convenient context. Second, Freud afforded no role for the client or clients to participate democratically or even actively in the planning of that therapy and the choice of its targets. Therapeutic communities specifically encourage the active and democratic participation of their members and use the social environment to effect personal change.

We can see the influence of Freudian theory on the therapeutic community approach in the community meeting where problems are 'talked out' and in the special friendship where the child is given the opportunity to form a new parent–child relationship, talk out and grow again. However, the predominant emphasis of the special friendship is not about events that occurred in the child's early life, but on today's events. The child's past may be reflected upon, as the child begins to appreciate that current problems are often repetitions of past problems.

Behaviour therapy

Behaviourism and its various divisions are poorly understood. Strictly speaking we incorrectly use the term 'behaviour therapy' as it is used to identify the application of Pavlov's classical conditioning theory. Contemporary behaviourism (Skinner 1972; 1977) has long since moved away from terms such as conditioning, behaviour modification, stimulus and response. The term 'behaviour' is generic including cognitions, thoughts and feelings. Contemporary behaviourism sees individuals as acting on their environment to produce or avoid consequences, which in turn act to maintain that behaviour (Blackman 1982). Punishment is a consequence that behaviourists have empirically shown merely suppresses behaviour and may lead to adverse side-effects for both client and therapist (Scherer 1990). It is here that both Freudians and behaviourists concur, but for very different reasons.

The community meeting procedure may equally be described by cognitive behaviourism and social learning models (Bandura 1971). Here the thoughts and feelings that may precede behaviour are revealed, approved or disapproved of by community members. Alternative thoughts, feelings or behaviours are suggested. Behaving in accordance with those suggestions will then gain the approval of the community. Learning is enhanced by the provision of a variety of social models, many of which are closely similar to the individual – one's peers.

A behavioural programme does not require the active participation of the client in the design of the programme or the choice of goals. Many contemporary behaviourists do look to the client, the client's parents or representative, and those who need to provide for the client – social workers, teachers, employers and society – for the goals of any programme and actively seek to involve those affected by the programme (Blackman 1979; Scherer 1979).

What behaviourists do, or should do, is objectively and rigorously evaluate behaviour change programmes (Scherer 1990). However, the method of evaluation is not the prerogative of behaviourists. Ironically it was first used by Brewer and Freud (1957). Hersen and Barlow (1976) argue that the Freudians made exaggerated claims for the importance of their method and the findings that emerged, bringing both into disrepute. Further they subsequently abandoned the method, failing to test their ideas. Today we can see the same error in the 'behaviour modifiers' (cf. Scherer and Brown 1984).

What does exist between the two predominant approaches is a level of antagonism based on ignorance and prejudice. It sometimes amounts to a blind moralistic crusade with character assassinations of principal proponents. So do particular theories guide the practice of therapeutic communities? Without rigorous evaluation the question is impossible to answer. Certainly the philosophy of an approach will guide the practitioner who chooses it, but the practitioner is equally likely to adapt that philosophy to suit perceived needs and use the approach to justify practice after the event. While theories are used post hoc and may not predict or be logically related to practice, this does not deny the validity or success of that practice. Defending their approach, practitioners often choose between theories, describing their stance as eclectic or common sense. Such a description also avoids evaluation of the approach, its goals and its success in meeting the needs of children.

What contemporary behaviourism cannot do, and psychoanalysis appears deliberately to fail to do, is state what should be the behaviours or skills of an individual. This is a social and political question. Contemporary behaviourism fails to describe the nature of the relationship that must exist between client and practitioner or the appropriate relationships that a child needs to enable development into adulthood. Freudian approaches claim that the client will transfer feelings of early relationships, often with parents, on to the therapist. If we are going to provide for children, rejected by their social and educational backgrounds, according to what model are we going to construct that provision?

Current demands of provision for children

Approximation to a normal life

The concept of normality is fraught with problems as illustrated by the title of Valentine's (1956) book *The Normal Child and Some of his Abnormalities*. While rejected in the 1960s and 1970s the concept of normality re-emerged with the Education Act 1981. It shifted focus of the term from the child to the environment. Rather than a generalized term, the Act gave it a more specific usage in education limiting it to the school or schools of the local education authority (LEA) concerned. The simple reality is that the 1981 Act presented a model of normal social development that reflects everyday life (see Newell 1983). The same concept exists in the Children Act 1989, where the LEA is obliged to provide a context as close as possible to the kind that parents would arrange for children. What is normal is the social environment in which most of the client's peers develop, within the cultural group from which the client came. Most children develop within a nuclear family with at least one parent, siblings and a host of others in some form of extended family. They will develop peers from the local environment or through school. The most obvious and logical provision is in foster homes and attendance at mainstream schools. However, these children have been rejected by one or both.

Maybe therapeutic communities offer a model that is not unreasonably distant from this ideal, substitute parental relationship with at least one adult, but probably two, who live in the same environment, are there before and after school and during the night; in a family group with siblings in a larger social environment not dissimilar to an extended family; with peers gained in the local environment and in class. Many therapeutic communities maintain links with parents and normal schools and seek the gradual integration of children to home and mainstream school, and did so long before normalization and integration became the vogue.

The location and design of the building and employment structure of many residential contexts mitigate against the provision that therapeutic communities choose to make. Most residential communities are located in the heart of the country. Most children come from urban areas. Children live in dormitories or large adjacent rooms. Single rooms exist but are typically provided for the child with specific needs such as enuresis. House-parents live in separate flats somewhere in the vicinity or increasingly off-site. Staff work shifts. Parents do not do this: their bedrooms are adjacent. Parents may work by day but are usually there after school, through the night and in the morning. The design of residential establishments needs to be radically rethought to provide the normal life experience of childhood; a house with its own kitchen, dining-room and garden. The trend towards shift work of child-care staff needs to be rethought. Working split shifts and 'sleeping in' your own accommodation is not excessively demanding.

It is what married women with families do every day. With adequate support, community living can be immensely free and rewarding. Around are a ready supply of baby sitters and a safe environment for their children to play in and an ample supply of friends to drop in for a chat. What is demanding about residential work is the problems presented by children and young people with special needs. The pressure created by the hours should not be confused with the pressure created by the work itself. Communal living provides considerable support and guidance for staff, who are not alone or isolated like foster-parents and will find release from unbearable circumstances within moments rather than days.

Individualized assessment and provision

This is the principal requirement of the Education Act 1981, coupled with an annual review of that provision. Therapeutic communities have long since maintained annual case conferences that may set generalized goals. However the therapeutic community uses day-to-day experiences to prompt the targets of therapy that are met within months if not weeks or days. Contemporary behaviourism argues that annual review of programmes is insufficient. Programmes should be rigorously evaluated while in progress. Programmes are typically established for weeks rather than months or years. On completion of a programme the child's needs should be reassessed before proceeding to the next target of the child's needs. The therapeutic community performs a similar function but fails to do so in similarly systematic or recorded manner.

Informed consent and confidentiality

It is taken for granted that no intervention in the life of an adult can be taken without the informed consent of that adult other than under special circumstances. No such assumption is taken with children. Rather the opposite, that as children are incomplete adults, yet to mature, they are incapable of autonomy. Children were the chattels of their parents, to be seen and not heard, with no right to participate in the decisions affecting their lives and no right to own or dispose of property. This position has radically changed since the Law Lords' ruling in the Gillick case (Children's Legal Centre 1985) and may now be seen embodied in the Children Act 1989. The ruling presented a radically new perception of parental duties, which includes all those in the role of '*loco parentis*' be they teachers or care workers. The control by parents over the person or property of the child existed only so long as it was required. The Lords ruling rejected a specific age at which a child became an adult. Instead a child was perceived as gradually acquiring the understanding and ability to take decisions affecting his own person or property and participate in decisions affecting his family or school. Should children so wish, they have the right, as any other person, to seek confidential advice and give informed consent to interventions into their lives. The person giving advice is bound by the normal expectations of confidentiality. The person making the intervention is responsible for ensuring that the child understands before consenting and that the intervention is for the benefit or protection of the child. The duty of parents is to enable children to acquire the skills and experience required to take their decisions through a protective and supportive relationship.

There is a striking parallel between the Lords' perception of the parent-child relationship and the therapeutic community procedures. The community meeting, special friendship and 'in care' relationships fulfil the Law Lords' expectation but predate it by several decades. The community meeting is a complaints procedure that long predated the Children Act 1989.

The future of therapeutic communities

There are and will continue to be children who need residential provision for some part of their development. When applied to their needs, the therapeutic community approach has typically come under the remit of special education. The survival of this provision has been seen in two forms: as part of a continuum of provision and in resource centres.

As part of a continuum of provision

Many LEAs have eschewed the notion of a continuum of provision from main-stream day schools to residential special education. The aim is to co-ordinate provision and select from the continuum as a child's needs are met and reassessed. In practice the continuum has merely been to encompass provision under one administrative umbrella. Provision within the different components of the continuum has hardly changed and children do not move along the continuum. The major problem is that there is no real continuity for the child, especially in the supportive relationships that a child needs to enable him or her to benefit from different types of provision for different needs. Each move may be more damaging than the benefits of the therapy provided by the move. It may be more beneficial to move the provision to the child, than the child to the provision.

There is a place for residential therapeutic communities within a continuum of provision by maintaining their role of preparing children for integration to main-stream schools and providing support from special friends who are themselves supported and guided by the establishment of which they are a part. With the Education Act 1971, special schools assumed responsibility for the education of children at a local psychiatric hospital. This enabled a gradual integration from psychiatric hospital, through residential school to the local mainstream school and then home.

The Children Act 1989 requires local authorities to present children and their parents with real alternative choices. A residential therapeutic community may be one of those choices.

Resource centres

In the late 1970s the Warnock Report (1978) opened the possibility of preserving the expertise of special schools through the concept of 'resource centres'. The aim was to retain the resources and expertise of special schools and enable their use in mainstream education. Such centres with specialist staff could provide expert advice, resources and support to teachers in mainstream schools, parents and foster-parents at home. Short-term residential provision could be made available for children rejected by mainstream schools and homes with an aim to provide respite care and then integrate. The Warnock Committee report reached consensus on the future of provision for children with physical disabilities, but did not appear to do so for children with emotional and behavioural disabilities. Some special schools have extended their provision to provide day services and support. However, the concept of the resource centre has not been extensively developed.

The therapeutic community approach may be successful for children with emotional and behavioural difficulties. However, to transfer it to mainstream schools would be to challenge the traditional authority of the mainstream school. What is required is a radical change in the philosophy of mainstream education and the social structure of mainstream schools. Any hope that children may be encouraged to participate in the responsibility for the organization of mainstream schools was lost in the withdrawal of pupil representation on school governing bodies.

It is now apparent that children with emotional and behavioural disabilities present the greatest demands in integration and place the greatest stress on foster-parents and mainstream education. Emotionally disabled children may survive the experience of integration but there is little evidence to show that their needs are met. Hence segregated special provision remains a reality for emotionally disabled children. If therapeutic community provision is to continue its contribution to education and social work then it must meet the most valid criticisms made of it.

Training

The vast majority of staff involved in therapeutic communities have learnt their practice by living in the community. The community meeting not only serves to teach appropriate social skills to children but also serves to enable staff to learn the methods of the approach. It may be that the best practical training is on the job learning by trial and error and observation of colleagues. However, learning by doing the job alone is likely to be haphazard, incomplete, imbalanced and biased. Specific training programmes serve to identify the skills required of practice and place that practice within a wider context of other approaches and developments. Identification of the key elements of practice also serves to identify targets for evaluation of practice. Evaluation of practice and training enables its evolution.

It is only recently that resources have been made for in-service training. Previously termed 'Baker days' in education (after the former UK Education Secretary), many are yet to make full use of this opportunity. Several establishments have provided in-service training and annual conferences for some years (Lane 1980). The Warnock Report (1978) recommended that resource centres should undertake research and provide training. There are two dangers of formal training. First, training can be used by traditional authority as a means of ordering the actions of the organization. Second, no amount of training will equip an employee with all the skills required of employment. It is equally important to train people to evaluate their procedures and performance.

Evaluation of practice

Special education has been severely criticized for failing to show any evidence for the validity of its practice (Topping 1983). This criticism is harsh on three grounds. First, the goal posts have only recently moved. Rigorous research of practice hardly exists in any area of social provision from education to social work and nursing. The absence of evidence by today's standard does not invalidate practice, it merely fails to support it. Second, the training and resources have not been made available to enable applied research. In research establishments and universities, applied research has always received a lower status and vastly inferior resources to pure research. Third, until recently there has not been a suitable method for practitioners to evaluate practice while undertaking it. The simple choice was between making the provision or taking the time to evaluate it. Contemporary behaviourism contends that this is a case of the chicken and the egg. Objective and rigorous methods of action research and evaluation are now available, applicable while making provision and do not require extensive resources or prior training (Scherer 1990). However, few practitioners are trained in these methods. If the therapeutic community approach claims to innovate good practice then it must evaluate and substantiate that practice. Since the early 1980s the approach has failed to grasp this opportunity.

Conclusion

Residential special education and children's homes are becoming the dodos of the education and social work worlds. However, the alternative provision, 'integration', does not appear to be working for children with emotional disabilities. Truancy and suspension rates are increasing. Referral rates to residential special education are recovering. Emotionally disabled children and adolescents are understandably mistrusting of adults and society. Their problems have usually emerged from early disturbed social relationships, emotional, physical or sexual abuse. Their inability to relate normally has resulted in behaviour that society has found offensive and rejected. It takes a long time to win the trust of emotionally disabled people and help them to learn the behaviour that society finds acceptable. One method that has found and shown success is the approach of therapeutic communities. Here meaningful personal relationships are established that enable children to develop self-control through participation in their own social control. Without therapeutic residential provision the choices presented to children are substantially reduced.

Therapeutic communities have innovated and pioneered practice that today conforms to the demands of good practice. By rejecting therapeutic community provision because it has evolved through residential special education and child care, we may be killing the goose that lays the golden egg.

Applied research establishments, education and social services departments, and therapeutic communities, have failed to evaluate this type of provision objectively or rigorously identify the successful elements of its practice. Trends in education and child care tend to be set by Committees of Inquiry and Acts of Parliament. Often they reflect the prevailing morality of society more than any objective evidence. If therapeutic communities do make provision that meets the needs of children with emotional and behavioural difficulties, will we one day need to reinvent the wheel that is today the therapeutic community?

The 1980s witnessed greater care and attention in the assessment of children's needs and a trend towards integration. In the 1990s may we witness the same care and attention in the evaluation of provision and a trend towards integrating provision into mainstream education and child care as well as integrating children?

Acknowledgements

My gratitude is expressed to the children and colleagues from whom I have learnt, to Bob Hogg, Roston Owen, John Hobley and David Lane for their comments; and to Rhiannon Beaven, who repeatedly tests my commitment.

References

Bandura, A. (1971) *Social Learning Theory*, Englewood Cliffs, NJ: Prentice Hall.
Berne, E. (1975) *Transactional Analysis in Psychotherapy*, London: Souvenir Press.
Blackman, D.E. (1979) Ethical standards for behaviour modification, *British Journal of Criminology* 14: 420–48.
Blackman, D.E. (1982) Psychologists and the community: influence and counter influence (British Psychological Society Presidential address), *Bulletin of the British Psychological Society* 35: 334–41.
Brewer, J. and Freud, S. (1957) *Studies on Hysteria*, New York: Basic Books.
Bridgeland, M. (1971) *Pioneer Work with Maladjusted Children: A Study of the Development of Therapeutic Education*, London: Staples Press.
Browne, D. (1991) Millbrook Grange. Consultancy: a consumer's view, in W.R. Silveira (ed.) *Consultation in Residential Care*, Aberdeen University Press.
Children's Legal Centre (1985) Landmark decision for children's rights (the Gillick case), *Childright* 14: Briefing Supplement.
Hersen, M. and Barlow, D.H. (1976) *Single Case Experimental Designs: Strategies for Studying Behaviour Change*, New York: Pergamon Press.
Lane, D.A. (1980) *In House Training and Development: The Royal Society of Health Scheme*, London: Professional Development Foundation.
Newell, P. (1983) *Ace Special Education Handbook*, London: Advisory Centre for Education.
Owen, R. (1973) Selection and training of staff for a residential school for the maladjusted, *1973 Conference Proceedings*, London: King Edward Hospital Fund.
Owen, R. (1974) Millbrook Grange: a new therapeutic community for adolescent girls, *Journal of the Association of Workers with Maladjusted Children* 2: 3–12.
Pugh, D.S. and Higson, D.J. (1989) *Writers on Organizations*, 4th edn, Harmondsworth: Penguin.
Scherer, M.B. (1979) Resolving ethical problems in behaviour modification, *Behaviour Modification with Children* 3: 7–11.
Scherer, M. (1990) Using consequences in class, in M. Scherer, I. Gersch, and L. Fry

(eds) *Meeting Disruptive Behaviour: Assessment, Intervention and Partnership*, Basingstoke: Macmillan.

Scherer, M. and Brown, B. (1984) Eliminating exclusion time out, *NCSE Research Exchange* 3(4); see also *Behavioural Approaches with Children* 8: 127–33.

Skinner, B.F. (1972) *Beyond Freedom and Dignity*, London: Cape.

Skinner, B.F. (1977) *About Behaviourism*, London: Cape.

Topping, K. (1983) *Educational Systems for Disruptive Adolescents*, London: Croom Helm.

Valentine, C.W. (1956) *The Normal Child and Some of his Abnormalities*, Harmondsworth: Penguin.

Warnock Report (1978) *Special Education Needs*, London: HMSO.

Wills, W.D. (1969) *The Hawkspur Experiment*, 2nd edn, London: Allen & Unwin.

Wills, D. (1973) Planned environment therapy – What is it? *Studies in Environment Therapy* 2: 9–21.

Wills, D. (1979) Planned environment therapy: a concise description. *Studies in Environment Therapy* 3: 59–61.

10

The Child Guidance Clinic:
problems and progress for the 1990s

ROY HOWARTH

The past

The history of the delivery of psychiatric services to children begins in 1909 in Chicago, where William Healy established a centre to investigate the antecedents of juvenile delinquency. The publication in 1915 of the results of studies of 800 cases in *The Individual Delinquent: A Textbook of Diagnosis and Prognosis* was influential in the setting up of what became known as Child Guidance Clinics from 1922 onwards in the USA. By 1927 Britain's first clinic, the East London Child Guidance Clinic, was opened, and soon after the first training clinic, the London Child Guidance Training Clinic, was started in Canonbury in Islington (Cameron 1956; Kanner 1959).

Thereafter there was a slow expansion of the service, with forty-six Child Guidance Clinics in Britain by 1939, mostly local authority based with very few child psychiatry clinics in hospitals (Warren 1971). After the Second World War (1939–45) concern about the effects of loss, separation and stress on individuals, family life and child-rearing led to Blacker's survey of the mental health services. The resulting recommendations (Blacker 1948) included suggestions for a greatly increased nation-wide service of Child Guidance Centres administered by education authorities, and also an expansion of the hospital-based child psychiatry clinics. The National Health Service, (NHS) in 1948 incorporated responsibility for child psychiatric services, so that finances for the already identified need for increased numbers of child psychiatrists slowly became available. The following forty years have seen the gradually increasing practice of child psychiatrists having a base in an NHS facility, and providing sessions to the local educational authority Child Guidance Clinic, Special Schools and Social Services Departments (Hersov 1986). It has also been a period during which the academic and scientific basis of child psychology and psychiatry has been laid down; treatment approaches have become more varied, though still subject to fashion and faith (Parry-Jones 1989).

Parallel to these developments the Educational Psychology Service had been established in Britain when Burt took up the first post with the London County Council in 1913; education authorities throughout the country later followed suit (Howells 1965). The Child Guidance and the Educational Psychology Services have worked in varying degrees of closeness from time to time and place to place. Generally speaking educational psychologists have given a proportion of their time to interdisciplinary collaboration with psychiatrists and psychiatric social workers in the Child Guidance Clinics; in some areas they co-ordinate or lead the team at the clinic on behalf of the local education authority. There has, therefore, developed an organization and system of delivery of child psychiatric service which is now both hospital and community based.

The hospital service takes the form of Child and Adolescent Psychiatry Departments, clearly set in and run by the NHS, but district hospital services outside the main cities often have a very limited staff and can provide little more than a liaison service to the hospital paediatricians.

The community service takes the form of Child Guidance Clinics, the subject of this chapter.

The present

Community Child Guidance Clinics provide the greatest part of the specialist provision for children, adolescents and families where there are emotional, behaviour and relationship problems. Referrals of children and families come from teachers, family doctors, community social workers, health visitors and other professional workers in the local community. Usually the referral process has become much less formal than to the hospital child psychiatric services, and many clinics accept parents and young people referring themselves. The interventions on offer are largely informed by psychodynamic and family systems theories, with some loosely applied behaviour modification principles. In recent years the recognition of the importance of attempting to widen the delivery of service has lead to many clinics also providing some consultation to teachers, social workers and primary health care workers in their district.

Clinics are housed in a variety of settings and buildings; most have been traditionally education authority administered and many still are. The personnel in these clinics are drawn from the disciplines of child psychiatry, clinical child psychology, child psychotherapy and community psychiatric nursing – all employed by the health authority – and from the disciplines of educational psychology and teaching employed by the education authority; frequently the numerically largest number of staff members are drawn from psychiatric social work sometimes employed by Social Service Departments and seconded to the clinics, sometimes employed by the education authority (and rarely by the health authority as family therapists).

The numbers and balance of personnel in the clinics varies greatly in different parts of the country, and even between contiguous local authorities. Often there is a part-time psychiatrist, one or two psychiatric social workers and sessions from the educational psychologist. Where multi-disciplinary teams exist they have the advantage over individual professionals in potentially covering a broader range of knowledge about normal human development and behaviour as well as pathology and deviance. By working not only under the same roof but also in close interaction at times, members of these teams learn from one another and ideally potentiate the overall expertise of the Unit's assessments and treatments.

However, such teams being a loose confederation with often ill defined areas of, or lines of responsibility and management structure, can also become infected with professional rivalry and power-struggles. Even when working together well as a team it is still possible for it to function poorly in relation to the other agencies in the community, eg schools, family doctors, Social Services Departments. For example, when a team becomes inward-looking, its members become pre-occupied by their own limited area of work and communicate infrequently, in the wrong form or inappropriate language with colleagues in other institutions who are also involved with the same children or families.

In addition the Child Guidance Clinics evolved like most social institutions as society's response to deal with pressing problems, with little evaluation over the subsequent years of the real effectiveness of the treatments and recommendations provided.

Biological evolution leads to the perpetuation of genes in their fleshly forms whose interaction with the environment is successful in the survival game. At the social organizational level we would hope to develop the institutions which are most useful to the majority of individual members of society. Unfortunately social evolution in some respects mimics its biological counterpart and perpetuates the selfish gene in the form of ways of working within organizations which are more to do with habits and beliefs than responses to social needs. Moreover, organizations are better able than vulnerable individuals to protect themselves from the ravages of a harsh environment. So aspects of an institution which once served a useful purpose may no longer do so, but linger on like the human veriform appendix.

From time to time, therefore, it is a good idea to use that other faculty of human beings, the ability to think ahead and make predictions on the bases of past experience, to help us decide what direction to choose rather than continue to follow the imperative just to keep going in the same old way.

Applying this principle to the community Child Guidance Service what can we anticipate for the 1990s?

The future

In order to consider the direction in which the Child Guidance Service might usefully progress, it is necessary first to assess the needs of the communities being served.

Some knowledge of normal variations in child and family psychological development is important for people in different roles in relation to children and young people, but who would not see themselves as experts in that field. So parents, including those who foster or adopt, nursery workers, child-minders, local authority children's homes' staff, teachers, social workers, family doctors, community medical officers, paediatricians, nurses and health visitors all require access to a body of information about the normal development and maturation of children and families.

When things are thought to be going wrong, concern about children's development, their emotional state, relationships and behaviour is experienced by these adults in a variety of settings: in the family home and children's homes, pre-school day centres, schools and special school units, hospitals, surgeries and clinics.

There are therefore four main groups who might need child psychiatric or child guidance service:

1   parents and family
2   the health service (hospital and community)
3   the schools (mainstream and special, nursery, primary and secondary)
4   the Social Services Departments (fieldwork, residential and day care, assessment centres and in relation to the Courts).

Parents and family

The principal needs are ease of access to different levels of psychosocial service. What deters parents and young people seeking advice or help for themselves is physical and psychological distance between them and the service providers (Cottrell et al. 1988; Subotsky and Berelowitz 1990). So ease of referral process, including self-referral and walk-in clinics make for better uptake of a service. Closeness to living and working places and some flexibility of times of clinics clearly also improves uptake and follow-up. Integration with other well-used facilities such as in a health centre or in a quite separate unit have advantages and disadvantages for some potential users of a psychiatric service.

Often people complain that child psychiatric services are not client orientated enough. The level of intervention, from simple one-off advice through to intensive family or individual therapy, seems to them sometimes to be determined less by their need and more by what the clinic wants to provide (Bailey and Garralda 1989; Burck 1978). Young parents and single parents, sometimes isolated from their families, often have a need to learn about normal child development, what to expect from their first child (and what not to expect of him or her), management of common behaviour problems and when to seek more help.

We can expect continuing and perhaps increasing numbers of single parents or serial partnerships – with a need to think about the different ways of bringing up children to provide as complete as possible a family life and social relationships. Fluctuating finances and other strains on adult relationships are set to continue or increase through the 1990s, so more children who present to Child Guidance Units are likely to have parents who need counselling about their own relationship as well as how to maintain their parenting and ensure the continuity of care of their children.

The present wide difference in timing between physiological puberty, which is gradually occurring earlier than in previous generations, and 'social' adolescence, which is tending to be prolonged by the difficulties in becoming financially independent and the pressure to remain in full-time education, is likely to be exacerbated. So more young people in their late teens are probably going to be more appropriately counselled in adolescent facilities than in adult psychiatric clinics.

The NHS practitioners, school teachers and social service workers all have similar needs of a Child Guidance Service but with differences related to the settings in which they work. Each group of workers, in addition to their own training courses, require some in-service training or updating resource in their working district to maintain their knowledge of the field of child development and disorders of child and family life. These primary care providers also need to be able to turn to others who specialize in child and family psychiatric problems for consultation about children in their care and, as for parents, ease and speed of referral without the expectation of long delays before at least diagnostic assessment is provided.

The health service

In the hospital service, psychiatric liaison with paediatricians is established in some centres, and the level of satisfaction suggests that it should become more widespread (Black 1989). Similarly, consultation or liaison work between Child Guidance members and family doctors, community medical officers or health visitors might be expected not only to improve the delivery of psychosocial care to children and families but also to enhance the mutual respect and trust between Child Guidance teams and other community health workers.

The schools

Schools often rely on the educational psychologist and educational social workers to mediate between individual teachers who identify a child with emotional or behavioural problems and the Child Guidance Clinics. In many instances there is a reluctance to refer to the clinics because of concern about labelling or stigma; there are frequently complaints of lack of contact or communication with the clinic staff.

Increasingly the educational psychologists are heavily involved in the processing of the assessment of special education needs. In urban areas especially the educational social workers are struggling with school attendance and other social problems. The diminished morale of teachers, together with the burden of establishing the National Curriculum in a workable form, is likely to continue well into the 1990s, and one can predict a greater need for more support and guidance concerning the management of children in the schools and higher rates of requests for individual children to be assessed and 'treated' by the Child Guidance Clinics. The fact that many, perhaps the majority of these concerns about children, will be seen by parents as largely a school-based problem with little they can or wish to do about it, means that more direct involvement of Child Guidance in the schools may be necessary (Dowling and Osborne 1985), though this brings with it various dilemmas in ways of working (Dupont and Dowdney 1990).

The Social Services Departments

Social Services workers sometimes already have good working relationships with Child Guidance Clinic staff. The increased rate of reporting of suspected cases of physical and sexual abuse in recent years has already changed the pattern of requests to the clinics (Black 1989). It is expected that, however the local authority organizes its child protection services, Child Guidance personnel will continue to be increasingly involved in the assessment and treatment programmes for these children and their families. As research and experience throws new light on family dysfunctions, failure-to-thrive due to relative neglect or emotional abuse can be predicted to be another area where social workers will call on others to join them in the investigation and management. Social workers also take the brunt of problems surrounding the increase in family breakdown. Not only the fall-out in the form of having to make arrangements for child care, but also the disputes over custody and access in which they have to mediate. They are likely to need more help from other psychosocial agencies, including Child Guidance, in the future as the demands on their resources outstrips the possibilities of their own specialist expansion.

Similarly limitations in local authority finances are likely to continue to restrict work with delinquent and pre-delinquent young people, and those involved in drug, alcohol and solvent abuse. Again there will be a heavier demand on other services for joint work with these adolescents and their families and possibly an increase in the number of young people requiring psychiatric reports as part of their preparation for appearances in court.

Summary of needs

The Child Guidance Service is a resource for children and adolescents, parents and primary care workers which will provide expertise about normal child and family social development and their disorders. There should be ease of access to and speedy response from the resource, with a flexible range of responses – from information giving, through advice and consultation to psychological and psychiatric treatments with a good system of communication with the resource. If these are some at least of the predicted needs, and if we did not have the existing Child Guidance Clinics, how could they be met?

It is evident that many people are involved in helping children and parents to deal with emotional problems or behaviour difficulties. However, there does seem to be a need for a group of professionals who have a more thorough and broader knowledge of child development and psychiatric disorders and who attain a special level of experience by working in the field exclusively.

Could such a group meet the needs by working from a hospital base? It has been argued (Black 1987) that child psychiatrists and associated teams should be based in NHS premises. However, the criterion of being within easy reach of families, schools and places of work so that initial access is simplified and continuing regular attendance if necessary is facilitated, would not always be met by a hospital team in many parts of the country. So some form of community clinics are necessary in perhaps most areas.

If there is a need for a group working at least part of the week in a community setting, does such a group need to operate together in a separate team (Child Guidance model)?

Children and families with psychological problems present to, or are identified by workers in health, education and social services in a variety of settings. A case can, therefore, be made for mini-psychosocial teams in each of these three main agencies.

An advantage would be that the teams would be close to the primary care providers and therefore close to the source and time of referral, and also available to families who may be willing to go only to that particular agency for help. For example, parents who go to a Social Services Department for support for their rehousing may also talk while there about concerns about one of their children who is bed-wetting and seems depressed and withdrawn, but are reluctant to be referred to the Child Guidance Clinic. Given our present resources of Child Guidance personnel, such a dispersion of specialist services seems impossibly uneconomical.

In fact, at times of economic stringency, there is a tendency for each service to withdraw to its own area of work and to try to look after its own interests, for it is unlikely that help provided to one service by another will continue if funding is reduced. For example, a district health authority that has largely relied on its Social Services Department to employ psychiatric social workers to provide family therapy in the district, will face a sudden loss of service to hospital, GPs and community doctors if the Social Services Department has to withdraw its psychiatric social workers to cover statutory duties because of cuts in staff.

In these circumstances each of the main services (health, education and social) will want to ensure some basic provision for the psychosocial aspects of the work within its own organization which it can manage and control.

Thus *Social Services Departments* will need to have some social workers trained in family therapy practice as well as others skilled in child protection functions (and ideally once more some trained in child care and development).

Education authorities will need to keep educational psychologists and possibly education social workers under their management. They will also need to maintain a body of specialist advisory teachers who have had further training in the management and teaching of children with emotional and behavioural disorders. The main responsibility for the psychiatric care of children and adolescents appropriately lies with *the health authorities*. They will need to continue their management of child psychiatrists, child psycho-therapists, and child psychiatric nurses to meet the NHS's obligations.

These employment and management arrangements would provide only a basic minimum for each service to offer some sort of psychosocial provision in each of their agencies independently of each of the other services.

It is clear that each of the main services needs input from the others in order to provide something more than the basic minimum service. No one discipline or agency can encompass the whole of human development and pathology within its theories and practice. So a collaborative model would seem to be the one of choice when local authority and district health finances permit.

The personnel provided by health, education and social services when they collaborate at the present time form the Child Guidance Clinics, and it looks as though a system of Community Clinics on Child Guidance lines is needed to meet the needs as outlined above.

The next question is what changes in the present practices of Community Child Guidance Services would be necessary to meet the needs.

There is now some empirical knowledge about what happens when development is interfered with by environmental events and experiences. 'Natural experiments' and epidemiological studies have also begun to throw light on aetiology, or at least on strong associations of psychiatric disorders and learning characteristics of children with family and school dysfunctions (Rutter 1985). Some interventions developed to counteract these disorders are beginning to have some scientific evaluation (Patterson et al. 1982; Kolvin et al. 1981; Pellegrini and Urbain 1985).

However, the most commonly used interventions in Child Guidance practice are least well evaluated in outcome research (Kazdin 1988; Weisz et al. 1987). In particular the intensive psychodynamic psychotherapies of individuals or groups and the application of systems and other theories to treat whole family groups have little empirical support. The application of learning theory and cognitive psychology in behavioural and cognitive therapies has produced some evidence of the possibility of efficacy (Yule 1985), but this has relied so far largely on laboratory-style studies or work with adults. So far therefore there is justification only for a small proportion of time in Child Guidance Clinics being expended on the various intensive or long-term psychotherapies. It is not that we know that most psychological treatments do not work; we just have little idea yet about which specific aspects of child and parent behaviour are influenced by what specific interventions.

As a way of spreading knowledge about child and family development and disorders, and giving away some of the non-specific skills of counselling, the trend is already for there to be more emphasis on consultation with the various primary care workers in the health, education and social services. There is some evidence for the usefulness of this form of liaison work (Mannino and Shore 1975; Ritter 1978), and it can be expected to continue and extend with perhaps more involvement by Child Guidance staff in specific in-service training groups or workshops for colleagues in these other services.

If the need for a more flexible range of treatment responses is to be met there will need to be an increase in the clinics of brief interventions with focused work towards specified goals. Such a change would have to be achieved largely by gradual changes in the working practices of staff already in post, while maintaining the strengths of their previous training. This training in many cases will have been with longer-term unfocused interventions in mind, and a small number of children and families with long-standing entrenched problems will probably continue to need these approaches.

It is unlikely that these busy community clinics will in the 1990s have the time or expertise to carry out their own scientific evaluation of this core of individual and group therapy; but it must be done. Greater emphasis will have to be placed on treatment outcome studies in the teaching hospital departments and the increasing number of university academic departments of child psychiatry and clinical psychology. Secondment of academic staff to Child Guidance Clinics, or close collaboration between the community clinics and academic departments, could transform the service. To achieve this, much encouragement and facilitation will be necessary from both sides; but with the new generation of more widely trained child psychiatrists, psychologists and social workers now entering the service, it should be possible in the foreseeable future.

How are the clinics to cover this range of activities?

First, some diversion of the present clinic staff-hours from therapy to consultation and liaison with others, as already suggested, would be necessary. Another strategy is to have a variable response to referrals or requests for help. In other words it will be necessary to have some sort of continuum of service. One which might be adopted would be a range of responses from the following list.

1 Consultation only – about general issues or problems in the consultee's own working practice.
2 Consultation only – about a specific child or family (unnamed so that confidentiality is not breached), so that the consultee can continue to work with the child or family with increased confidence.
3 Acceptance of referral of a child or family with a view to diagnostic assessment in order to make a recommendation or give advice to the primary care provider (with perhaps continuing supervision or further consultations).
4 Acceptance of referral leading to treatment of child and/or family.

One of the practices of some Child Guidance Clinics which has come under criticism in the past is that of multi-disciplinary assessment and treatment of cases. Some complex multi-problem cases clearly still need this approach, but the majority do not (Eisenberg 1969; Tizard 1973).

The time taken to organize the necessary interviews and carry them all out followed by a professionals' meeting to share findings, give their conclusions to the family and perhaps embark on open-ended co-therapy is clearly prohibitively expensive for anything other than a teaching or research programme, or for very complex cases.

The balance between making best use of the expertise of staff of different disciplines, and making the best use of a limited amount of time, has tended to be in the direction of using special expertise, that is, assigning cases to staff members who are considered to have special training in particular aspects of therapy. In the light of the lack of scientific trial of the therapies, the balance should be pushed in the opposite direction in the 1990s while awaiting evaluation of specialist interventions. Some clinics have already moved towards the position where all experienced staff members of all disciplines are regarded as having sufficient knowledge and expertise in child and family assessment to take on any case referred. This may be for a relatively brief screening diagnostic interview to determine if and what sort of further intervention is called for. The possibilities are then for the same person to continue to provide whatever intervention is needed, recruiting someone else in the clinic to supervise or join if some extra specialism is required, or transferring the case to someone else in the clinic for treatment after the assessment. Where this method of working is used, the initial diagnostician most frequently engages with the child and/or family and continues to work with them if it is necessary.

It is then very important to maintain the standards in general child and family assessment within the clinics, by making it possible for staff to watch or discuss each other's work, and to keep one another informed of developments.

Staffing

Whatever changes in the balance of working practices within the clinics, there will continue to be inadequate staffing to respond to the potential numbers of children and adolescents with emotional and behavioural disorders. The epidemiological studies of recent years indicate average rates of about 10 per cent of children and young people with psychiatric disorder, varying with age, school and city or country life (Rutter et al. 1970; 1975). Few, if any, districts have the number of psychiatrists recommended by the Royal College of Psychiatrists, or the levels of other disciplines required to provide a comprehensive service (Royal College of Psychiatrists 1985). So there needs to be continuing efforts to achieve these suggested levels.

In the mean time various ways of involving alternative sources of 'helpers' under supervision needs to be encouraged, with built-in evaluation of projects so that there is feedback to clinics and local authorities about what is useful and what is not. Various innovative approaches have been attempted mainly in the USA using para-professionals not only in schools but also as befrienders of children, adolescents and parents, and as supervised counsellors and caseworkers. The initial enthusiasm for the programmes has not been maintained to the same degree, and it remains unclear what roles para-professionals might play beyond a non-specific befriending one (Rafferty 1975).

Hetznecker and Forman (1974) provide an inspiring description of the conversion of a traditional Child Guidance Clinic into a Community Psychiatry Clinic, using para-professionals in clinic and schools; in Big Brother–Little Brother and parent education programmes; and consultation to schools and social agencies (Hetznecker and Forman 1974). There is scope for the Child Guidance Clinics to try out and evaluate more initiatives on these lines, for example the New Pin Project (Pound and Mills 1985).

How should the Child Guidance Clinics be administered to facilitate a flexible response to their communities?

The Education Authorities have so far funded the administration of the clinics in most areas, and consequently have had the major voice in their running and philosophy. In the past the education authorities took this responsibility because teachers felt the need for help and support with children with emotional and behavioural problems with whom they spend more than six hours a day for many days a year.

Of the other disciplines, medicine in particular had not in the past shown much interest in 'maladjusted' children. However, the emergence and development in relatively recent years of a branch of medicine with paediatric and general psychiatry roots, called child and adolescent psychiatry, is gradually growing strong enough for the health authorities to take a more active role, not only in the provision of clinical personnel, but also in the whole administration and management of the community Child Guidance Clinics.

In fact a more persuasive case can now be made again for the Child Guidance Clinics to become the community arm of the child and adolescent psychiatry services (Court 1976). However, it may be too soon or inappropriate for the Health Service to carry the full financial burden of the Clinics, and an intermediate or alternative model may be necessary. In this model the health authorities would assume their share of accommodation, administration, secretarial, clerical, furnishing and equipment costs of the community aspect of child and adolescent psychiatry, that is make a contribution to the Child Guidance Service beyond the salaries of a small number of usually part-time staff.

Similarly, in districts where Social Services Departments wish for a share in the assessment and treatment resources of Health and Education Departments, they should be prepared to second social workers on a permanent or long-term basis to the Child Guidance Clinics and also to share the funding of the running of the Clinics. These contributions from the other two services would free the education authorities to take only their fair share of the costs of the Child Guidance Clinics, and would encourage the Clinic not only to have a community-wide remit to schools and school-age children, but also to have collaboration between them for the management and administration of the Child Guidance Clinics.

A small management committee consisting of management representatives from Health, Education and Social Services Departments, and the budget holder from each Child Guidance Clinic in the district would act as the intermediary body between the three services and the Child Guidance Clinics. The functions of such a committee would be to hold the budget allocated from the three services and to manage the funding and staffing of the Clinics in the district. Such committees could be similar to or the same as those needed for other joint ventures between local authorities and district health authorities, such as services for physically and learning disabled people.

The clinical staff of the district would benefit from their own multi-disciplinary organization (in addition to each discipline's professional body), perhaps to be called something like a Child and Family Mental Health Group. This would act as a forum from which to influence the management committee on the direction in which Child Guidance Clinics should be progressing, which aspects of the service could be curtailed and which initiatives should be essayed. Similarly, the community health councils, parent–teacher associations and other parent groups or local watch-dog bodies would be encouraged to feed information to the management committees to ensure responsiveness to the consumers of the Child Guidance Service.

Roles, relationships and responsibility of disciplines within the Child Guidance Units

In order to function efficiently and meet the needs of its local children and families, the Child Guidance Service has to have not only a workable administration by its parent bodies, but also a clear and agreed internal structure. It is unlikely that the district health authorities will have the finances to run Child Guidance Clinics as the community branch of the hospital and community child psychiatry service in the 1990s, and it is in any case questionable whether the model of organization used by hospitals is appropriate for a community setting.

For the foreseeable future, therefore, we are likely to require ways of structuring the clinics to facilitate collaboration of the multi-disciplinary personnel and a system of lines of responsibility acceptable to each discipline and each of the parent services (health, education and social). Various strategies have been adopted to try to overcome or avoid the potential problems of the uncertainty of primacy among the senior members of each discipline in a clinic (Brunel Institute of Organization and Social Studies 1976). For example, the system of Team Co-ordinator (rotating between senior clinic staff) used by the Inner London Education Authority for its fourteen Child Guidance Units before its dissolution in March 1990 still contained the germs of discontent and inter-discipline conflict with consequent occasional undermining of clinic effectiveness. With the introduction of increased accountability of doctors in the NHS and funding of secondary health care units becoming dependent on their use by the referring general practitioners and district health authority, consultant child psychiatrists will wish to be more in control of what goes on in their name. Similarly, educational psychologists and the principal social workers will increasingly feel the pull of the strings of their managers, who will want them to account clearly for the value of their work in the Child Guidance Clinics. In order to do so the educational psychologists and social workers will feel the need for control over some aspects of the work of the units.

One way to deal with this is to designate as child and adolescent psychiatry the part of Child Guidance work which is carried out by NHS employees (child psychiatrists, psychotherapists, clinical child psychologists and nurses) with any seconded or co-opted social workers or others. For that aspect of the work of the Clinic carried out by NHS employees, the consultant psychiatrist would have medical responsibility for the assessments and treatment as in other areas of the NHS. This part of the work of the Child Guidance Clinic would be with children and adolescents whose behaviour or emotional state had become handicapping. The treatment or intervention provided might be with the individual or family, or in a group of children or young people. The other parts of the work of the Child Guidance Clinics such as intellectual or developmental assessments, preventative counselling or consultation, and other forms of liaison and teaching, would be seen as the primary focus and responsibility of the other major disciplines in the clinic.

In this way liaison and consultation with teachers, or the counselling of pre-morbid youngsters with problems in school or clinic, or the running of groups for children with less severe behaviour problems than the psychiatric group, would be the responsibility of the educational psychologist. Any other members of the team (eg psychiatrist or social worker) might participate and at times be the main worker on a project in this part of the work of the clinic, but would be responsible to the educational psychologist when doing so. This section of the work of the Child Guidance Clinic might be termed the Schools Psychosocial Service or Education Guidance Service.

Similarly liaison and consultation with social workers in the various community settings – fieldwork teams, children's homes, and so on – would be the responsibility of the most senior psychiatric social worker in the clinic. This aspect of the work would also include the Child Guidance Clinic's response to requests for the assessment and treatment of child abuse cases referred by the Social Services Department of the local authority. It would also include any specialist service that the Unit was able to provide for children where family breakdown has occurred, such as counselling children of divorced parents, and conciliation work with separating parents, and advising in cases of disputed custody and access.

Again, any other team member of different disciplines might join the psychiatric social worker in this work, but would then be responsible to the psychiatric social worker in charge. This part of the work of the Child Guidance Unit might be called the Family Guidance Service. In this way the areas of expertise would be more clearly defined, and the lines of responsibility both within the Clinic and with the external bodies would be better acknowledged. It would mean also that the ownership of the records of clinical activity, the gathering of statistics and the provision of stationery and other supplies would be the responsibility of each of the parent services. So for the child and adolescent psychiatry section of the Child Guidance Clinics, supplies, statistics and records would be the responsibility of the health authority. For the School Psychosocial Service or Education Guidance Service part of the Child Guidance Clinic, these functions would be the responsibility of the Education Department; and for the Family Guidance Service part of the clinic they would be the responsibility of the Social Services Department (or Education Department if the Education Department employed the PSWs).

Obviously internal referrals between the different sections of the clinic would need to occur if a change in therapeutic intervention was called for. For example, a family might be seen in the Family Guidance section for conciliation work with a divorcing couple and associated support in some family sessions for the three children. If one of the children develops handicapping psychosomatic and depressive symptoms, he might be referred to and registered in the child and adolescent psychiatry section as well for assessment, and especially if additional or alternative treatments were then recommended. There would also then have to be an agreement within the Clinic about whether to run more than one intervention concurrently or to provide one at a time. With this model the old title might be dropped as no longer describing the activities or the joint service. Something like Family and Educational Guidance Centre with Child and Adolescent Psychiatry Clinic might be chosen instead.

In these various ways the needs of the children and families and their primary care workers in a local community in the 1990s are more likely to be attended to and sometimes met.

Postscript: but what if . . .?

If we are hopeful, however tentatively, of influencing the evolution of services by anticipation, then it is tempting to take a step further. Local Community Clinics are where the buck stops. There is rarely any other place to refer on to after an assessment; this is where the proposed treatment plan usually has to be carried out. Despite all the strictures about evaluation of treatment, psychological therapies are destined to be the interventions of choice for behavioural and emotional disorders and relationship problems, and will increasingly be carried out by people other than psychiatrists, especially in the Community Clinics. Psychiatrists, like other medical doctors, tend to be illness oriented and better trained than other disciplines in a broad approach to diagnosis and assessment as well as in psychopharmacology. Drug treatment in child psychiatry may become more available and useful (Rutter 1986) but it will probably continue only to contribute to the treatment of a small range of conditions more often dealt with in hospitals. From the point of view of the optimal use of resources, therefore, the time may approach where child psychiatrists will be encouraged to work mainly in the hospital service with conditions which utilize their medical and general psychiatric training such as psychological problems presenting as physical symptoms, psychoses, physical disability, and chronic and life-threatening disease including those congenital or metabolic disorders leading to major learning disability and effects on social and personality development. It is then not too great a leap to the recognition that the child psychiatrist's branch of the evolutionary tree may die out; while another shoot of paediatrics – perhaps developmental neurology – strengthens itself by absorbing and incorporating the investigation and management of the emotional and behavioural aspects of disorders.

Such changes if they were to occur might stimulate development in the psychologist's part of the evolutionary tree. At the present time clinical child psychologists are a small professional group, and can be employed by Health or Social Services when their value is recognized and funding is available. There is a lot to be said now for educational psychologists and clinical child psychologists joining forces (Court 1976; Rutter 1986), and perhaps linking with psychologists working with adults to form an independent District Psychology Service. The possibility then arises for a further alternative metamorphosis of the old Child Guidance Service into a Primary Community Child Psychology Service with clinical, social, educational and developmental components. But such possibilities are not even stirring among the social institutional 'genes' at the moment, and nourishment in the form of potential funding is nowhere to be seen, so we had better leave further futuristic fictional fantasies to the twenty-first century.

References

Bailey, D. and Garralda, M.E. (1989) Referral to child psychiatry: parent and doctor motives and expectations, *Journal of Child Psychology and Psychiatry* 30: 449–58.
Black, D. (1987) The future of Child Guidance, in J.A. MacFarlane (ed.) *Progress in Child Health*, vol. 3, London: Churchill Livingstone.

Black, D. (1989) Consultant manpower in child psychiatry, *Bulletin of the Royal College of Psychiatrists* 13(1): 32–5.

Blacker, C.P. (1948) *Neurosis and the Mental Health Service*, Oxford: Oxford Medical Publications.

Brunel Institute of Organisation and Social Studies (BIOSS) (1976) *Future Organisation in Child Guidance and Allied Work*, Uxbridge: Brunel University.

Burck, C. (1978) A study of families' expectations and experiences of a Child Guidance Clinic, *British Journal of Social Work* 8: 145–58.

Cameron, K. (1956) Past and present trends in child psychiatry, *Journal of Mental Science* 102: 599–603.

Cottrell, D., Hill, P., Walk, D., Dearnaley, J. and Ierotheou, A. (1988) Factors influencing non-attendance at child psychiatry out-patient appointments, *British Journal of Psychiatry* 152: 201–4.

Court, S.D.M. (1976) *Fit for the Future: Report of the Committee on Child Health Services*, London: HMSO.

Dowling, E. and Osborne, E. (1985) *The Family and the School: A Joint Systems Approach to Problems with Children*, London: Routledge & Kegan Paul.

Dupont, S. and Dowdney, E. (1985) Dilemmas in working with schools, *Newsletter of the Association for Child Psychology and Psychiatry* 12: 13–16.

Eisenberg, L. (1969) Child psychiatry: the past quarter century, *American Journal of Orthopsychiatry* 39: 389–401.

Healy, W. (1915) *The Individual Delinquent: A Textbook of Diagnosis and Prognosis*.

Hersov, L. (1986) Child psychiatry in Britain: the last 30 years, *Journal of Child Psychology and Psychiatry* 27: 781–801.

Hetznecker, W. and Forman, M.A. (1971) Community child psychiatry: evolution and direction, *American Journal of Orthopsychiatry* 41: 350–70.

Hetznecker, W. and Forman, M.A. (1974) *On Behalf of Children*, New York: Grune & Stratton.

Howells, J.G. (1965) Organisation of child psychiatric services, in J.G. Howells (ed.) *Modern Perspectives in Child Psychiatry*, Edinburgh and London: Oliver & Boyd.

Kanner, L. (1959) The Thirty-Third Maudsley Lecture: trends in child psychiatry, *Journal of Mental Science* 105: 581–93.

Kazdin, A.E. (1988) Promising approaches to treatment, in *Child Psychiatry*, Oxford: Pergamon Press.

Kolvin, I., Garside, R.F., Nicol, A.R., MacMillan, A., Wolstenholme, F. and Leitch, I.M. (1981) *Help Starts Here: The Maladjusted Child in the Ordinary School*, London: Tavistock.

Mannino, F.V. and Shore, M.F. (1975) The effects of consultation: a review of empirical studies, *American Journal of Community Psychology* 3: 1–21.

Parry-Jones, W.H. (1989) Annotation: the history of child and adolescent psychiatry: its present day relevance, *Journal of Child Psychology and Psychiatry* 30: 3–11.

Patterson, G.R., Chamberlain, P. and Reid, J.B. (1982) A comparative evaluation of a parent-training program, *Behaviour Therapy* 13: 638–50.

Pellegrini, D.S. and Urbain, E.S. (1985) An evaluation of interpersonal cognitive problem-solving training with children, *Journal of Child Psychology and Psychiatry* 26: 17–41.

Pound, A. and Mills, M. (1985) A pilot evaluation of Newpin – Home-visiting and Befriending Scheme in South London, *Newsletter of the Association for Child Psychology and Psychiatry* 7(4): 13–15.

Rafferty, F.T. (1975) Community mental health centres and the criteria of quantity and universality of services for children, *Journal of American Academy of Child Psychiatry* 14: 5–17.

Ritter, D.R. (1978) Effects of a school consultation programme upon referral pattern of teachers, *Psychology in the Schools* 15: 239–43.

Royal College of Psychiatrists (1985) Providing a district service for child and adolescent psychiatry: medical manpower priority, *Bulletin of Royal College of Psychiatrists* May: 94–7.

Rutter, M. (1985) Family and school influences on behavioural development, *Journal of Child Psychology and Psychiatry* 26: 349–68.

Rutter, M. (1986) Child psychiatry: looking 30 years ahead, *Journal of Child Psychology and Psychiatry* 27: 803–40.

Rutter, M., Tizard, J. and Whitmore, K. (1970) *Education, Health and Behaviour*, London: Longman.

Rutter, M., Cox, A., Tupling, C., Berger, M. and Yule, W. (1975) Attainment and adjustment in two geographical areas, *British Journal of Psychiatry* 126: 493–509.

Subotsky, F. and Berelowitz, G. (1990) Consumer views at a Community Child Guidance Clinic, *Newsletter of the Association for Child Psychology and Psychiatry* 12: 8–12.

Tizard, J. (1973) Maladjusted children and the Child Guidance Service, *London Educational Review* 2: 22–37.

Warren, W. (1971) 'You can never plan the future by the past': the development of child and adolescent psychiatry in England and Wales, *Journal of Child Psychology and Psychiatry* 11: 241–57.

Weisz, J.R., Weiss, B., Alicka, M.D. and Klotz, M.L. (1987) Effectiveness of psychotherapy with children and adolescents: a meta-analysis for clinicians, *Journal of Consulting and Clinical Psychology* 55: 542–9.

Yule, W. (1985) Behavioural approaches, in M. Rutter and L. Hersov (eds) *Child and Adolescent Psychiatry: Modern Approaches*, Oxford: Blackwell Scientific Publications.

School support: towards a multi-disciplinary approach

PETER GRAY AND JIM NOAKES

Introduction

There has been considerable interest recently in developing services within local education authorities (LEAs) to support mainstream schools in dealing with problems of difficult behaviour. The term 'support' merits further consideration. A brief review of the literature suggests a range of activities, from permanent or temporary off-site placement to 'whole-school' approaches to mainstream curricular and pastoral development. As the financing of support services to schools and local authorities is increasingly under scrutiny (following recent legislation requiring 'local management of schools'), consumer attitudes to different types of support are becoming increasingly relevant.

With behaviour difficulties, removal of 'the problem pupil' (by the provision of alternative placement) is often the kind of support schools ask for (Gray and Noakes 1987). This provides satisfaction and relief in the short term: a problem which has been stressful and time-consuming 'disappears'. However, places available in alternative provision are finite and schools become frustrated when places are filled and there is no support available for new problems. Inevitably, while outside provision is limited, further support of this type can be released only by reintegrating children: a process which can be beset with difficulties, particularly when placements are remote from the child's originating school (see Gray and Noakes 1992). Such difficulties can be prevented only by adequate planning *before* segregation, which reduces the chances of a quick and easy solution.

Another form of support popular with schools has been additional staffing. Provision of extra help in the form of additional teaching or welfare assistant time has been a growth industry in many LEAs since the Education Act 1981. However, more recently, as financial constraints have been imposed by government on the amount of resources that any LEA can maintain centrally, ceilings have been introduced. The idea that more and more outside resources can be drawn upon to provide support to schools is no longer tenable. It is increasingly a matter of ensuring that the support available can be fairly distributed and accurately targeted at the most needy situations.

The need to release resources from one school and reallocate them to another, however, is beset with as many difficulties as making space in a segregated provision. Both the schools and children become dependent on the presence of the resources in order to keep the problem manageable. There is rarely a clear plan aimed at effecting the sort of genuine change that would reduce the need for additional help. As a result, the limited number of resources that an LEA maintains cannot easily be made available for more urgent needs that may arise. Again, an adequate turnover and redistribution of resources can be achieved only if there is a clear plan or contract between schools and resource providers when resources are first allocated (Gray 1986). This requires a degree of work which may reduce the appeal of a potentially immediate solution.

While external management and direction of support may be less popular with schools, there is some evidence that this increases the chances of redistribution of support. External management also ensures that there is some overview of relative priorities *across* schools within an area. However, anyone based in a particular school but managed externally has to tread a lonely path in no man's land with often conflicting loyalties and accountabilities. There are in fact several major advantages to support staff being based together 'off-site' in a team covering a number of schools, despite the reduction in 'accessibility'. Coulby and Harper (1985) summarize these as follows:

1 If support service resources are not tied to specific schools, they can be used flexibly according to varying needs across an area.
2 As part of a team, support staff are more likely to develop in their particular role, rather than simply be subsumed into an individual school system.
3 An outsider is not necessarily bound by existing school organizational hierarchies and can therefore provide support at a variety of levels (pupils, teacher, senior staff, etc.)
4 Difficult behaviour usually gives rise to conflict (eg between school and parents) and it is easier for an outsider to be seen as having a neutral perspective.
5 The 'expertise of the outsider', despite its problems, carries with it an aura of credibility which is sometimes necessary.
6 An outsider support service is more likely to be in regular contact with a range of other agencies and can assist in fostering productive liaison between agencies and schools.

A danger inherent in having outside support services, however, is that they can proliferate, resulting in potential confusion for 'consumers' (schools and families) and for the services themselves. There is currently a range of services involved in school support of some form or other (eg educational psychology, educational welfare, behaviour support teachers, social services and child guidance). While such services individually are increasingly making attempts to develop their *internal* coherence, this may still not tackle the problems inherent in external support.

In this chapter, we intend to explore some of the issues that may arise between different support services in the area of emotional and behavioural difficulties and consider in more detail the need for a coherent multi-disciplinary approach. We shall argue that such an approach is facilitated by clear structures and indicate from our experience how these assisted with moves towards more coherent support for schools within one LEA. In our view multi-disciplinary support services are a realistic aim towards which we should seek to progress. There are, of course, alternative models of support other than those already mentioned including 'whole school approaches'. Although the advantages of such approaches have been described elsewhere (eg Dessent 1987), it is as yet unclear how far they seek to replace or complement traditional off-site support structures. In our view any support system must be judged largely by its ability to assist with tackling problems in the context within which they occur.

EBD: the network of services

The number of relevant support services surrounding schools is extensive (see Table 11.1; also Johnson et al. 1980). Children with serious emotional or behavioural difficulties (EBD) often come to the attention of a variety of these, either in succession or simultaneously. However, it is rare that responsibility for such problems is eagerly embraced by any particular agency. Behaviour difficulties are characterized by an atmosphere of stress which derives from perceived challenges to people's personal effectiveness and control. Support workers themselves are not immune to such feelings.

However, even when responsibility is accepted by an agency or an individual, freedom from interference cannot be guaranteed. A detailed plan may be made which can be disrupted by the introduction of a new agency which fails to consult those already involved. Moreover, where an attempt is made to include other agencies and ascribe functions to them, contributions do not always follow the expected pattern.

Coherent multi-disciplinary responses in fact require joint planning and a mutual understanding of what various services can practically offer. However, the potential barriers are considerable. Patterns of service vary both within and between authorities. Mutual accessibility of services may be restricted by geographical distance between bases and formalized referral systems. Organization and administration tends to differ across departments (Education, Health and Social Services). Area boundaries are not necessarily conterminous and there may be differing policies and pressures. At a case work level, there may be conflicts in perspectives or models of working that can be confirmed and reinforced by the focus and traditions of particular services. Thus Reid (1986) cites Skinner et al.'s (1983) attempt to outline some of the differences in outlook between social workers and teachers. Reid draws attention to the tendency of social workers to emphasize family rather than individuals as clients, to see 'inadequacies' in terms of family resources rather than family or parental morality, and to put less emphasis on schools as being necessary (or in some cases positive) environments for child and adolescent development. A distinction might also be drawn between medical personnel and educational psychologists: the former tending to consider behaviour and educational performance as deriving primarily from 'within-child' factors (eg 'hyperkinesis', 'dyslexia', 'minimal

Table 11.1 Members of agencies or institutions who may be involved with children with EBD

Education	Social Services	Health	Other
Mainstream school staff	Fieldwork social workers	Child Guidance team	Juvenile bureau (police)
Education welfare officers	Residential/day care	Clinical medical	Probation officers
Educational psychologists	social workers	officers	
	Foster-parents	General practitioners	Private sector clinics and individuals
Behaviour support service	Observation and assessment staff	Hospital out-patients staff	
On-site or off-site provision	Court officer	Health visitors	
Other specialized educational services	Social Services alternative project staff (eg IT, etc.)	Adolescent psychiatric unit staff	
Administrators		Paramedical staff (eg physiotherapy, speech therapists)	

brain dysfunction') and the latter focusing more on relevant curricular factors and the possibilities of change.

Fundamental variations between professional support services can in fact occur in relation to any number of the following areas:

1 *The client* Although there is a trend among services now to broaden their focus, there is still a tendency for different client emphases. Thus, Child Guidance personnel stress the privacy and confidentiality of their relationship with parents and children. Educational support services, on the other hand, may see their major client as being teachers and schools.

2 *Nature of investigation* Services differ in the types of questions they may ask. Questions relate to differing models and views about causes. Behaviourally oriented services attempt to clarify in observable terms the problems raised by those voicing concern. Psychodynamically oriented services may focus on identifying 'pathological' behaviour and relating this to developmental disturbance. There may be a difference in status given to historical as opposed to present-day events.

3 *Types of explanation* Views of causation may differ. These relate partly to the client focuses of different agencies. Those predominantly involved with family stresses and pressures may come to see schools as destructive and uncaring. Those who work more closely with schools may identify with their compensatory aspirations and emphasize the negative aspects of family background. A particularly strong identification with the child's perspective may encourage a view that all ills are due to parental, school or neighbourhood inadequacies.

4 *View of concern* Agencies vary as to the extent to which they see concern as legitimate. Some services tend to insist on clear evidence to substantiate reports. Others may accept reports without challenge, on the basis that their source is regarded as 'respectable', or that there is 'no smoke without fire'.

Agencies also have different thresholds for what they consider a problem. This relates to the type and range of their responsibilities. Failure to attend school may be considered a minor problem by those involved in 'last-ditch' attempts to keep a family together. An isolated disruptive incident, however bizarre or offensive, may not be seen as a priority by a service which deals with difficulties of a more persistent nature.

5 *Ideas about change* Those holding strong views about internal causation are unlikely to believe that change can be easily achieved, at least without considerable specialist input at an individual level. Services, on the other hand, who think that environment has a significant part to play in the development and maintenance of behaviour, are likely to have greater belief in the viability of change, especially if they have a strong community rather than clinic focus. Commitment to change is likely to be strongest where a service considers that an environment in which they have a direct concern (eg school or family) contributes to the occurrence of the problem and is amenable to alteration in some way.

Beliefs about change are also in part dictated by the extent to which any agency ultimately has responsibility for tackling the problem. Services have varying accountability in this respect which relates to the extent of their statutory duties.

Working within a multi-disciplinary context: 'unilateral' or 'multilateral' approaches?

In the face of the possible complications and territorial disputes involved in multi-disciplinary work, any service may be tempted to adopt a 'unilateral' position. Clear rules for the particular service may be specified, outlining the criteria for involvement, the types of problems deemed appropriate to tackle and the methodology that will be used. Although service members may feel more confident about defending their ground in this context, their accountability is perhaps more limited than it seems. Criteria can be set that increase the changes of success (eg dealing with less complex cases). Failure to achieve the desired outcome may be attributed to the service's methodology being inappropriate 'in this particular case', with subsequent 'cross-referrals' to other agencies who might offer an alternative.

A 'multilateral' approach, on the other hand, would seek to offer greater flexibility, with service responses being informed by as well as informing other agencies. Regular negotiation and clarification of respective responsibilities, both at an organizational and individual casework level, would be necessary to ensure that services could be sure of their relative contributions and be able to evaluate these. Moreover, some obligation would remain among professionals to continue an interest in cases where preferred methods had been relatively unsuccessful in their own terms.

The advantages and disadvantages of these two approaches can be summarized as follows.

The *unilateral approach* has greater internal and external predictability. The skills involved with a particular service can become well-practised and all members, including clerical and administrative staff, can become familiar with what the public may legitimately expect. There is no continuing need to redefine one's service to the consumer. The limits of the service are acknowledged explicitly and there are fewer grounds for frustration and disappointment if the service withdraws after an agreed period. The disadvantages of the approach are the lack of incentive for development of skills and the dangers of over-generalizing particular techniques to situations where they are inappropriate. There are dangers too of passing more complex problems on elsewhere and missing the opportunity to improvise and develop solutions through joint work with other services who may have a concurrent interest.

A *multilateral approach* has the advantage of being able to match service responses more closely to particular needs. It is difficult for services working unilaterally to do this unless they have a well-informed 'intake' system. Types of need which are not covered by existing patterns of service can be more easily identified. New responses can be developed and shared and new skills learned. Fuller use can also be made of the resources and skills that are available among services area-wide.

On the other hand, once a service loosens its boundaries, there are increasing strains on what might constitute 'service policy'. There are dangers of losing direction and of ending up reacting to other people's cast-offs. Developing new skills requires time and energy and a willingness to ignore certain status considerations.

In our view, the unilateral approach, though attractive, is untenable if professional responses to the full range of emotional and behavioural difficulties are being considered. However, the move towards a truly multi-disciplinary way of working (which amounts to more than traditional case-conference gossip-mongering) will have to be a gradual one. In the next section, we will explain how moves were made in one LEA towards providing more coherent support for teachers of children with EBD.

Steps towards a unified support service: experience within one LEA

LEAs usually have a range of peripatetic services which tend to be separately organized. The Warnock Report (1978) recommended unification of these into 'Special Educational Needs Advisory Services'. The position of the educational psychology service within this has been unclear and there have been continuing rivalries between educational psychologists and special needs advisers over management responsibilities.

Unfortunately, while these may be important in status terms, they do not usually lead to productive working. In the fight to establish management hierarchies, it is sometimes forgotten that the main purpose of setting up more unified services is to enable professionals to work together more effectively rather than to enforce respect.

In the particular LEA in which we worked, we were perhaps fortunate that some locational integration of services had been achieved early. In the late 1960s remedial advisory staff, educational psychologists (EPs) and Child Guidance personnel moved together to purpose-built premises. The Child Guidance Team (psychotherapists, psychiatric social workers, psychologists and psychiatrists) subsequently moved into a separate centre, following an increasing distinction between school and family-focused work. The remaining professionals included EPs, remedial advisory staff and the staff of a part-time off-site unit based in the building which had officially provided an assessment facility for children referred to the EPs. In the absence of any alternative day special facility for children with EBD in the borough, however, this unit had been under pressure to provide a 'relief' placement for mainstream schools.

Until about 1983, services had worked to some extent in parallel (and sometimes in opposition!). Relations between the services were not always smooth. Some resentment was expressed by the remedial advisory staff against educational psychologists encroaching on their traditional domain of learning support in mainstream. EPs were perceived to be adopting a narrow behaviourist view of curriculum. On the other hand, following the Warnock Report (1978), EPs were becoming increasingly frustrated with rubber-stamping special school placements that had already been advocated by other support services. Unit staff complained of the lack of support that they received from other services in dealing with some of the more difficult children that they were expected to manage.

Moves towards more functional integration of services were facilitated by a number of developments: first, the LEA, following the Education Act 1981, issued clear guidelines to schools which attempted to clarify responsibilities for children with special needs and pointed to good practice in involving parents early in both assessment and intervention, and in working with support services *in partnership*. Second, within the building, area teams were created that covered geographical 'patches'. These initially included an educational psychologist, a remedial advisory teacher and a clerical assistant. Finally, a new teacher was appointed to take charge of the 'unit', who sought to improve contact with mainstream schools and provide support for children with difficult behaviour *within the mainstream context*. This approach linked unit staff more closely with the types of service being offered by the newly created 'Teams'.

The LEA guidelines were particularly useful in so far as they provided a common framework for all the constituent services. Although the guidelines involved a number of stages in the assessment and provision for children with special needs, three levels of involvement could be clearly differentiated (see Table 11.2). Level I could be characterized as mainly preventive, providing a forum for consultation and in-service training to schools and assistance with system change. Level II was typically individual casework with aims shared by parents, teachers and support workers, usually over a specified period. The number of such cases was limited to enable effective working within the service's resource capacity. Level III involved the LEA deciding that an individual's difficulties were exceptional across the borough and that therefore provision of additional resources was a priority. Support services were involved in providing formal advice to the LEA on this issue and, in some cases, supervising the resources allocated following formal assessment under the Education Act 1981.

Teamwork in practice

The structures outlined above assisted in a number of ways. At Level I, exchanges of information between team members arising from informed contact with schools helped provide a clearer picture of specific needs in the areas of learning and behaviour difficulties. It was possible for different professional disciplines to consult with each other and collaborate on in-service and project work. Team discussions of caseloads ensured greater joint responsibility, even when particular team members were working independently on cases. Team members' awareness of each other's finite capacity restricted the tendency to off-load and stimulated discussion about ways of keeping case involvements finite.

At the level of statutory work (Level III), there was a particular need for coherence. Without any alternative day provision for children with EBD, the team had to deal with some extremely difficult cases (and it is these that expose any shortcomings in a service's quality of response!). It is perhaps fruitful to provide some examples of work at this level where a team approach was beneficial.

Case study: Wayne

Wayne was 10-year-old who had already attended four different schools within the borough before being brought to the attention of Team 'A'. School records indicated that each school had been glad to see the back of him. Each had

Table 11.2 Levels of responsibility and involvement with children with special educational needs (adapted from LEA Guidelines)

	Whose responsibility?	Characteristics of service involvement	Example activities (behaviour area)
Level I	School and parents	Informal advice Project work In-service training	Consultative visits to schools (regular) Advice to teachers on possible methods of collecting data/tackling problems Developing school rewards/sanction system In-service training courses for schools
Level II	School and parents together with (named) support service(s)	Individual casework • with aims and objectives clarified • agreed by/involving all relevant parties • formal 'referral'	Individual/group interviews with child, teacher(s) and parent(s) Information collection from variety of sources Analysis of problem and formulation of intervention Possibility of individual sessions (limited withdrawal)
Level III	School and parents together with (named) support services(s) Overseen by LEA officers	Individual casework (as above) and consideration of resource issues • Access to additional resources on/off-site • 'formal assessment' • statements (Education Act 1981)	Documentation of success/problem areas of interventions tried Innovative use of additional resources with a view to removal of these when success criteria achieved Supervision/training of additional staff (eg welfare assistants) Monitoring and review

requested the assistance of the EP shortly after he started, but alternative courses of action (school transfer) were negotiated before programmes could be put into practice. There was a history of diverse contact between school and family, with a tendency for behaviour to be justified by parents as a reasonable reaction to inappropriate work requirements or hostile teachers. Wayne had already been subject to several exclusions from school and prosecutions by the police for alleged neighbourhood offences. Following a 'last straw' exclusion when Wayne had to be physically removed from the classroom by his headteacher, a meeting was held to which parents were invited; this was chaired by a senior education officer. The meeting was repeatedly disrupted by Wayne, who had arrived independently at school, bursting into the room demanding to know what was going on.

In this very difficult case, the educational psychologist was required by the LEA to co-ordinate formal assessment of the child (under the Education Act 1981) over a period with the aim of determining whether Wayne would be able to succeed in mainstream with reducing support or alternative provision would be needed. Additional teacher resources had been allocated to the Behaviour Support Service and it was planned that Wayne should be taught at the centre and reintegrated over a period into his primary school. The teacher allocated was expected during the course of the programme to develop from an individual contact role to that of a formal observer in the classroom. The teacher had worked only in mainstream classrooms and needed training and support in both of the roles envisaged. The behaviour support teacher was able to provide this by designing a token economy system for the allocated teacher to use with Wayne at the centre during individual teaching sessions and by organizing regular supervision meetings. These included in-service sessions on particular techniques, assistance with analysis of Wayne's day-to-day behaviour, and with implementing programmes agreed.

The behaviour support teacher in turn worked closely with the educational psychologist in formulating the overall management plan; specifically the phasing of the reintegration process, setting reasonable time limits for each stage, and deciding the contingencies for success and failure. Any changes to the programme were discussed and agreed jointly. In addition, he was able to monitor on an occasional basis and supplement the observations of the allocated teacher, and provide therapeutic sessions on an individual basis with Wayne in a particular area of identified need (temper control).

The educational psychologist was able to liaise closely with the LEA over the nature and use of the additional resource, discuss the practicalities of the formal assessment process and clarify these with parents. He was also able to identify particular needs for the programme to tackle and discuss in detail with the behaviour support teacher how this might be achieved, as well as participate in regular reviews of Wayne's progress on the programme.

As already stated, the parents considered that many of the difficulties presented were due to inappropriate work set. The team were able to draw on the resources of their advisory teacher for learning difficulties who made a thorough assessment of Wayne's basic educational skills and devised a suitable programme of work which the teacher was able to continue at the centre and parents were able to support with a home-based programme. This was a vital step towards securing improved parental collaboration and could not have been guaranteed if assessment was dependent on another service's 'unilateral rules'.

In this case there were further benefits of a team approach with joint responsibility. Different team members were able to support each other when things seemed to be going wrong and, when necessary, step outside of their narrow role definition and relieve pressures on an individual member. By sharing a problem in this way, considerable levels of expertise were built up within the team. By pooling experience from a range of disciplines, creative solutions to difficult problems were engendered. Most importantly, the knowledge of the problems experienced by individuals within their own particular role definition was understood by all members of the team, which prevented the 'buck passing' that can be only too common with cases of this kind.

The school benefited here from consistent and coherent support at times of difficulty and from the opportunity to anticipate and plan for problems that might occur, rather than responding without preparation to crises.

Case study: Tracy

Tracy was a secondary-aged pupil who had experienced considerable domestic turmoil after the death of her father and who moved schools frequently at junior age. In her first year at secondary school, she had been suspended pending action by the LEA and her mother had moved into our borough to provide another start at a new school. On her first day there Tracy was sent home for swearing at a senior member of staff.

Following an initial attempt by the behaviour support teacher to help Tracy change her behaviour, it became clear that she was able to control her own actions to a greater extent than had been imagined and was also rather good at manipulating the behaviour of adults; this had resulted in a lack of clear and consistent limits being set for her by significant adults. Her mother and new stepfather did not want to participate in any programme to control Tracy at school, preferring to consider alternative causes for any difficulties. They proposed a variety of medical explanations (premenstrual tension, pubertal abnormalities, psychiatric illness) which needed adequate investigation before returning to the management issues. During this period, Tracy continued to test the limits by becoming involved in increasingly disturbing incidents (smearing faeces, alleging unsubstantiated sexual abuse, 'suicide attempts') as well as a range of confrontations with staff.

Involving the educational psychologist created the opportunity, with parental permission, to liaise effectively with hospital consultants who became involved, in order to clarify the reality of any physical condition and its implications for Tracy's behaviour. In the meantime, it was possible for the behaviour support teacher to implement and maintain a management programme over a lengthy period of time, providing the option of a weekly withdrawal session as part of this strategy and jointly analysing with the team psychologist some of the more bizarre incidents that occurred. With the level of stress and the variety of explanations that were being proposed by Tracy, her parents and her teachers, it was particularly important to have a means of standing back and considering what was actually happening.

During times of particular difficulties, it was possible for the team to access the expertise of colleagues across teams which proved particularly valuable when stress levels were high. It was also possible to use colleagues not directly involved in the case to carry out a monitoring role when there was a need to clarify reported behaviour.

Tracy was a child who put considerable pressure on the complexity of the secondary school system and on the network of welfare services that surround it. Although it was not always possible to prevent diversions from the process of tackling her school behaviour, the maintenance of a consistent approach by at least some of the services helped the school adhere to clearer limits and expectations than might have been the case.

Case study: Kevin

Kevin was a child who had been placed in an integrated assessment nursery apparently because of delayed language development. The nursery had expressed serious reservations about his ability to cope in a mainstream infants school. Investigation had clarified that the main concern was now about his behaviour. There were major difficulties whenever compliance was required, with Kevin screaming, running away, and kicking or hitting adults who tried to restrain him. Although special educational needs continued to be stressed, his language development had in fact almost reached the level that would be expected of a boy his age.

It was possible as a team to clarify the legitimate focus of support and ensure that any additional resources allocated following Kevin's formal assessment were directed towards developing compliant behaviour rather than simply avoiding the need to conform to the requirements of the normal infant school routine. The learning support teacher was able to draw on her cumulative experience to help clarify the organizational expectations of reception classes and the wide range of individuals that can be found within them. This was instructive for the behaviour support teacher whose experience had been predominantly with the secondary age range. He in turn was able to support the educational psychologist responsible for organizing and reviewing the infant behaviour programme, by sharing in the responsibility of training and managing the welfare assistant involved and attending meetings with school and parents where necessary. Once the programme was completed successfully, it was possible to involve the learning support teacher again in reviewing Kevin's educational progress which had been considerable as compliance had been increasingly achieved. This helped reinforce the class-teacher's view of the programme's success and direct attention towards more normalized teacher expectations.

The infant school, which had anticipated considerable management difficulties, experienced some initially but was able, with the guidance of the support team, to use the welfare help constructively so that compliance was achieved and maintained even after the resources allocated were withdrawn. Without support, both they and Kevin could well have become dependent on the welfare assistant to avoid trouble. The release of welfare assistant time assisted allocation to another infant school where there was a more pressing problem.

Practical benefits of teamwork

The practical benefits of teamwork can be summarized as follows, from our experience.

1 *Easier access to the resources of other disciplines*   Workers attempting to involve people from other professional disciplines traditionally have to negotiate the complexities of varying referral systems. Each discipline tends to reserve the right to make its own assessment of the problem and judge its priority level in comparison with other commitments and responsibilities. While this may be to some extent inevitable (since services have to be realistic about their own resources), teamwork assists with clarifying the level of input that is actually required by different disciplines. This may range from minimal to intensive over a clearly defined period. Awareness of the current demands on others within the team may assist any service worker in stepping beyond his or her official role when necessary, ensuring greater flexibility. On the other hand, even minimal adherence to an official role within a jointly planned strategy can have significant effects (for example, being present at a meeting in a 'consultant' role, or carrying out a follow-up assessment).

2 *Professional development*   The skills of any particular professional discipline are not (and should not be) fixed. Working together with others encourages team members to develop new skills which can most easily be learned through observation (for example, in joint interviewing) or participation in programme planning. Members of different services have a chance to pool their skills. Advisory teachers who have often had a more substantial teaching background are able to benefit in turn from the perspectives of educational psychologists who have traditionally been involved with children in a wide range of contexts. Access to skills, knowledge and materials builds up a bank from which all members are drawn. Ongoing membership of individual professional groups ensures that these joint resources continue to be supplemented from outside.

3 *Support*   While any individual discipline may have its own support arrangements, some of the more intractable problems tend to need creative thinking which goes beyond the usual range of responses that are offered by a particular professional group. A well-designed behaviour modification programme may not be the best solution for a child in a school which is very resistant to the notion of behaviour change. Ways of changing attitudes or increasing commitment may need to be considered carefully with the support of other groups (eg family workers) who may deal regularly with situations where there is no *professional* requirement to change. When dealing with emotional and behaviour difficulties, the best-laid plans can go wrong, and with some cases at least, it is unrealistic to think that you can go it alone.

4 *Effectiveness*   There is no doubt that services working in parallel can easily duplicate each other's activity, which, if ineffective, can be frustrating (at the very least) for those dealing directly with the problem. Differing contributions, on the other hand, can easily lead to agencies being 'played off' against each other, with a resulting reduction in effectiveness for both. Such problems can be avoided if programmes are jointly planned, or at least if consultation

between services occurs early on. Although this may seem time-consuming for the hard-pressed support worker, such consultation tends to lead to better planning and less likelihood of interference.

Conclusion

In this chapter, we have given an overview of the benefits of closer collaboration between services in the welfare network. We have also described briefly the beginnings of 'teamwork' in school support within one particular LEA. Currently, teams are often limited to a small number of professional groups. Any attempt to include other support services in such a framework is clearly likely to be a slow process, considering the risks and uncertainties involved in breaking down professional and administrative barriers. We would like to conclude by suggesting some elements that, in our view, would assist progress towards a wider multi-disciplinary approach:

1 locational integration
2 co-terminosity
3 joint accountability
4 equitable distribution of power and responsibility
5 evaluation of effectiveness.

These elements are now described in detail.

Locational integration

Sharing of ideas and perspectives and acknowledging current limitations is a necessary first step towards formulating a joint approach to problems. Although a common institutional base does not guarantee that professional groups work effectively or harmoniously together, the chances of inter-professional discussion are at least increased by the greater proximity and accessibility of different group members.

Co-terminosity

Rarely do Health, Social Services and Education Departments have common geographical boundaries within local areas. This means that a member of one professional group may need to be in contact with several members of another over concerns within his or her 'patch'. Making boundaries co-terminous increases economy in inter-professional contact and the likelihood of coherence in approach.

Joint accountability

Many problems currently fall through the welfare net, and this is more likely to happen when case responsibility is not clearly agreed. An allocation system is necessary therefore, with one or two individuals assuming responsibility for work with each case or problem. Allocation may be on the basis of particular skills or interests (or a need to develop these), or on the basis of resource capacity. Allocation may also be dictated by official role (for example, the requirement on educational psychologists to submit written advice to LEAs and parents in formal assessments under the Education Act 1981, and the requirement on Social Services to call case conferences in the event of an incidence of child abuse). These are all reasonable criteria.

However, there is a danger with allocation that particular professional groups or individual workers may be continually saddled with the more intractable problems. It may not be too harsh to state that, in some cases, professional groups seek to define their official role in a way that protects them from taking on such difficulties. Where there is a perceived lack of parity in responsibility between individuals or different professional groups, harmonious multi-disciplinary structures are unlikely. While qualitative differences in role and the need for allocation must be acknowledged, there is a need to preserve a sense of joint responsibility. This can be achieved only by teams of professionals accepting that they are accountable as a unit for the total range of support services that they offer. Team accountability is not incompatible with individual day-to-day responsibility. It can be assisted by regular well-structured team meetings and by clear agreements about supervision arrangements when particularly complex cases are taken on.

As exemplified in Table 11.2, there are a number of levels at which services need to work in order to provide adequate support. As support services take on a greater share of responsibility, they become more accountable for their contribution. This accountability needs to be shared equitably, and all team members must therefore acknowledge the need to contribute to the planning and monitoring of more complex problems.

Equitable distribution of power and responsibility

In an ideal world, it may be desirable for power to be equally shared, not only among professionals but also within the communities with whom they work. In practice, there are differences in pay and formal status, both between professional groups and within them, which tend to conflict with such democratic ideals. Such differences may on the one hand lead to the view among less well-paid professionals that higher salaries should be linked with greater stresses and uncertainties. On the other hand, highly paid professional groups may seek to preserve their differential status by presenting themselves as specialized consultants with little responsibility for day-to-day planning. For example educational welfare officers and educational psychologists may not agree that an equal share of responsibility for intractable non-attendance cases is equitable. While differences in pay and formal status exist, progress towards truly multi-disciplinary structures is unlikely, unless such differences are explicitly related to an overall managerial consultative structure.

Another barrier is the lack of parallel internal structures. While some agencies have explicit managerial structures (eg social services), others have greater traditions of individual autonomy and professional equivalence. Emphasizing team as opposed to professional boundaries can pose a threat to the managerial structure of particular groups, unless this is recognized by the inclusion of a multi-disciplinary management tier. However, those members of multi-disciplinary teams who have experienced a tradition of equivalent status within their own professional group may resent the existence of a 'management body' that includes senior members of other professions whose management status they do not accept.

Again the exact status relationships need to be clarified if multi-disciplinary structures are to be viable at a wider level. Even with clear hierarchical relationships, there is a danger that some of the creative benefits of inter-disciplinary contact will be sacrificed to preserve people's positions within the hierarchy.

Informal status relations can do something to offset the effects of 'official' differences. Good experiences of work with members of other professional groups where both labour and credit are equally shared can also increase the chances of further collaboration. However, these efforts continue to be vulnerable to structural and managerial reorganization and cannot therefore be seen as a solution to the problem.

Evaluation of effectiveness

The arguments we have put forward in favour of multi-disciplinary teams are that they ultimately provide a more coherent service to the consumer. There are too many 'grey' areas where services have overlapping responsibilities for distinct contributions to be possible. At present, there are plenty of reasons why incoherence is maintained (including status, convenience and personal comfort). However, the professional identity of all groups within the welfare network, at least, urges effectiveness in the provision of support for those that need it.

The notion of multi-disciplinary work is nothing new. The need for collaboration has been urged by the Court Report (1976) and Committees of Inquiry following notable incidents of child abuse. A truly multi-disciplinary team has long been the aspiration of the Child Guidance movement (as endorsed particularly by DHSS 1974: Circular HSC (IS)9). What such early attempts at multi-disciplinary co-ordination have lacked, however, has been a systematic evaluation of the effectiveness of such collaboration which is certainly not proven (cf. Shepherd et al. 1966). There are a range of new initiatives, for example welfare service liaison groups in secondary schools; joint-funded education and Social Services projects; portage services; which are attempting to provide more co-ordinated support to schools and parents. These need to be evaluated systematically and critically to establish what elements and styles of multi-disciplinary contact are most useful and in order to provide a stimulus for further rapprochement. Not only is periodic research necessary but also service recipients (parents and schools) need to be involved in their management to enable a more regular dialogue on service organization.

References

Coulby, D. and Harper, T. (1985) *Preventing Classroom Disruption: Policy, Practice and Evaluation in Urban Schools*, Beckenham: Croom Helm.

Court Report (1976) *Fit for the Future: Report of the Committee on Child Health Services*, Vol. I, London: HMSO.

Dessent, T. (1987) *Making Ordinary Schools Special*, Lewes: Falmer Press.

DHSS (1974) Circular HSC (IS) 9 *Child Guidance*, London: HMSO.

Gray, P.J. (1986) From gatekeeping to planning: the link between statutory work and the development of special educational resources, *Educational and Child Psychology* 3(2): 46–54.

Gray, P.J. and Noakes, J.S. (1987) Time to stop taking the easy option, *Times Educational Supplement*, 10 April.

Gray P.J. and Noakes, J.S. (1992) *Planning Reintegration*, in A. Miller and D.A. Lane (eds) *Silent Conspiracies*, Stoke-on-Trent: Trentham Books.

Johnson, D., Ranson, E., Packwood, T., Bowden, K. and Kogan, M. (1980) *Secondary Schools and the Welfare Network*, London: George Allen & Unwin.

Reid, K. (1986) *Disaffection from School*, London: Methuen.

Shepherd, M., Oppenheim, A.N. and Mitchell, S. (1966) Childhood behaviour disorders and the Child Guidance Clinic: an epidemiological study, *Journal of Child Psychology and Psychiatry* 3: 39–52.

Skinner, A., Platts, H. and Hill, B. (1983) *Disaffection from School: Issues and Interagency Responses*, Leicester: National Youth Bureau.

Warnock Report (1978) *Special Education Needs*, London: HMSO.

12

Change in natural environments: community psychology as therapy

NEIL HALL

Introduction: the nature of community psychology

Rappaport (1977) claimed that 'Community psychology is interested in social change, particularly in those systems of society where psychologists are active participants'. These systems clearly include the family, schools, social care, hospitals, and the courts. He added that community psychology is concerned with the quality of relationships that diverse individuals and groups of people have with their varying environments. It is thus a perspective, in Rappaport's terms, of 'cultural relativity, diversity, and ecology: the fit between persons and environments'.

What this chapter will seek to demonstrate is that, as Levine and Perkins (1987) suggest, 'community-oriented psychologists are interested in creating new services consistent with the ecological perspective . . . [and in the] search for resources instead of a search for psychopathology'. It is Heller's (1990) contention, formulated from a wide-ranging review of recent community psychology, that those themes which 'highlight the importance of social and environmental factors in behaviour, and the necessity of conceptualizing intervention from a proactive and preventive stance, have become "mainstream"'.

The above was written about community psychology in the USA. Loxley (1978) is well recognized as a noted contributor to the promotion of community psychology in Britain, especially within the realms of educational psychology. He regarded the role of psychologists not so much as therapists, rather as 'client advocates' within the community (eg the local authority) and primarily as 'facilitators', not as 'change agents'. However, it will be proposed here that there are psychologists currently working in the community, who are providing a specific range of child and adolescent services, and that the nature and significance of their work, to the people and systems receiving such interventions, is more rightly referred to as therapy. This, of course, does not obviate the roles Loxley proposed, rather it is contended that these have been extended. Such a process explicitly demands a multi-disciplinary approach and, concomitantly, a preparedness for becoming involved in community groups and services. As an example, this could mean that educational psychologists, working for a local authority, did not work solely within the Education Department, but also contributed to projects in other areas, such as the Social Services Department, the Department of Youth and Community Services, the Directorate of Law and Regulation, and so on.

Equally, there are many, less formally constituted groups, not necessarily of professionals, but of local people who serve to represent the views and aims of particular sections of their community. As Loxley points out, 'Educational psychologists are in a good position to be mediators in some matters concerning community needs and public policy'. In this context, we must be especially clear about the term 'community'. Heller suggests that it 'is used in at least two generally recognized ways: As a locality, a community is a territory or geographic area – a neighbourhood, town, or city. As a relational concept a community is defined by the qualities of human interaction and social ties that draw people together'. It is in the latter arena that most community-based psychologists are working and at a variety of levels of input.

Community psychology: child and adolescent services

Background

In Britain little overall attention has been given to the development and practice of community-based psychological services for children and adolescents. In the early 1970s Bender (1972; 1976) was another significant advocate of the practice of community psychology in Britain. In developing his own team of community psychologists in the London Borough of Newham, he effectively led other British psychologists in the development of their own community-based services, some of which were solely for children and adolescents (eg Brown 1981; Barlow 1982). According to Bender (1976), 'Community psychology is an attempt to fuse two traditions, the psychological and the sociological/political'. As will be exemplified, the use of psychological approaches to, and or interpretations of, child protection, juvenile justice, and mental health services clearly illustrates this fusion. But what of progress since then?

The provision of an adequate community psychology service, probably irrespective of the client group or the spatial context, will depend both on how a community's psychological needs are assessed and how resources are determined which would be considered sufficient to meet those needs. In relation to children's services there is no specific literature which points to the most efficacious method for determining either the nature, or the level, of input to which a community-based psychological service should aim.

However, psychology services have generally been provided with reference to three major areas of children's lives: the school (but rarely the work/training setting for older adolescents); the family (although, mostly on an individual basis, without much incorporation of the whole family); and the community (which, essentially, refers to interventions for those who have committed, or are at risk of committing, offences; and/or because they are in need of protection from abuse and neglect).

Traditionally, the first area has been provided by a service from educational psychologists, and the second area from clinical psychologists. The third area has not been comprehensively serviced by any one particular group of professional psychologists. Throughout the 1980s, however, a gradually increasing number of professionally trained psychologists has been employed by (or seconded to) Social Services Departments. As a professional group they have been most closely associated with developing family- and community-based child and adolescent services. It is clear from a recent report, *Psychologists and Social Services* (British Psychological Society 1990) that the nature of work undertaken by psychologists working wholly, or closely, with Social Services/Social Work Departments is very much in the domain of the community psychologist. This work is outlined below and described in more detail later.

Some examples of practice

Community-based clinical psychology services for young children (pre-schoolers), particularly preventive work in relation to the screening and assessment of developmental and behavioural problems, are discussed by Bidder and Hewitt (1986). As an example of a community-wide service development they reported on how South Glamorgan Health Authority specially appointed 'child development advisers', working in league with clinical psychologists, to offer home-based services for children with behaviour difficulties. They also provide an interesting focus on various aspects of preparing mothers and fathers for parenting. Overall, however, it is somewhat unnerving to note the general paucity of such fundamental work in Britain. Iscoe and Harris (1984), Gesten and Jason (1987) and Heller (1990) provide considerable research evidence, mostly American, on the demonstrated effectiveness of community interventions in, for example, reducing child maltreatment, promoting levels of child health, and in providing services at a preventive level.

A range of community psychological services has been described by Hall (1987). This kind of input, provided by a group of educational and clinical psychologists working for the Children's Teams of Birmingham's Social Services Department, none the less remains a comparatively scarce resource. Moreover, there are few other groups of psychologists working in the community who have, as a major portion of their work, child and adolescent clients who have been abused and/or neglected (Hall 1990a). Interventions with these clients include home-based initiatives with families who are working towards rehabilitation; staff training programmes in day nurseries and children's homes; support groups for foster-parents; individual therapy for a range of psychological trauma; and a wide variety of generalist and specialist consultative services to social workers who are operating from a variety of care settings – secure accommodation, independent living units, adoption and fostering units, day care centres, juvenile justice centres, field social work teams, and so on.

Halpern (1990) reports on many community-based early interventions which specifically engage 'lay family workers', most of whom share the same culture as those they are serving. These workers are able to act as so-called 'culture brokers' assisting in the negotiation so often necessary between professional workers and parents. It is apparent that this specific example of an anti-discriminatory practice may still have much to achieve, such work is only incompletely a part of the British agenda for many community interventions with children and adolescents.

Services for adolescents, especially for those youngsters who are at risk of being admitted to residential care and or committing offences, have been described by Brown (1986), particularly as these have developed as primary prevention programmes (eg managing violence, survival skills, substance misuse). However, research evidence relating to the effectiveness of community-based, non-custodial interventions for young offenders is somewhat equivocal, according to Hollin (1989). Those interventions which most receive the attention fall within the general purview of intermediate treatment (IT)/juvenile justice centres yet, as Cawson (1985) notes, psychologists are rarely involved in this potentially demanding work. Certainly, psychologists have a role to undertake in the management of groups, behavioural change programmes (as in social skills training or SST), and promoting, and evaluating, the development of self-esteem; all of these factors being central to IT work. Preston and Carnegie (1989) and Feldman (1989) have described various British community-based psychological approaches (including several American projects).

Occasionally posts have been established which are specifically entitled 'community psychologist': a very small proportion of these have been targeted at work with children and adolescents. Wilson (1988) provides information about an innovative sample of the community projects he has developed and implemented in Glasgow. This has included training staff in counselling skills, for use with voluntary groups working with young people misusing drugs; helping to develop a 'Befriending Scheme' within the context of an Intermediate Treatment Centre; being a member of an Urban Aid Planning Group; and also undertaking various interventions with individual children and families.

The impact of criminological and legal factors

As indicated above, psychology services are provided at a variety of levels of input: directly to individuals and to groups of clients (including families and other carers where applicable); to the staff groups of particular establishments, as noted above; and to policy and research groups. Moreover, in the larger urban areas, and particularly within the inner cities, much of the work is likely to be determined in nature by the impact, sometimes demand, of various court proceedings. As Hollin (1989) exemplifies, the developing role of psychologists in legal and criminological work is integral to many of the various psychological therapies provided within the community.

Assessment and therapeutic interventions are undertaken in response to wardship proceedings of the High Court, care and criminal proceedings of the Juvenile and Crown Courts and, frequently, in terms of pre-and post-sentencing orders in the context of the work of the juvenile justice centres. Many of these interventions necessarily involve the development of close working relationships with a local authority's Directorate of Law and Regulation (or Solicitors' Department) and often a range of other legal and criminological agencies. This can include Guardian ad litem, court welfare services, Probation and After Care

Departments, the police, the Prison Service, and other solicitors. In many cases, where a child, or a parent, resides in alternative accommodation to the family home, this will additionally involve liaison with the staff of bail and parole hostel accommodation, and other rehabilitation centres and projects (including for children foster homes, residential family support centres and children's homes).

The nature of community-based therapeutic work in relation to the above is, therefore, very closely related to a network of other resources. The quality and outcome of any psychological input in these contexts undoubtedly depends on the development and maintenance of relationships between what is often a widely varying set of professionals (and untrained workers), different establishments, their staff groups, and the philosophies inherent in their work. Psychologists can undertake many roles in these community-based interventions. An essential pre-requisite for any psychologist working in the community is the ability to demonstrate both a willingness, and the necessary skills, for creating an ethos of multi-disciplinary team work, that is, a jointly developed and implemented therapeutic intervention (Hall 1988).

The role of the family in service development

Furthermore, the values that psychologists attribute to the role of the family, in their various community interventions, could be viewed as a determining factor in the nature and quality of those services. The implementation of a community-based child and adolescent service should relate directly to how a psychologist conceptualizes not only the role of 'the family' in connection with the need and provision of such a service but also the very nature and value of the family for a child's long-term psychological and social development. Psychologists can clearly be differentiated according to the kinds of involvement they determine for those members of the family beyond the referred child. This will easily be exemplified in relation to the resources that are used within the community to help maintain a child within their natural environment, and whether or not places are sought in local, alternative care settings which actively encourage the participation of parents and members of the child's family. There are clear expectations that, with the implementation of the Children Act 1989, a greater number of psychologists will be explicitly involving parents in a 'partnership', in terms of remediating difficulties which are, or may be, preventing a child from remaining permanently within their family home. As present, it is contended (Vetere and Gale 1987) that, probably, a majority of psychologists have a poorly defined understanding of the theoretical foundations of the psychology of the family. That there are enormous implications, arising from such a notion, for psychologists providing community-based services for children and adolescents, has yet fully to be researched.

Community psychology and Social Services Departments: psychological services for children and adolescents

A broader outline of those inputs that psychologists provide to the children's establishments and services of some Social Services Departments (SSDs) should indicate what is being undertaken in the community. Some of this work is preventive, for example in just one area of work, in Birmingham, a Leaving Care curriculum has been produced by a children's home staff group working with a psychologist, and Gregory and Tweddle (1979) earlier demonstrated how independence skills training in residential care could be enhanced by using behavioural objectives. Much, however, still remains crisis-led, as in the identification of, and response to, child abuse. This latter area, and others, will be considered in the following sections. All the interventions referred to have some connection with a local authority's Social Services Department.

Community psychology and child protection services

The Trinity Road Project, a jointly sponsored West Birmingham Health Authority and Birmingham Social Services Department facility, was established as a fully multi-disciplinary child protection centre in 1987, to provide a variety of community services for children, their families, social workers and other professionals throughout the City of Birmingham. Within the staff group there are three psychologists who currently provide separate, but co-ordinated, inputs to the Project: a clinical psychologist (top grade) who works there two sessions per week, and two educational psychologists (seconded from two of the Birmingham Psychological Services, to work for the Social Services Department) who work respectively two and five sessions per week. (Other psychologists have supported specific casework interventions.) The psychologists' inputs vary from direct client contact (individuals and families), staff training, consultation, and research and development. A range of psychological therapies, approaches, and projects have been implemented.

The clinical psychologist initiated a research project, with pre-school children, using a specially developed video which has been designed to help the very young understand the nature of inappropriate touching (Adams and Gifford 1992). Aspects of an approach to some of the family-based work at the Project has been presented in Hall (1988). Further psychological and evaluative studies have also been started, by several members of the staff, and external bodies (eg the Universities of Aston, Birmingham, and Lancaster), including the following:

1 'Effectiveness Evaluation'   This is a research study of the Project, since its inception, which examines how parents and professionals view the services they have received.
2 'The use of a behavioural-objectives-based curriculum for intensive work with parents and their pre-school-aged children'.
3 'INTERACT: a computerized system for the analysis of trends in child abuse'.
4 'The relationship between children's cognitive and emotional development in the context of their experiences of psychological trauma'   The results of this study are to be used to devise specific therapeutic approaches for working with children and significant adults.
5 'The sexual development and behaviour of young children'   Both as a review of contemporary research and as a set of training materials.

6 Children's Drawings   To establish whether abuse can be identified from the drawings of children of differing ages.

The work of two American psychologists, Newman and Lutzker (1990), who describe a community-based, professionally supported, 'in-home' programme for parents at risk of abusing their children, was of particular use at the inception of the Trinity Road Project. Their intervention – referred to as 'Project 12-Ways' – was based upon social learning theory, and utilized an eco-behavioural approach (which merges the two disciplines of ecological psychology and behavioural analysis within a community setting). Such work represents a significant attempt to remediate several factors known to contribute to child abuse and neglect, and covers a range of parental, child and situational characteristics.

Psychologists in Britain have only hesitantly been involved in child protection work and, certainly, rarely within the community or at a level which is fully multi-disciplinary. Community-based approaches to child abuse within the family will always be rightly regarded as high-risk strategies if adopted by a local authority's Social Services Department. Hall (1988) has described two kinds of psychological input within the setting of a day nursery, and which have been incorporated into the work of the Trinity Road Project. Both interventions relied upon the explicit use of legal controls (wardship orders) for the therapeutic work, as explicated by Dale et al. (1986). In each instance both the mother and the father were actively implicated in the physical, sexual and emotional abuse of their children.

In this approach an attempt was made to create a 'core team' of professionals, comprising a day nursery social worker (officer-in-charge), a field social worker and a psychologist. (Other 'teams', in working with school-aged children, have consisted of a probation officer, field social worker and a psychologist, or two social workers and a psychologist.) The purpose of this was to provide a forum for the parents, within the day nursery environment, which would enable their parenting behaviours to be discussed.

It was further hypothesized that, by allowing the parents sufficient opportunity to discuss their own childhood experiences, they would be facilitated in understanding how the local authority constructed its concerns about the parenting of their children. Each of the parents knew of the day nursery as a place where their children had always received positive adult contact from the staff. Moreover, each parent, separately and as a couple, was offered the opportunity of staying throughout a day, sometimes for the greater part of a week, to work alongside their children, nursery staff (where appropriate), and/or to socialize with other parents attending the unit. Therefore, attendance at the nursery came to assume a considerable significance for the family. Not to attend required a sufficiently adequate reason. The reinforcers for attending were clearly related to receiving professional support for the parenting of what they defined as their 'difficult' children. Apart from what might be termed as a therapeutic training element, the team also provided structured inputs on the nature of the parents' interpersonal relationships, their childhood experiences and development, and the opportunity to reflect on the upbringing of their own children. At other times a senior clinical medical officer, who was a member of the Trinity Road Project, and who also had a specialist, community-wide responsibility for children at-risk, provided sessions on various aspects of child health and physical development.

In Lutzker and Newman's Project 12-Ways, the use of 'In-Home Services' is seen as central to the programme, given the seeming reluctance of abusing parents to attend clinic-based services – through recalcitrance or fear of stigma. Such an intervention could consist of, for example, various parent training exercises, stress reduction, personal fitness programmes, home safety routines, or problem-solving approaches. From the Trinity Road Project a variety of home-based interventions are provided. The work of Herbert (1988) has proved useful, as has Goldstein and Keller (1987). All of the inputs are, however, based upon the collection of detailed behavioural observations of interactions between parents and children, and significant other persons. These are collated and analysed for later discussion with the parents and, where appropriate, the children too. On occasions these behavioural observations will be video-taped (or, sometimes, only the verbal interactions will be audio-taped). Narrative, hand-written recordings are made, on a specific time-sampling basis, and are made available for the parents. Such data are invaluable for comparing parents' stated theories of their behaviour with samples of their actual behaviour. Such work has two main benefits: it is always received extremely well by judges, magistrates, barristers, and so on, and has a powerfully, disclosing effect upon parents.

Community psychology in educational and social settings

To further the theme of child protection, but within the schools' context, it is important to note the few British, community-based initiatives. Probably the first local authority-wide programme to be developed by a psychology service was implemented in the Metropolitan Borough of Oldham (Fingleton et al. 1988). Joint work with the local NSPCC Centre, in Rochdale, was an essential factor in the success of this endeavour (for an example of one of their joint productions see Rochdale Child Abuse Training Committee 1987). Birmingham Education Department has constructed its own programme, led by the city's chief psychologist, and based upon specific materials (eg Braun 1988) developed co-operatively with the Community Education Development Centre, Coventry, to train a group of educational psychologists and social workers to undertake a city-wide, schools-training initiative.

Also a team of educational psychologists, working for the Social Services Department in Devon, have written about the child protection work that Schools Psychological Services could undertake in the community (Billinge et al. 1990). Moreover, various psychologists have had their work widely utilized in several community settings, for example KIDSCAPE/TEENSCAPE (Elliot 1986; 1989; 1990) has been incorporated into a range of schools-based programmes, as in Crampton-Smith (1987). Tattum and Lane (1989) present various psychological approaches to the problems of bullying, and the victims of such behaviour, which could form the basis for whole-school approaches. Rouf and Peake (1989), from their different perspective of a community-based educational psychology service, have produced resources for working with children who have been sexually abused. Lane (1990) has provided a model of school-focused support.

In relation to other community-based schools programmes, Allen and colleagues (1976), working in the USA, developed a social problem-solving curriculum. Their whole-school approach aimed at enhancing the psychological functioning of all children, although specific inputs were provided for those children already identified as having particular emotional and behavioural difficulties, sufficient to enable them to remain within the mainstream setting. Teachers were given a skills-based input to help them deal with various aspects of classroom management, particularly in relation to academic and disciplinary problems, with the aim of developing appropriate within-school strategies to prevent referrals to external agencies. Allen et al. (1976) argue that 'The model integrates the preventive orientation of community psychologists with the empirical operations of applied behaviour analysts'. Several British examples are now available; one notable programme, 'Preventive Approaches to Disruption', was developed by a group of practising educational psychologists (Chisholm et al. 1986).

A schools-based mental health programme was formulated by Levy (1989), a clinical psychologist, and a colleague (a community psychiatric nurse), both of whom were then working for a Community Mental Health Resource Centre. They were interested in forming a group, for which they would run a ten-session, once weekly course, at which sixth form students, who had volunteered to do so, could discuss aspects of mental health which typically concern their age group, particularly in the context of their leaving home to live away as university students. The group was run as an educational intervention given, as Levy argued, that mental health therapies are mostly sophisticated educational programmes and, therefore, the initial point for such an intervention should be the educational system. Topics for discussion were donated for each meeting by the group leaders, based on the information given in the initial broadsheet advertising the group. Evaluation of pre- and post-course knowledge and awareness showed clear gains in the sixth formers' understanding of the nature of mental health issues affecting young people, but it is recognized that a longer-term study needs to be undertaken.

Clearly, schools are only one part of the community environment. For community psychologists the challenge is to deal with the relationships between the schools and the wider community. Rapoport (1987) describes a range of large-scale, community-based, action-research projects for schools and their local communities in the United States. These have involved, to a much larger extent than any British projects, the use of parents and also multi-disciplinary teams of community workers, and have focused upon the teaching of social problem-solving skills to children as a preventive measure in relation to school adaptation. Priestley et al. (1978) were early developers of this approach in Britain, for children in a range of contexts. Spence (1980) also produced several research studies to support her Social Skills Training initiatives.

A much smaller 'Schools Project' was developed by a group of juvenile justice social workers and a psychologist working for Birmingham Social Services Department, in an attempt to prevent an increase in the crime rate among the 10–12-year-old age range within a particular neighbourhood (Hall 1987). Junior and secondary schools were selected from within the local community, as were members of the local police force. Discussions were held in relation to a range of criminological and legal matters, especially the types of offences that are knowingly (and unknowingly) committed by children of their age group. Didactic methods of teaching were used alongside more dramatic techniques of role-play and simulation. A central factor in the sessions was obtaining the children's varying social and moral perspectives on the types of crimes that are committed and what would constitute the feelings of the victims. Certainly, the children were sufficiently enthused and inspired by these inputs to raise their awareness into thinking of community crime prevention schemes in which they could participate.

In relation to a community-based project created for a group of 'shy adolescents', Jackson and Marzillier (1982) comment that 'The nature and extent to which adolescents have difficulties in relating to their peers have been under-investigated'. The authors describe how the advocacy of a social skills training (SST) programme for such a client group has been shown to be partially effective for modifying social inhibitions. Of great importance for such work is the notion that the environment for training should be as similar as possible to the one in which the adolescents are to apply their newly learnt skills. Consequently, Jackson and Marzillier's innovatory work also included the setting up, and evaluation, of a therapeutically-run youth club for shy adolescents. The following topics were incorporated into the SST programme: eye contact, facial expression, voice intonation, conversation initiation, conversation continuation, termination conversation, listening skills, requests, refusals, complaints, and dealing with teasing. As a control, a group of behaviourally similar adolescents were introduced to the same topics but, unlike the experimental group, they were not offered modelling, behaviour role-play and other feedback elements to them as a part of the training.

Even though there was a substantial number of statistically non-significant effects, Jackson and Marzillier (1982) were able to demonstrate that, as a consequence of their intervention, 'On average the youngsters had significantly extended the range of their social activities by the end of the club'. Equally, there was also a recognition of the need for a controlled experimental evaluation of the effectiveness of the youth club, in addition to an evaluation of the psychological impact of the SST groups.

The work of the Manchester-based Youth Development Trust (eg McDermott 1986) signals an innovatory example of providing a community mental health service; '42nd Street' is a project for young people, aged between 15 and 25, who are experiencing various forms and levels of stress. Manchester City Council and the Social Services Department provides financial support for the project. Professional psychologists are not employed within 42nd Street: the project has its own formal counselling service, utilizing a dynamic psychotherapeutic approach. Staffed by three social workers, and utilizing several other volunteers, young people with a very wide range of mental health needs have presented themselves to 42nd Street. As in other community-based work there is a need for close liaison and co-operation with a range of agencies and other services. The work presented to date exemplifies a model worthy of further research and evaluation. 42nd Street appears to offer a basis for much needed community-based therapeutic interventions.

Community psychologists and adolescent sex offenders

Therapeutic work with adolescent sex offenders, within community settings, is inseparably linked to legal and care proceedings. Adolescents do not present as self-referrals. The motivation for change and, or therapy is provided externally, and this is a major factor of the initial engagement process (Wilson and Shine 1990). Psychologists who work in the community with those adolescent clients who have appeared before a court will often be intervening on a co-working basis with a member of a Social Services Department. The child's allocated field social worker is usually the most obvious professional with whom to work. It is not unusual, however, for an adolescent offender, who is the subject of a Supervision Order, or who is directed to a residential care establishment, to be without an allocated social worker. In the latter instance, the establishment can usually provide a specified 'key-worker' who can take on a role within a joint therapeutic intervention. With such work, the psychologist is frequently in the position of facilitating a social worker in the development of particular therapeutic skills (eg behavioural approaches, elements of interviewing and assessment skills, aspects of counselling, or other specific inputs).

One particular example, of a jointly developed intervention, (for an adolescent male who had sexually assaulted a middle-aged woman), was produced by a juvenile justice social worker, a psychologist and other members of the Trinity Road Project (Hall 1990a). The seemingly unprovoked attack occurred in the context of the boy's peer group. Of central importance to the intervention was the existence of a suitable adult male role model, sufficient to help the boy change a particular set of his existing cognitions. These included constructs about the roles of women and men; the nature of emotional, social and sexual relationships; his concept of morality, particularly in relation to 'guilt and shame', 'right and wrong', and 'individual rights', his understanding of sexuality, and the various related components of sexual preference, sexual fantasies, sexual contact and personal experience.

While much of the therapeutic input was undertaken at a juvenile justice centre, home visits, to work with the boy's family, were also a main element of the intervention. The overall programme included a set of written exercises; discussion sessions; drawing; participative evaluation; use of videos; and role-play. A major task for the boy was to provide a highly detailed behavioural analysis of the offence. Therapy sessions were used to facilitate particular cognitive changes. A simple reinforcement schedule was employed throughout the whole programme. An overall aim was to develop a framework of social and moral judgement for this boy, sufficient to enable him to consider how to prevent any further offences.

Ryan et al. (1987) have produced a model for the identification of commonalities inherent in adolescent sexual offending, which has informed the work at the Trinity Road Project. The authors have constructed a framework – a 'sexual assault cycle' – to enable them to gain a clearer understanding of those cognitive, behavioural, psychological, and situational factors which have contributed to sexual offences. Moreover, Becker et al. (1987) have provided details of how adolescents exemplify sexually offending behaviour in many ways similar to adults. Such information, from both studies, has been of particular value for a range of therapeutic work with these adolescents and their families.

Psychologists in Britain have rarely reported specifically on work of this nature, although Wilson and Shine (1990) have commented on those adolescent sex offenders who would most benefit from some form of psychological intervention. Hall (1990a) has explained the nature of his work – undertaken jointly with social workers and, at times, other members of Birmingham's multi-disciplinary child protection project – with six male clients, one child of 8 years old, and five adolescent boys aged between 13 and 17. Three of the older boys had appeared before the Juvenile Court on charges relating to their sexual offences. In consequence, two were received into the care of the local authority and were placed in children's homes. The other three youngsters remained at home, one being given a Supervision Order (plus IT clause) as outlined above. The younger child was living at home.

The 17 year old lived at home with his birth parents, younger brother (15) and much younger sister (6). He was accused of sexually abusing his sister, a case which was found proven against him. This resulted in his removal to a children's home. He attended a special school.

All the young people had social workers allocated to them. Information is given below, as an example of the various elements and staff involved. The work was essentially twofold, first the family, and children's home, focussed (but excluding the young girl), and second, for the girl who had been abused.

The first part of the work was undertaken in six stages:

1 family meetings with mother, father, and two brothers
2 meetings with the brothers
3 individual sessions with the boy
4 separate meetings with each of the parents
5 joint meetings with a residential social worker, the boy, and a psychologist
6 liaison meetings with the school.

This work involved two specialist child protection social workers, residential social workers, the year tutor, and a psychologist. Various techniques were developed from structural family therapy, applied behavioural analysis, play therapy, non-directive counselling programmes (including psychosexual counselling).

The second part to the work was undertaken in four stages:

1 individual interviews for the girl (with the female social worker) to determine the specifics of abuse
2 play therapy
3 play sessions, including the mother, to develop self-protection strategies
4 liaison with school, to help the child develop her trust of another adult.

This work involved the field social worker, class teacher, and a psychologist in a consultative role.

The young man remained in residential care until he approached his nineteenth birthday. His sister continued to live at the family home. Preventive work is ongoing, for both of them. For the girl the input is centred upon monitoring her emotional development and in continuing to provide her with self-protection strategies. For the boy the aim is to extend his self-understanding as someone who has the potential for re-offending, notwithstanding having developed a sense of self while in care, sufficient to recognize, and act upon those triggers which previously occasioned sexually abusive behaviour. Both the brother and sister continue to need their own social work support and the oversight of a psychologist.

Conclusions

Overall, the most significant inputs from community-based psychologists have been in relation to several aspects of children's developmental assessment, child protection, and juvenile justice services for adolescents. Probably, this could also be said to illustrate the different ways in which 'the family' has been directly involved in various community-based resources. Such work has only gradually become more apparent, as more clinical and educational psychologists have provided community-based services to their local Social Services Departments or Social Work Departments. Of course, this situation may alter radically, as a consequence of the implementation of various pieces of legislation, for example the National Health Service and Community Care Act 1990, the Children Act 1989, and the Education Reform Act 1988.

Psychologists working with the families and children who are referred by Social Services Departments or Social Work Departments (and this, at present, is mostly because of concerns about child abuse and neglect), cannot possibly do so without direct reference to the social and economic, and cultural and political circumstances in which they are functioning. To attempt not to include these factors is to ignore the basic environmental influences which impinge daily upon people's lives. Work within community settings is committed to accounting for these factors and enabling them to be utilized for the purposes of therapeutic change. Heller (1990), however, appropriately comments that 'social change is more easily recommended than accomplished, because social problems are woven into the fabric of society and reflect longstanding political and economic policies'. Of direct relevance to the work outlined in this chapter, Guishard (1990) has provided an example of how an attempt can be made to understand the psychology of two obvious examples of these social problems – racism and child abuse – and, moreover, how professionals working in the community can better develop an anti-discriminatory service. What is further required is that British psychologists produce sufficient research and evaluation studies which exemplify the effectiveness of their community services.

What also seems apparent, from the information contained within the British Psychological Society's Report (1990), neither clinical nor educational psychology professional training courses provide an adequate preparation for working in many of the settings as outlined above. The Report comments on those areas that should be incorporated into a professional training course. Hall (1990b) has suggested a specific curriculum, for the training of educational psychologists, which might offer an appropriate preparation for the kinds of community-based services psychologists could offer to Social Services Departments and, possibly, other departments of the local authority. Further developments in this area are to be welcomed.

Finally, Brown (1986) has suggested that community psychologists need 'to make available as much knowledge as possible about how communities can use their expertise with good effect'. What has to be accepted is that for communities to receive adequate therapeutic interventions psychologists will need actively to seek other professionals with whom to work. Community psychology services have been shown above mostly to be one part of a wider, multi-disciplinary endeavour which aims to meet the varied needs of many children and adolescents.

References

Adams, J. and Gifford, V. (1992) Taking Care with Toby and the Puppet Gang, Nuneaton: George Elliot Hospital, N.E. Warwickshire H.A.

Allen, G.J., Chinskey, J.M., Larcen, S.W., Lochman, J.E. and Selinger, H.V. (1976) *Community Psychology and the Schools: A Behaviourally Oriented Multilevel Preventive Approach*, Hillsdale, NJ: Lawrence Erlbaum.

Barlow, N.T. (1982) Implementing a challenge to care, *International Journal of Behavioural Social Work and Abstracts* 2(1): 17–30.

Becker, J.V., Cunningham-Rathner, J. and Kaplan, M.S. (1987) Adolescent sexual offenders: demographics, criminal and sexual histories, and recommendations for reducing future offenses, *Journal of Interpersonal Violence* 1(4): 431–45.

Bender, M.P. (1972) The role of a community psychologist, *Bulletin of the British Psychological Society* 25: 211–18.

Bender, M.P. (1976) *Community Psychology*, London: Methuen.

Bidder, R.T. and Hewitt, K.E. (1986) Child health, in H.C.H. Koch (ed.) *Community Clinical Psychology*, Beckenham: Croom Helm.

Billinge, M., Blayney, C., Woods, R. and Benfield, P. (1990) Child abuse and educational psychologists, *Division of Educational and Child Psychology Newsletter* no 38, Leicester: British Psychological Society.

Braun, D. (1988) *Responding to Child Abuse: Action and Planning for Teachers and Other Professionals*, London: Bedford Square Press.

British Psychological Society (1990) *Psychologists and Social Services*, Leicester: BPS.

Brown, B. (1981) Constructing psychological services in Social Services Departments, in I. McPherson and A. Sutton (eds) *Reconstructing Psychological Practice*, London: Croom Helm.

Brown, B. (1986) Services for adolescents, in H.C.H. Koch (ed.) *Community Clinical Psychology*, Beckenham: Croom Helm.

Cawson, P. (1985) Intermediate treatment, *Journal of Child Psychology and Psychiatry* 26(5): 675–81.

Children Act (1989) London: HMSO.

Chisholm, B., Kearney, D., Knight, G., Little, H., Morris, S. and Tweddle, D. (1986) *Preventive Approaches to Disruption*, London: Macmillan.

Crampton-Smith, F. (1987) Paper presented to the Association for Behavioural Approaches with Children, Hillscourt Education Centre, Birmingham.

Dale, P., Davies, M., Morrison, T. and Waters, J. (1986) *Dangerous Families: Assessment and Treatment of Child Abuse*, London: Tavistock.

Education Reform Act (1988) London: HMSO.

Elliott, M. (1986) *KIDSCAPE: Good Sense Defence for the Young*, London: Kidscape Press.

Elliott, M. (1989) Bullying: harmless fun or murder?, in E. Roland and E. Munthe (eds) *Bullying: An International Perspective*, London: Fulton Books.

Elliott, M. (1990) *TEENSCAPE: Personal Safety Programme for Young People*, London: Kidscape Press.

Feldman, P. (1989) Applying psychology to the reduction of juvenile offending and offences: methods and results, *Issues in Criminological and Legal Psychology* 14: 3–32.

Fingleton, K., Samson, A., Hazell, A., Ridley, R. and Marsland, P. (1988) *Child Protection: Two 2-day Courses for Teachers*, Oldham: Child Protection Training Group, Oldham MB.

Gesten, E.L. and Jason, L.A. (1987) Social and community interventions, *Annual Review of Psychology* 38: 427–60.

Goldstein, A.P. and Keller, H. (1987) *Aggressive Behaviour: Assessment and Intervention*, New York: Pergamon Press.

Gregory, P. and Tweddle, D. (1979) Teaching independence in community homes, *Social Work Service* 19: 48–52.

Guishard, J. (1990) *The Psychology of Race and Child Protection*, Birmingham: Trinity Road Project.

Hall, N. (1987) Psychologists in Social Services Departments working with children and young people, Paper presented to 'Psychologists in Community Settings', University of Birmingham.

Hall, N. (1988) Working with parents who abuse their children, *Educational Psychology in Practice* October: 131–40.

Hall, N. (1990a) Psychological interventions in a multi-disciplinary child protection project, Paper for submission to *Educational Psychology in Practice*.

Hall, N. (1990b) Educational psychologists in training: applying psychology to the work of Social Services Departments, Paper for submission to *Educational Psychology in Practice*.

Halpern, R. (1990) Community-based early intervention, in S.J. Meisels and J.P. Shonkoff (eds) *Handbook of Early Childhood Intervention*, Cambridge: Cambridge University Press.

Heller, K. (1990) Social and community intervention, *Annual Review of Psychology* 41: 141–68.

Herbert, M. (1988) Behaviour modification of children with aggressive conduct disorders: the use of triadic model interventions in home settings, *Issues in Criminological and Legal Psychology* 12: 46–57.

Hollin, C. (1989) *Psychology and Crime: An Introduction to Criminological Psychology*, London: Routledge.

Iscoe, I. and Harris, L.C. (1984) Social and community interventions, *Annual Review of Psychology* 35: 333–60.

Jackson, M.F. and Marzillier, J.S. (1982) The Youth Club Project: a community-based intervention for shy adolescents, *Behavioural Psychotherapy* 10(1): 87–100.

Lane, D.A. (1990) *The Impossible Child*, Stoke-on-Trent: Trentham Books.

Levine, M. and Perkins, D.V. (1987) *Principles of Community Psychology: Perspectives and Applications*, New York: Oxford University Press.

Levy, B. (1989) A mental health initiative in a sixth form college, Paper presented to the Association for Child Psychology and Psychiatry, University of Birmingham.

Loxley, D. (1978) Community psychology, in B. Gillham (ed.) *Reconstructing Educational Psychology*, London: Croom Helm.

McDermott, A. (1986) *Principles into Practice: A Developmental Study of a Community, Mental Health Service*, Manchester: Youth Development Trust.

National Health Service and Community Care Act (1990) London: HMSO.

Newman, N.R. and Lutzker, J.R. (1990) Prevention programmes, in R.T. Ammermon (ed.) *Children at Risk: An Evaluation of Factors Contributing to Child Abuse and Neglect*, New York: Plenum.

Preston, M.A. and Carnegie, J. (1989) Intermediate treatment: working with offenders in the community, *Issues in Criminological and Legal Psychology* 14: 69–77.

Priestley, P., McGuire, J., Flegg, D., Hemsley, V. and Welham, D. (1978) *Social Skills and Personal Problem Solving*, London: Tavistock.

Rapoport, R.N. (1987) *New Interventions for Children and Youth: Action-research Approaches*, Cambridge: Cambridge University Press.

Rappaport, J. (1977) *Community Psychology: Values, Research, and Action*, New York: Holt, Rinehart & Winston.

Rochdale Child Abuse Training Committee (1987) *Teachers Don't Just Worry, Do Something*, Rochdale: RCATC.

Rouf, K. and Peake, A. (1989) *Working with Sexually Abused Children: A Resource Pack for Professionals*, London: Children's Society.

Ryan, G., Lane, S., Davis, J. and Isaac, C. (1987) Juvenile sex offenders: development and correction, *Child Abuse and Neglect* 11: 385–95.

Spence, S. (1980) *Social Skills Training with Children and Adolescents*, Windsor: National Foundation for Educational Research.

Tattum, D.P. and Lane, D.A. (1989) *Bullying in Schools*, Stoke-on-Trent: Trentham Books.

Vetere, A. and Gale, A. (1987) *Ecological Studies of Family Life*, Chichester: Wiley.

Wilson, M. (1988) *Community Psychology in Easterhouse*, Glasgow: Strathclyde Regional Council.

Wilson, P. and Shine, J. (1990) Characteristics and potential treatment needs of sexual offenders, *Issues in Criminological and Legal Psychology* 15: 50–8.

Index

Barnardos, 15
Barrett, C.L., 57
Bartak, L., 24
Basalisco, S., 142
Bayley, J., 149
Becker, J.V., 245
bedwetting, 54, 208; *see also* enuresis
'Befriending Scheme', 238
Behavior Problem Checklist, 158
behaviour
  anti-social, 22, 122, 168
  disruptive, 139, 145
  modification, 21, 193, 194, 203, 230
  phobic, 164
  problems, *see* emotional and/or behavioural
    difficulties
  therapy, 47, 56, 57, 164, 209
    and the therapeutic community, 193–5
Behaviour Support Service, 227, 228
behavioural
  approaches, 4, 12, 13, 14, 17, 24, 27, 40,
    41, 42, 54, 123, 180, 241, 245
  management, 41, 43, 74, 240
  perspective, 18
  programmes, 72, 194, 238
behaviourism, 193–4
Bender, M.P., 236
Bentovim, A., 13
bereavement, 28
Berecz, J.M., 128
Berelowitz, G., 205
Berg, I., 26, 56, 125, 126
Berger, M., 24, 41, 58
Berman, J.S., 57
Berne, E., 193
Berryman, E., 125
Besag, V.E., 145, 148, 149
Beutler, L.W., 46
Bidder, R.T., 237
Billinge, M., 242, 243
Bion, W.R., 9
Birleson, P., 162
Birleson's Depression Scale, 162
Black, D., 28, 206, 207
Blacker, C.P., 202
Blackman, D.E., 194
Blagg, N.R., 25, 31, 41, 43, 49, 50, 51, 56,
    122, 123, 124, 125, 129, 131, 132, 133,
    134
Bolton, D., 30
Bornstein, B., 124
Boston, B., 3, 7
Bowlby, J., 8, 9
Bradley, C., 51
Braun, D., 242
breast cancer, choice of treatment for, 51
Brewin, C.R., 51
Brickman, P., 43
Bridgeland, M., 179, 192
Briere, J., 109, 110

Bristol Social Adjustment Guide (BSAG), 25
British Psychological Society, 6, 237, 247
Broadwin, I.T., 120
Brown, B., 236, 238, 248
Browne, 189
Bryce, G., 124, 128
bullying, 19, 138–54, 181, 186, 242
  a case study of intervention, 151–3
  causes of, 144–7
  definition of, 140–4
  a framework for intervention, 147–50
  model of, 138, 139, 147,
  systems approach to, 147–8
  'bullying structure', 143
Burck, C., 205
Burden, R., 12, 13, 17, 146, 150
Burke, A.E., 26, 57

Cain, B., 125, 126
Callias, M., 14, 26, 27, 30, 31, 40, 46, 48, 50
Cameron, K., 202
Cantrell, R.P., 130
Carkhuff, R.R., 46
Carnegie, J., 238
Carpenter, C., 130
Carr, J., 26, 27, 31, 40, 48, 50
Carralda, M.E., 205
Casdagli, P., 149
Casey, R.J., 57
Cawson, P., 238
change
  evaluation of, 54,
  maintenance of, 5, 14, 41, 43, 44, 45, 130,
    131
  methods of reporting, 49
  motivation for, 245
  psychological processes of, 53
'change agents', 235
Chapel, J.L., 130
Chapman, G., 123
characteristics of social context, 53
Chazan, M., 144, 145, 148
Child and Adolescent Psychiatry Departments,
    203
child
  and adolescent psychiatry services, 212
  and adolescent therapy
    practice of, 31–2
    theoretical perspectives of, 6–14
  and family/adolescent therapy services, 16,
    235
  characteristics, 26, 27, 47–8, 51, 57, 241
    effect on treatment outcome, 23
  guidance, *see* Child Guidance Clinics
  development of, 202–5
  health services, 19
  protection
    issues, 19, 20, 111, 207, 208, 236, 241,
      242, 246, 247

Index compiled by Anna Leeming